Technology and War

From 2000 B.C. to the Present

Martin van Creveld

THE FREE PRESS
A Division of Macmillan, Inc.
NEW YORK

Collier Macmillan Publishers
LONDON

The Free Press
A Division of Macmillan, Inc.
866 Third Avenue, New York, N.Y. 10022

Collier Macmillan Canada, Inc.

Printed in the United States of America

Library of Congress Cataloging-in-Publication Data

Van Creveld, Martin L.
    Technology and war / Martin van Creveld.
        p.   cm.
    Bibliography: p.
    ISBN 0–02–933151–X
    1. Military art and science—History.   2. Military history.
3. Technology—History.   I. Title.
U27.V27 1989
355'.009—dc 19   88–16405
                                                                        CIP

For Dvora
to whom this book owes a lot
and I, everything

The one thing more important than opulence is defense.
ADAM SMITH

CONTENTS

Contents

PREFACE

THE PRESENT BOOK, which has been several years in the writing, could never have seen the light of day without the assistance of many people who at various moments gave their advice, read drafts, or engaged me in discussion. Unlike the ideas behind some of my other books, the idea underlying this one was my own. However, I would have thrown in the sponge many times had it not been for the consistent support of Andy Marshall, head of the Office of Net Assessment, Department of Defense. Also supportive of my work, and as patient in bearing with my numerous periods of despair, has been Dr. Steve Canby, defense analyst in Washington, D.C.

I have had the usual numerous splendid arguments with my good friends, Stephen Glick, Seth Carus, and David Thomas, whose expert knowledge and well considered counsel were of greater value than I can ever repay. The same applies to Eado Hecht, Amnon Finkelstein and Lt. Col. (Res.) Moshe Ben David, three students who gave as good as they got. Detailed criticisms and constructive advice in regard to part or all of the study have been offered by Zeev Bonen of Israel Weapon R&D Authority, Gen. (Res.) Franz Uhle Wettler, and Fred Reed; I am grateful to all of them. Finally, thanks are due to my son Eldad, who although young in years often made telling points in discussion, and to my stepchildren Adi and Yoni Lewy who helped create the kind of atmosphere in which research can be conducted and work done. Much of what merit this book may have is due to all of them, whereas its faults are mine alone.

At one stage of its development, the present study was supported by a grant from the Ford Foundation.

LIST OF ACRONYMS

AWACS	Advanced Warning and Control System
BMD	Ballistic Missile Defense
ELINT	Electronic Intelligence
EMP	Electro Magnetic Pulse
ENIAC	Electronic Numerical Integrator and Calculator
FLIR	Forward Looking Infra Red
HUD	Head Up Display
ICBM	Inter Continental Ballistic Missile
MAD	Mutual Assured Destruction
MIRV	Multiple Independent Reentry Vehicles
MOS	Military Occupation Specialty
SALT	Strategic Arms Limitation Talks
SDI	Strategic Defense Initiative
SLBM	Submarine Launched Ballistic Missile
TERCOM	Terrain Contour Matching
WWMCCS	World Wide Military Command and Control System

Introduction

THE PRESENT VOLUME rests on one very simple premise which serves as its starting point, argument, and *raison d'être* rolled into one. It is that war is completely permeated by technology and governed by it. The causes that lead to wars, and the goals for which they are fought; the blows with which campaigns open, and the victories with which they (sometimes) end; the relationship between the armed forces and the societies that they serve; planning, preparation, execution, and evaluation; operations and intelligence and organization and supply; objectives and methods and capabilities and missions; command and leadership and strategy and tactics; even the very conceptual frameworks employed by our brains in order to think about war and its conduct—not one of these is immune to the impact that technology has had and does have and always will have.

In this book, my aim is to present a historical analysis of the role technology has played in the development and transformation of war. Unlike the vast majority of the very numerous works that have been written on the subject, however, the present study will not focus solely on the evolution of weapons and weapon systems and their effect on combat. On the contrary, it assumes that behind military hardware there is hardware in general, and behind that again there is technology as a certain kind of knowhow, as a way of looking at the world and coping with its problems. War is impacted by technology in *all* its forms; with the result

1

that, subject only to the limits of the available space, all will have to be taken into account.

To use a simple analogy, military technology affects warfare like waves spreading from a stone thrown into a pond. The disturbance is strongest at the point of impact; the farther the ripples spread, the weaker and less noticeable they become. And the farther they go, the more likely they are to lose their identity by becoming intermixed with ripples thrown up by other stones or reflected back from the pond's banks. Similarly, weapons and weapon systems make their power felt principally during combat, but war consists of much else besides. Apart from tactics, there are operations, strategy, logistics, intelligence, "C^3" (command, control, communication), and organization, to mention but a few. Naturally, all of these are affected by weapons, but all are also strongly influenced by other kinds of hardware, as well as by technology in its abstract sense. Thus we must begin by taking into account such mundane things as roads, vehicles, communications, timekeepers, and maps, and end by considering the most complex problems of technological management, innovation, and conceptualization.

To emphasize the way in which the study attempts to deal with the whole of technology as it is used in war, rather than dealing with weapons and weapon systems alone, its structure does not follow traditional lines. It is not divided into such chapters as "the age of edged weapons" and "the age of gunpowder." Instead, its organization is intended to reflect the development of technology as a whole. Accordingly, Part I starts slightly before 2000 B.C. and ends around 1500 A.D. Though this period can be subdivided in many ways, it is dominated by a single unifying theme. From Archimedes' pulleys to Leonardo's crank-driven war machines, most technology—and military technology in particular—derived its energy from the muscles of animals and men. Hence I call this era the Age of Tools.

Part II deals with the Age of Machines, beginning in the Renaissance and ending around 1830. Its unifying theme is that technology, with military technology in the van, had now reached the point where a dominant role began to be played by machines deriving their energy from nonorganic sources such as wind, water, and of course gunpowder. As one might expect, such a shift could not take place without important repercussions being felt in the realm of tactics. On the other hand, the impact of firearms on such spheres as strategy, logistics, military organization, and communications was much more limited. Thus, one purpose of this section is to put the so-called gunpowder revolution into its proper perspective.

Part III opens in 1830 and ends in 1945. Its theme is the rise and employment in war of technological systems, pioneered by the railway and the telegraph. Instead of operating on an individual basis as before, machines came to be integrated into complex interacting groups whose parts depended for their functioning—their existence, even—on precise coordination with all the rest. The outstanding characteristic of the age was that technology itself became subject to the phenomenon loosely known as organization, which previously had been applied only to human beings.

Finally, Part IV focuses on the present age, which opened in 1945. Although that year marked the dropping of the first atomic bomb, in retrospect the advent of cybernetics and feedback seems to be even more important. Hence this section opens by examining automated war—war waged with the aid of machines that are not only linked to each other in systems, but are capable, within limits, of themselves detecting changes in their environment and of reacting to those changes.

Of course, the framework outlined here is arbitrary to some extent. For one thing, considerable overlap exists. At sea, even more than on land, machines deriving their energy from nonorganic sources—such as wind and water—were in widespread use long before 1500 A.D., and possibly even before 2000 B.C. And though the invention of firearms justifies the name given to the period between 1500 and 1830, animate sources of power in the form of horses did not disappear but continued to play a very important role that lasted well into the twentieth century. Similarly, the development of automation is not limited to the last four decades. Rather, it dates back at least as far as the famous centrifugal device designed by James Watt to regulate the speed of his steam engine. Finally, all military-technological developments did not proceed at the same pace, and the periods of military and nonmilitary technological history did not necessarily coincide.

However, in other ways our scheme has much in its favor. By and large, Part I may be identified with the period in which the most important raw material used for the construction of technological devices, including many military-technological devices, was wood, and when technological progress was so slow that many of the devices in use at the beginning had hardly changed in the end. During the period discussed in Part II, the process of innovation accelerated, and metal tended to replace wood as a raw material for military technology in particular. The third period witnessed the institutionalization of innovation and, in regard to raw materials, a shift to steel. Finally, the decades examined in Part IV have been marked by a still-accelerating trend away from steel towards sophisticated alloys, ceramics, and other synthetic materials. Thus, on the whole the system of classification here adopted is probably as good as any that may be found. In any case, the organization offered here is not intended to put history into a straitjacket but simply to provide a framework for thought.

Each part of the book, in turn, consists of five chapters. Proceeding more or less in chronological order, each of the first four chapters in each part studies the impact of technology on one aspect of warfare: field warfare, siege warfare, the infrastructure of war, naval warfare, and others. The fifth chapter in each part, however, deals with one selected theme that does not fit into this chronological sequence. The four themes chosen for investigation are, in order of their appearance, irrational or disfunctional technology, the rise of professionalism, the invention of invention, and real—as opposed to make-believe—war. Taken as a whole, the book is therefore arranged around a combination of chronological and thematic principles.

The definition of technology itself raises problems when applied, sometimes within the space of a single paragraph, to civilizations as different from each other as ancient Rome and pre-Columbian Peru, medieval China and the present-day United States. Whether Technology with a capital t exists at all, or whether there are as many different technologies as there are places and times, is a question that must be answered. The answer is affirmative in so far as there have probably never been humans who did not produce and use certain implements to serve certain purposes and do certain kinds of work. Yet one must recognize that technical implements ranging from a simple shell to the most sophisticated supercomputers have but little in common; and that even identical implements are capable of being understood and used in entirely different ways in the hands of different societies.

As an extreme example, consider the problem of "irrational" technology. These are devices that do not derive their usefulness from the "work" that they do, nor do they "operate" on the basis of the laws of nature. Though irrational technology appears strange to the modern mind, it did not appear extraordinary to the Greeks who coined the original term. The Greeks believed that all crafts were invented in heaven and taught to men by the gods. The word *techne* itself, far from standing simply for the rational transformation of "scientific knowledge"—which, of course, did not exist in that form—into practical capabilities, carried overtones that were partly theological and partly magical in origin. Accordingly, not only is Greek mythology full of accounts of automatons that worked of their own accord, but such devices were built and displayed in temples where their movements were regarded as proof of the god's presence. The secularization of classical civilization during Hellenistic times caused such "irrational" overtones to weaken, but they were never entirely discarded. To return to the question of definitions, this book will assume that there is a kind of Technology equally applicable to all times and places, Technology in the abstract, but that in practice many different technologies exist.

At this point a warning may be justified. Undoubtedly, we are justified in thinking of our own age as a technological one *par excellence*. This is not only because modern technology governs our life to a great extent—after all, the impact of horses and chariots on society can be as great as that of motor cars and tanks—but also because rapid technological change has caused our minds to become preoccupied with the benefits that it may bring and the harm that it may do. Hence, there is a danger of projecting our obsession with technology backward into history and to assume that, just because something appears to be true today, it always has been true and will be true and must be true.

There are precedents to illustrate the dangers of such an approach. Observing the states of his time struggling for mastery, Hegel concluded that states had always constituted the supreme human creation. Watching contemporary society divided into oppressors and oppressed, Marx and Engels deducted that all history was nothing but a class struggle. Nor is the same phenomenon unknown in our field. Scarcely had the German Chief of Staff Schlieffen decided that a flank attack across Belgium was the only way for Germany to win World War I before he projected that principle backward into history from the battle of Cannae on, often doing violence to the facts. And Basil Liddell Hart, having made up his mind that World War I should have been fought by the indirect approach, lost no time in proclaiming that approach to have been the single principle behind all victories won by all commanders in all past wars; not surprisingly, in successive editions of his work, he was forced to expand his definition of the concept until it became virtually meaningless.

Since it is imperative that history be approached from *some* point of view, to a certain extent this kind of thing is inevitable; but only to a certain extent. It would be a mistake to think that, because present-day society is often obsessed with the impact of technology on every aspect (including the military aspect) of its life, this obsession has always been shared by all people everywhere. It would be erroneous to believe that, just because technology represents a very good starting point for thinking about war, it therefore represents the only or even the best starting point. Merely because technology plays a very important part in war, it does not follow that it alone can dictate the conduct of a war or lead to victory. Seeking truth, we must always begin by trying to recognize the limitations of our labor, or else serious misunderstandings will certainly result and thought itself may become impossible.

A final word about the purpose of this work. By far the most important insight it is possible to gather from knowing and understanding the past is that what is should not be construed as what has always been, nor as what necessarily must be, nor as what can be. In comparison to the ability to leap over one's own shadow, as it were, any other benefits that history may bring must take second place; nevertheless there are many lessons, explicit as well as implicit, buried in the pages that follow. Finally, may this work excite the interest, and arouse the pleasure, of the reader; in this age, when so much is read and written solely for its "information content," this surely is not an unworthy goal.

PART I
The Age of Tools, from Earliest Times to 1500 A.D.

CHAPTER 1

Field Warfare

WHEN AND WHERE did technology begin? Our knowledge of any period before the invention of writing derives almost exclusively from archeological remains, and it is indeed precisely for this reason that such periods are known under the name of prehistory. To serve as the foundation of our knowledge about prehistory, tools and implements had to be made of materials sufficiently durable to survive for hundreds of thousands if not millions of years. Since the most important material that can meet this requirement is stone, prehistory is commonly divided into the three Stone Ages—the paleolithic, the mesolithic, and the neolithic. Had there been, during these ages, any civilizations based mainly on tools made of materials other than stone—wood, say, or horn or bone— then in all probability we would have remained more or less ignorant of the fact.

Whatever the exact nature of the earliest tools, clearly they must have been made of natural materials, easily located in man's immediate environment and requiring no more than a few comparatively simple operations to perform useful service. Almost certainly, the technology based upon these materials was initially unspecialized for either military or nonmilitary purposes, if indeed one may apply these terms to a period when organized warfare as we understand it may itself have been unknown. A stone hand-ax must have been equally useful for chopping food and for breaking an enemy's head when occasion arose. Similarly a sharp flint blade could have served equally well for carving up a piece of meat and for settling a score with one's neighbor. If the customs of stone-age peoples who have survived into the present world constitute any guide, then activities such as warfare, the pursuit of personal quarrels, hunting, and even certain kinds of ceremony and sport overlapped, with the result that the tools employed in one for the most part also served in each of the others.

The history of technology is, nevertheless, in part the development of growing specialization. Even in prehistoric times, there must have been the recognition that some tools were more suited for some purposes than for others. It is thought that, after spending a long time as a gatherer, man gradually added hunting to his activities, and it would not be unreasonable to suppose that the tools employed for this purpose—harpoons, javelins and spears of the kind still employed by primitive peoples—were sometimes directed against his fellowmen in a more or less organized manner. We need not consider whether it was warfare that gave rise to weapons or, as is sometimes asserted, weapons that were responsible for the emergence of warfare. The two probably evolved together, each one driving the other and in turn being driven by it. Limiting our attention to historical periods only, even the earliest civilizations such as are described in the Bible or in the Epic of Gilgamesh already possessed some tools that were specialized for war: weapons.

Around the year 2,500 B.C., the great Chinese, Indian, Sumerian, and Egyptian civilizations all possessed a great variety of tools, made of naturally-occurring materials, which provided the foundation of their material life. These tools for the most part were hand-held; however, pictures in Egyptian tombs also reveal important exceptions to this rule. The sledge, consisting of parallel wooden beams permanently joined at a fixed distance from each other so as to carry some heavy load, had already been invented. So had the wheel in its earliest form—namely that of rollers put between a load and the ground. Together, these inventions represented an enormous technological advance, not only because they themselves could support much heavier loads than could human backs and shoulders, but above all because they both demanded and made possible teamwork on a large scale. Organization, which very quickly grew to truly monstrous dimensions, was added to hardware and put to work in a purposeful way. As the construction of the Egyptian pyramids demonstrates, the amounts of energy that organization could make available were entirely unprecedented, indeed almost unlimited, compared to anything that went before.

Though it was surrounded by rituals and ideas about magic that would have appeared strange to our modern notions of rationality, surviving evidence in the form of weapons, drawings, and literary texts shows that organized warfare was already quite familiar to every one of the above four civilizations. Certainly there is no reason to think that military organization lagged behind its nonmilitary counterpart. Indeed, to judge by later periods in which armies often served as models for civilian institutions, the reverse may well have been the case. Though obviously not all the technologies available were suitable for military purposes, the conduct of war demanded many different tools, some of which were unique to it whereas others were also employed in other tasks. Apart from stone, the main materials in use were of vegetable or animal origin, such as wood and wickerwork for spear-shafts and shields, hides and sinews for slings, body-cover, and the like. However, it was during this period that metal in the form of copper and bronze was being introduced in the most advanced centers. Unlike stone, wood, and materials of animal origin, neither copper nor the other constituent of bronze, tin, could be found everywhere. This, plus the fact that working them into serviceable form required comparatively complex processes, caused copper and bronze to remain expensive for a long time. Initially only those implements which were considered most important for life were made of metal, weapons being among the earliest. Thus, they literally represented the cutting edge of contemporary material civilization.

By far the most important, and for a long period the only, source of energy employed in technology (apart from fire) was man himself. Muscle was applied to material in order to do work, which is why we can speak of the Age of Tools. The idea that technology might acquire its energy from sources other than man's body almost certainly could not have occurred before the neolithic revolution of perhaps 10,000 years ago, the period in which animals were first domesticated. Even then, it would seem that millenia elapsed from the moment in which the first animal was made to keep watch or yield milk or carry a burden to the time it was harnessed to a piece of hardware. Again, the inherent limitations of archeological method prevent us from saying exactly when this took place. It is possible, however, that the first use of animal-powered technology only occurred during the first half of the third millenium B.C. when the oxcart, a clumsy wooden contraption with heavy solid wheels forming an integral part of the axis, was apparently invented in Sumer. Unlike the sledge and rollers, which in principle could be harnessed to teams of men numbering in the hundreds and even thousands, the energy that could be applied to oxcarts was strictly limited. On the other hand, the oxcart unlike men could be used to carry heavy burdens, including presumably military burdens, over comparatively long distances measured in dozens, possibly even hundreds, of kilometers. Still, by no stretch of the imagination could the oxcart be regarded as a weapon of war. For this it was far too slow, cumbersome, and vulnerable.

Some time around 1800 B.C., the next great step forward was taken and the light chariot was invented. Drawn first by asses and then by horses—access to which now became a military factor of great importance, as it was to remain for thousands of years to come—the chariot represented an immense technological advance over the oxcart. What with its spoked, hubbed wheels turning around a fixed axle, its lightness, maneuverability, and strength, it constituted a finely balanced instrument that gave its possessors a measure of mobility unattainable by any other means. A relatively complicated piece of hardware, the chariot was difficult to make, requiring specialized craftsmen whose services could only be had at a price. Consequently, chariots were expensive to own and maintain, and tended to be confined to certain segments of the population. Where ownership was private, the introduction of chariots gave rise to warrior aristocracies and, often enough, to something akin to a feudal class like the one described, anachronistically, by Homer. Where ownership was public, as in the New Egyptian Kingdom, it helped in the establishment and maintenance of a strong centralized government.

Endowing its possessors with very great mobility, especially tactical as opposed to strategic mobility, the appearance of the chariot in itself would have sufficed to revolutionize combat. In fact, however, it was not so much the chariot on its own as its combination with the bow which proved decisive. The simple wooden bow was a very old weapon which showed some important affinities with "civilian" devices used for kindling fire and for boring holes as well as with certain musical instruments. Its emergence as a specialized tool took place at some unknown time and place, and for millenia it was employed for hunting as well as for war. It so happened, however, that the rise of the chariot was soon followed by—if indeed it did not coincide with—the invention of the composite reflex bow, a very different weapon. Made of wood, sinew, and horn glued together, with each material carefully coordinated with all the others so as to yield the optimum combination of strength and flexibility, the composite bow represented as great an advance over its simple predecessor as did the breech-loading rifle over the muzzle-loading flintlock musket. Capable of firing arrows rapidly to an effective range of 200–300 yards, its power and effectiveness remained unsurpassed for several thousand years.

Regardless of whether it was the simple or the composite bow that was employed, the introduction of the chariot led to revolutionary tactical changes. Descriptions, verbal as well as pictorial, from ancient Sumer, Egypt, and Vedic India show that warfare previously had been conducted by men on foot. Their principal armament consisted of thrusting, stabbing, or slashing weapons, which for the most part demanded that the troops be packed into dense, comparatively unwieldy, blocks so as to provide mutual cover and maximize their staying power. Provided only that the terrain was open and flat, the introduction of the arrow-shooting chariot put such formations on the horns of a dilemma, compelling them to carry out two contradictory movements at once. If the infantry stayed together they would come under long-distance fire to which they had no counter, and for which, moreover, they represented an ideal target. If, on the other hand, they took the opposite course and dispersed, they would easily be overrun.

Given such a military advantage, the expansion of the chariot-riding peoples was explosive. From their point of origin in the steppes of southern central Asia, they set out in all directions. Wherever they arrived, they defeated the natives, who were driven into forest and mountain regions where the chariots could not reach. It took no more than a few centuries for Northern India, Egypt, Asia Minor, and Europe to be overrun and conquered. Thus, at this early stage in its development, technology already represented an important factor, since it was capable of determining what armed forces could do and the way in which they did things. Too, technological superiority could make a decisive contribution to victory even when the technology itself was not markedly sophisticated.

Towards the end of the second millenium B.C., the discovery

of iron-smelting in what is today northeastern Anatolia gave the peoples who first mastered it a temporary military superiority. Contrasting sharply with deposits of tin, iron ore deposits are widely spread, so that access to them was relatively easy. On the other hand, extracting the metal demanded higher temperatures, hence a more sophisticated and expensive technology than did the extraction of either copper or bronze. In other respects, the appearance of iron represented an evolutionary rather than a revolutionary development. Though the new metal was useful because it was harder than the materials that it replaced and because it could be honed into a finer, longer-lasting edge, in itself it did not give rise to new kinds of weapons, let alone new sources of energy. Rather, daggers, swords, javelins, spears, and even chariots such as the ones mentioned in the Biblical Book of Judges now came to be made wholly or in part of the new material, as indeed were many implements in civilian life. Once again, the cost of iron was an important factor. If people bore the expense of using it, then the implements in question must have been considered critical to life.

Overlapping the period in which the use of metal was introduced, we find the beginning of the age of written records, or history proper. While the development of literacy was by no means linear—it even appears that there may have been places in which the art of writing was first developed, then lost, then rediscovered— by and large it led to more and more records being kept, and, in so far as some of these records have been preserved, to an enormous increase in our knowledge. As we progress in time, both military and nonmilitary technology on the whole tend to stand forth in greater and greater detail.

By 600 B.C., at the very latest, the most important weapons which in their endless combinations were destined to dominate warfare during the next two millenia had been invented and were in widespread use. Whatever the culture we look to—in Europe, the Middle East, Southeast or East Asia—we find ourselves confronted with a broadly similar array of weapons, a fact which indeed is not surprising since, after all, they were all based upon broadly similar raw materials and employed roughly the same sources of energy. Although some of the most highly developed peoples, such as the Persians, and some of the most primitive ones, such as the Britons, clung to the chariot until 300 B.C. and 50 A.D. respectively, on the whole it was on its way out. As a means of attaining battlefield mobility, it was replaced by cavalry in the form of horses and, in certain geographical areas, camels. Cavalry was more economical in manpower than chariots, since the same man could ride and fight at the same time. It was also more mobile, hence to some extent able to overcome the greatest drawback of chariots, namely their total inability to operate in anything but the most suitable terrain.

Throughout the Old World, the most advanced defensive devices carried by both horsemen and foot soldiers were now made wholly or partly of metal, even though leather, quilt, wood, and even wickerwork continued in widespread use as inexpensive substitutes. Out of these materials were made body armor, shields, helmets, greaves, etc., manufactured in an enormous variety of types and shapes and often decorated in outrageous forms in order to terrify the enemy. Battlefield offensive weapons were similarly limited. They consisted almost exclusively of the mace, ax, dagger, sword, spear, pike, lance, javelin, and dart, each of them again produced in an almost infinite variety of forms and reflecting not only different tactical requirements but also cultural traditions of every sort.

For long-range work all these cultures were limited to the sling and, increasingly, to the various kinds of bow, ranging from the simple through the composite to the crossbow. Around the time of Christ, the last-named device seems to have been familiar both in China and the Greco-Roman world, although in the latter it seems to have been lost and had to be reinvented in the Middle Ages. Some of the weapons could be used both by foot soldiers and by cavalry, whereas others were limited to foot soldiers only. All of them were already specialized for war and were clearly differentiated from nonmilitary implements, although obviously in many cases considerable areas of overlap existed.

Although the array of weapons available was thus relatively modest, the number and variety of different styles of warfare that they made possible was truly astonishing. As circumstances differed greatly from one place to another, a tendency towards regional and national specialization soon appeared. A single dominant military technology, such as has characterized the modern world since about 1500, did not emerge, though clearly some combinations were more effective than others. Around 500 B.C., Cretans, Greeks, Romans, Gauls, Nubians, Egyptians, Persians, Indians, Chinese, to mention but a few, each had their own favorite weapons and hence a distinct way of fighting battles. Almost two millenia later, the same still applied to peoples such as the Chinese, Mamluks, Byzantines, and West Europeans, some of whom showed further sharp regional differences. While this lack of uniformity was partly the outcome of difficult long-distance communications, clearly this was not the only factor involved. Even where daily communications did exist, as for example between Christians and Moslems in medieval Spain, the normal result was not the triumph of one style over another but the appearance of fresh and even more complex combinations. This was what happened, for example, when the Greeks began employing cavalry, light infantry, and archers to support their hoplites after about 400 B.C., and also when the Persian kings started incorporating Greek mercenaries with their distinctive armaments into their forces.

The Eurasian continent as a whole could be divided into three huge divisions—eastern, central, and western. During the age broadly known as antiquity, and indeed ever since, the most advanced sedentary peoples were located along the littoral of this mass where the combination of large rivers with a semi-arid climate both demanded and permitted the establishment of strongly governed "hydraulic" civilizations. Where there were rivers there was water transport. Where water transport existed, it was possible to engage in exchange and commerce on a massive scale, and also to build the first cities. China on the one hand, and the Mediterranean world on the other, took to foot warfare and the heavy metal-made arms and armor that it demanded, cavalry being regarded as an auxilliary arm though often an important, even decisive, one. In the center, however, where rivers were comparatively few, the spaces immense and terrain often open, a more nomadic style of life prevailed for centuries after it had turned into a marginal form of existence elsewhere. Such a lifestyle being incompatible with sophisticated, hence heavy, technology, the superiority of the horse-and-composite-bow combination was such that it has lasted until comparatively recent times. Although violent shifts in the borders between the three areas could and did take place in both directions, on the whole the division between them remained remarkably stable, itself an indication that no single military technology was capable of attaining absolute dominance. Thus, whenever the Romans had to operate in the open desert or in forests, they found that there were limits to their power, limits that went far to govern the extent of their empire. Conversely, attacks by nomads on densely populated, urban civilizations were for the most part confined to border raids.

To focus on the Mediterranean world, ancient field-warfare as described by Xenophon, Polybius, Julius Caesar, Josephus, or Ammianus Marcelinus, was a complex affair making use of many different arms and weapons. In both Greece and Rome the core of the army was formed by heavy infantry protected by metal body armor, helmets, and shields. The Greek phalangists' principal offensive weapon was the spear or the pike, the sword playing no more than an auxilliary role. What made the Roman legionaries so effective, however, was their reliance on a *combination* of javelins and swords. This put the enemy in an almost impossible position, since it made it equally dangerous to close the ranks or open them. At the beginning of their development, both types of formations—the phalanx and the legion—appear to have fought largely on their own. Later they came to be supported by auxilliaries that either were drawn from the lower socio-economic classes or belonged to allied nationalities. Grouped into their own units, these auxilliaries were armed with a variety of long-distance weapons such as bows, slings, and sometimes darts. Both light and heavy cavalry were employed to achieve tactical mobility, the heavy cavalry often covered with scale armor and armed with swords and lances. Beginning in the fourth century B.C. field warfare also made limited use of mechanical engines.

Occasionally during this period in history, one side or another was able to introduce a new device to which the other side had no reply. On the whole, however, such advanced Mediterranean peoples as the Greeks, the Romans, and the Carthaginians attained very similar technological levels. The complexity of much ancient combat meant that victory was less a question of obtaining superiority in any single weapon than of coordinating the various technologies in such a way as to mask their respective weaknesses and bring out their respective strengths. This, in turn, required a properly articulated organization as well as commanders who understood their business. Over time, this worked in favor of the more varied, complex, flexible technologies which prevailed over simple, more homogeneous ones. One good example is provided by the Macedonian armies, with their combination of phalangists and peltasts and heavy and light cavalry beating their Greek opponents. Subsequently the Roman legions, with their joint use of shock and fire, were able to defeat the simpler shock-oriented Hellenistic forces.

The balance between infantry and cavalry in the Mediterranean began to change in the fourth century A.D., the battle of Adrianople (378) forming a clear turning point. By the time of Justinian and Belisarius, around the middle of the sixth century, the principal strength of the Byzantine army had come to consist of its horse archers employing their typical hit and run, "swarming" tactics. Two and a half centuries later, even peoples such as the Franks, who had previously fought exclusively on foot, had taken to horse and turned into cavalrymen, although of a different type. We do not know the exact stages by which cavalry managed to win its dominance over foot soldiers. Undoubtedly many different factors were involved, technology being but one of them. Modern authors, however much they may differ in detail, are united in their opinion that, sometime between 500 and 1000 A.D., the stirrup and the high saddle—both of them originating in the peoples of the steppes and neither of them representing military technology, properly speaking—spread to Europe. Add the horseshoe, the origin of which is simply unknown, and the ascent of cavalry over the ancient infantry becomes at least understandable.

As the term "the age of chivalry" suggests, the high Middle Ages in Europe—and, for that matter, in the Middle East—were dominated by the horse to an extent unprecedented before or since. The population was divided into two classes, those who fought on horseback and those who did not. Horsemen constituted society while the rest counted for nothing, a fact well reflected in chess sets of the period where king, queen, bishop, and other major pieces have finely carved forms, but the pawns are represented by faceless stones. In Western Europe the horseman's principal weapon was the lance. Until about 1050 A.D. it was apparently waved overhead or held underhand, but later it grew longer and heavier and began to be couched under the arm. In the Middle East the most important weapon was the composite bow, which had attained its highest perfection and had indeed come to form the centerpiece of an entire science of archery. In both places, the training of horse-warriors started early and lasted a lifetime. However, much of the preparation consisted not of military training proper but rather of spiritual exercises designed to inculcate the cultural, religious, and social code that was chivalry, known in Arabic as *farsia*. In both cultures the superiority of the man on horseback over foot soldiers, particularly individual foot soldiers, was crushing to the point that warfare, properly speaking, took place mainly between knights. Everything else was regarded more in the nature of rebellion, police work, and butchery, and hence subjected to an entirely different set of rules. During the Crusades, as well as in Spain, the Christian and Moslem systems came into contact and clashed. The outcome was not the same in both places; so to claim that one of them was "technologically superior" would be absurd, the more so since we are dealing with an 800-year period lasting from 711 to 1492 A.D. during which an infinite number of shifts and changes occurred.

These considerations notwithstanding, the role of cavalry on the medieval battlefield, especially in Western Europe, has often been exaggerated. The horses themselves, as well as the armor worn by their riders (whether consisting of scale or mail or plate), were very expensive; hence they were limited to a fraction of the forces. Furthermore, there were certain things that horsemen could not do under almost any circumstances, such as engaging in siege warfare, or standing fast and holding terrain. For these and other reasons, battles from which infantry was completely absent were comparatively rare. Sometimes the knights themselves dismounted and fought on foot, a good example being Poitiers in 1356. On other occasions the infantry consisted of a motley array of peasants and town dwellers armed with a variety of make-shift weapons and even with agricultural implements. The infantry was able to play a dominant role, however, when properly organized and armed with the longbow, the pike, or (in the case of the Swiss) some combination of shock and missile weapons.

As in the case of ancient warfare, it is difficult to point to any important battle where victory was due solely or even principally to the clear cut effect of a superior weapon. Rather, the most successful armies were often those that combined perfectly ordinary infantry and cavalry weapons in such a way as to make the best possible use of both. It was a question of putting the enemy into the kind of contradictory situation where he was damned if he did and damned if he did not. Excellent illustrations of this principle are provided by those great warriors, William the Conqueror at Hastings, and Richard Coeur de Lion at Arsouf.

Apart from the rise of cavalry, at least partly due to technological factors, the transition from the ancient world to the Middle Ages also brought other changes. The Chinese after about 800 A.D., and the West Europeans after about 1300, began to manufacture steel in blast ovens. The product was much superior to that of the Romans both in quality and quantity, enabling far better weapons and armor to be made. During the eleventh century the crossbow was reinvented in the West. Although its power was increased by the substitution of a steel spring for one made of wood, horn, and sinew, and also by the addition of a winch for cocking, it was slow to load. But this disadvantage apart, it was a murderous weapon, more powerful than anything known to the ancients, and attempts were made to have it banned and declared fit for use only against heathens. Cheaper and better iron also permitted the replacement of mail armor by plate, culminating in the highly artistic, extremely expensive, suits produced in Germany and Italy between about 1450 and 1520. In spite of these and other examples of the rise in the importance of metal as a raw material for military purposes, wood and other organic substances remained essential. When it came to a clash, they were not necessarily inferior.

Despite the numerous and complicated developments described here, it is possible to argue that the technological changes introduced into field combat during the two millenia from about 500 B.C. to 1500 A.D. were frequently minimal. When everything is said and done, a sword remained a sword, a lance a lance, and a shield—a shield. A leather-clad Greek bowman of Homer's day may not have been easily distinguishable from a Norman in the eleventh century or, for that matter, from an English bowman in the fourteenth or the fifteenth. Though they may not have had stirrups, Persian and Byzantine horsemen around 500 A.D. strongly resembled medieval knights in that they wore armor (hence their name, cataphracts), and wielded a lance as their principal weapon. As if to illustrate the point, when Alexander the Great first crossed into Asia Minor he was presented with a suit of armor guaranteed to be of Trojan War vintage. He then actually wore this 900-year-old contraption in battle, until it became so battered that a replacement became necessary.

By the end of the Middle Ages, it is true, certain weapons had become obsolete and had all but dropped out of use. They included the spear (which was replaced by the heavier lance and pike), the battle-ax (likewise replaced by its larger counterpart, the halberd), the javelin, and the sling. However, such was the nature of the age that not even the disappearance of certain devices and their replacement by others necessarily constituted a sign of sustained technological progress of the type associated with the Industrial Revolution. This is demonstrated by the persistence into the 1400s of some extremely primitive weapons, like the mace, whose origins reach back into the earliest civilizations. Moreover, regression sometimes occurred. Knowledge of some technologically sophisticated weapon was lost, as in the case of the crossbow, and—an even more famous instance—Greek fire.

Thus, the period on the whole was marked not so much by the invention of altogether new weapons as by endless alterations and combinations of existing ones. As is to be expected, similarities in weapons often led to marked similarities in tactics. To take an extreme case, there is no indication that Saracen warfare as observed by the Crusaders around 1200 A.D. differed greatly from that practiced by Rome's Parthian enemies at Carrhae in 53 B.C. Moreover, there were strong resemblances between the Macedonian style of war in 300 B.C. and the Swiss style in 1400 A.D., as there were between Roman legionaries under Julius Caesar and Spanish sword-and-buckler men under Gonsalvo de Córdoba. Contemporaries, of course, were aware of these similarities. To them, they frequently meant that all history was contemporary history, freely to be culled for inspiration, examples, and even for outright models to copy. Thus, throughout the Middle Ages, the Roman military textbook of Vegetius was used as a handbook for commanders, Richard Coeur de Lion and his rival Philip Augustus being among its most prominent readers. Even more significant, sixteenth- and seventeenth-century commanders such as Machiavelli, Maurice of Nassau, and Gustavus Adolphus consciously sought to profit from the lessons of earlier armies, even to the point of directly imitating weapons and formations and tactics. So limited was military-technological progress that it was a matter of some doubt among early modern European experts whether "modern" armies could have stood up in a trial of strength against the best ancient ones. When the Chevalier de Folard published what was to become one of the most influential tactical treatises of the century in 1729, he cast it in the form of a commentary on Polybius. The perfection of firearms, and the subsequent dominance of the machine over the battlefield, finally caused all these older devices to be relegated to the scrap heap around the time of the War of the Austrian Succession. These developments, in their turn, contributed to the invention of military history as we now understand the term.

The essential unity of the period under consideration is also the result of the equality of maximum energy that could be utilized by all peoples. So long as the range of weapons is limited, everything pertaining to field warfare must necessarily be mobile. That meant that some forms of technology and large-scale organization, of the kind that was applied to civilian construction as well as to fortification, could not be employed on the battlefield. True, the chariot may be understood as an attempt to maximize the energy of horses, just as the phalanx represented an attempt to maximize that of men. Both devices were successful at first but, as massed power resulted in unwieldiness, they ultimately became self-defeating. Packing men into masses—such as the Greek phalanx, the Roman wedge, and similar formations employed by the early Germans—or using animals in teams, was a simple expedient equally available to virtually all peoples, whatever their relative degree of economic and material development as represented by the amount of horsepower available to them on a per capita basis. Thus, when it came to taking the field and fighting a battle, the maximum energy that could be usefully brought to bear was about equal. This was true regardless of the technological level that may have been reached in other fields, such as building, writing, or agriculture.

If this line of reasoning is valid, then it endows the period under consideration with yet another kind of unity. It helps explain how the Hyksos—the "shepherd-kings" whose material civilization was so primitive that we know hardly anything about them—were able to bring down the Egyptian Middle Kingdom; how, perhaps 300 years later, tabernacle-dwelling Hebrews employing trumpets as their weapon could vanquish the technologically much superior, urban-living, Canaanites; how Germans and Huns, the latter so primitive that they are reported to have eaten meat uncooked, could bring down the Roman Empire; and how, as late as the thirteenth century, the tent-dwelling Mongols could conquer China on one end of the Eurasian continent and come within a hair of overrunning Europe on the other. In all these cases, the decisive factor was mobility. Its importance while on campaign and during battle was such that the advantage of the "civilized" peoples over "uncivilized" ones was seldom decisive, never to be taken for granted. It lies in the nature of things, however, that nomadic tribes were unable to compete with sedentary civilizations when it came to siege warfare and fortification.

CHAPTER 2

Siege Warfare

THOUGH IT DIFFERS sharply from field warfare, fortress warfare and its technological foundations also dates back to neolithic times. However, so much has been written about the history of fortification, the process by which the earliest mud walls and palisades developed into the lofty and complicated stone structures dotting the countryside during the later Middle Ages, that not even a brief recapitulation appears in place here. Rather than retrace, we will bypass that evolution and focus on the things that all or most fortresses before 1500 A.D. had in common.

From time immemorial, fortifications have always fallen into three different types, here discussed in order of increasing strength and ability to resist assault. Of these the most elementary is represented by field fortifications, which may be defined as obstacles erected shortly before a battle and intended for temporary use while it is going on. Originally such fortifications may have been derived from hunting, where various devices were used since prehistoric times to trap animals and to limit their movements. Accordingly, these fortifications frequently took the form of pits or ditches. Sometimes, however, more sophisticated devices were employed. Stakes, either simple or joined together crosswise into *cheveaux de frise*, represent a very ancient invention. So does the caltrop, a contraption made out of four iron spikes joined to each other in such a way as to form a tetrahedron. Numerous devices of this kind were strewn on the ground, in the hope that the enemy's horses might step on them and become disabled.

25

Last but not least, temporary wooden fortifications were also developed at an early date. When the Normans landed in England in 1066, the first thing they did was to unload a prefabricated wooden tower and erect it on the beach.

While many of these devices were technically quite primitive, this should not be taken as proof of ineffectiveness. On the contrary, at the right time and place, field fortifications however simple could present a formidable obstacle, since they forced the enemy to divide his attention between dealing with them and protecting himself. Consequently they helped decide the issue in many engagements, including the famous battles of Crecy (1346), Poitiers (1356), and Agincourt (1415), in each of which the English archers resorted to stakes to protect themselves against the French knights' assault. The effectiveness of field fortifications, incidentally, also helps explain why their development has been so very slow, and why some of the devices in question, though essentially dating back into prehistoric times, have remained in use almost unaltered down to the present day.

Though the erection of field fortifications did not present a technical problem to any people that was even halfway civilized, tactically speaking they were effective only if the enemy could be persuaded to launch himself against them rather than transfer the fight somewhere else. To prevent such an outflanking movement from being made on a strategic scale, it was necessary to resort to fortifications of the second type and erect continuous barriers. Again, the concept of constructing long defensive lines consisting of ditches backed by earthen walls was not in itself very difficult. It did, however, require managerial and organizational skills and resources, and the ability to put thousands and even tens of thousands of men to work in a purposeful, coordinated fashion while simultaneously keeping them fed, clothed, housed, and policed. These were areas in which a number of ancient societies excelled, particularly so-called hydraulic societies that depended for their existence on the large-scale management of waterways in semi-arid regions.

At various times and to varying degrees, the Chinese, Sumerian, Hellenistic, and Roman Empires all invested heavily in the erection of continuous barriers, an art that the Romans in particular are said to have developed to a point which may never have been surpassed before or since. It has been said that the legions during late Republican and Imperial times consisted not so much of heavy infantry as of combat engineers, "Marius' Mules," who in addition to their stakes and saws and pickaxes and shovels and measuring instruments also happened to carry weapons. This equipment, and even more the quality of the organization by which it was put to use, enabled the Romans to carry out remarkable feats such as erecting a legionary camp in a single night or digging a trench right across the heel of Italy in order to contain Hannibal. It was a question of pouring sweat in order to save blood.

Barriers were sometimes built on a truly massive scale so as to protect entire provinces or even countries, as exemplified by the Roman frontier, or *limes,* and the Great Chinese Wall. The remains of such systems, particularly the Great Wall of China, are certainly very impressive. Nevertheless, their size should not mislead us in regard to their nature or cause us to overlook their limitations. In the first place, always and everywhere it was only the largest, politically most centralized, empires which were capable of building fortifications on such a scale, a consideration which does much to put into perspective their importance to the development of warfare. Second, even where lines were established and maintained, the economics of construction were such that military-technological perfection along their entire length was hopelessly beyond reach. Consequently, even the most powerful of the systems we have mentioned were far from impenetrable. In every case, their value was derived not so much from their intrinsic physical strength as from the patrols which guarded them, the signaling apparatus with which they were provided, and the garrisons which were stationed behind them and used to seal off any local penetrations. Even so, in almost every case the people they were designed to keep out—such as the Caledonians, or Germans, or Mongols—were rather backward culturally, which of course also meant that (except when they employed prisoners) their siege technology was undeveloped.

Where siege techniques had reached any real development, however, mere earthen ramps, or even walls made of stone like those constructed by Hadrian across northern England, were certainly insufficient to keep out a determined invader. In such a situation, economic considerations invariably dictated that only individual points, not large areas, could be surrounded by fortifications sufficiently powerful to enable them to be defended for any length of time. This is just the opposite from the situation today, when entire fortified belts may be expected to survive the worst enemy attacks even if individual strongpoints do not. Inevitably, in the period under consideration, the inability to fortify extensive tracts of land led to the erection of a closed ring or, to use the meaningful French term, an *enceinte*, as the dominant type of fortification.

Depending on whether the society in question was monarchical or democratic in character, and urban or rural, *enceintes* might protect citadels (often containing the principal public buildings of a town), entire cities, or individual castles belonging to feudal lords and serving as points of refuge for the surrounding population. One way or another, their existence implies that the relationship between open countryside and human settlement was different from the one to which we have become accustomed during the last few centuries. However great the superiority that an invader enjoyed in the field, and however numerous his victories in battle, a country was not really occupied until its fortresses had been reduced. These fortresses, accordingly, were designed to resist a siege, that is, to deal with a situation in which the surrounding countryside was overrun and one's own forces encircled by the enemy on every side. For this purpose, ring-like defenses, however well built, only represented the first step. What was needed, in addition, was room for supplies of various sorts, as well as a reliable source of water.

The technical problems associated with this kind of fortification are simple enough in principle. During neolithic times, villages were already located in inaccessible areas and surrounded by ditches, palisades, and sometimes by water-barriers which had bridges that were easy to remove. The first town to encircle itself with a complete belt of permanent stone fortifications is thought to have been Jericho around 5000 B.C., though the suggestion has recently been made that the structures in question were intended for flood control. The fortification of cities may have been practiced in Egypt as early as the Old Kingdom, but the interpretation of the evidence is once again uncertain. Be this as it may, fortifications belonging to the period 2500–1500 B.C. have been dug out in Egypt, Sumer, and Palestine. The first really detailed evidence concerning siege warfare dates to the period 1300–1200 B.C., whereas the Assyrian reliefs now at the British Museum show us that, by 850 B.C. at the latest, most of the basic principles of building a fortress were well understood. This included curtain walls with loopholes for shooting arrows, crenelation, parapets, reinforced gates, and towers projecting from the walls and serving to cover the base of curtain walls by interlocking fields of fire.

Lagging behind the eastern civilizations in this as well as in other respects, the Greek *poleis* that started emerging from about 800 B.C. were not fortified. Usually only the akropolis, a lofty hill in the center of town, was surrounded by a wall and served as a place of refuge in case of war. Shortly before 430 B.C., however, the Athenians took the advice of Pericles and constructed the long walls linking their city with the port of Piraeus, thus enabling them to wage a prolonged war in spite of the repeated ravaging of their hinterland. Other cities soon followed suit. A number of building projects on a comparable scale were initiated, with the result that by Hellenistic times at the latest the art of fortification already reveals a grasp of principles probably not surpassed even in the present day. The strongest fortresses, like those of Rhodes or Pergamon, consisted of multiple walls affording mutual cover and incorporated especially constructed vaults for archers, as well as sally ports. They also contained a system of internal communications so as to enable reinforcements to be rushed from one part of the perimeter to another. Self-contained forts within the system were capable of being sealed off from the remainder of the system, rather on the model of damage-control in modern warships; special, often quite elaborate, protection was provided for the weak points presented by gates.

In so far as the early Middle Ages constituted a period of darkness and the art of fortification declined (though many towns seem to have retained their old Roman walls more or less intact), some of these devices may have had to be reinvented from the year 1000 onward. However, apart from the fact that the strongest medieval fortresses consisted of castles rather than of town walls, few if any new elements were added. Medieval castles differed from Greco-Roman towns in that they centered upon massive stone towers, or donjons. These were surrounded by often multiple curtain walls that were provided with the usual covered galleries, buttresses, parapets, crenelation, machicolations, flanking towers, sally ports, protected gates, etc., all of which were in a state of constant development and tended to become more and more elaborate as time went on. Since the area enclosed by the walls of these castles was relatively small, it became practicable to surround many of them with a ditch, and since water was often more abundant in northwestern Europe than it was in the Mediterranean basin, many of these northern ditches could be filled with water either permanently or in preparation for a siege.

However, many medieval castles differed from ancient fortifications surrounding cities in one respect: their function was not only to afford protection and refuge, but also to dominate the surrounding countryside. This meant that, instead of being built in the plains, many of them were set up on the spurs of hills, which of course offered additional protection. From a tactical point of view, however, these were improvements in detail. For our purposes, the important thing to remember is that the basic principles of the *enceinte* and its counterpart, the siege, were everywhere maintained.

For reasons that will become clear in a moment, we do not know when and where the first specialized siege weapons originated. Siege warfare may have been practiced in Sumer as early as the third millenium B.C. Much detailed evidence also comes from Egyptian sources dating to the period 1300–1200 B.C. To judge from the reliefs, the Assyrian army that destroyed the Biblical Kingdom of Israel and came within a hair of doing the same to Judea already possessed quite an array of such siege devices amounting to a regular train. The equipment in use included ropes attached to hooks, crowbars, scaling ladders, rams, siege towers, and mantelets, the latter being a kind of wagon that was armored in front and could be pushed close to the walls so as to afford cover for archers. Mining, too, was practiced.

Unlike the fortifications which they confronted, the principal materials from which all these devices were made, in this as in all subsequent periods until the end of the Middle Ages, were organic, hence perishable. As a result, none has survived intact and our understanding of them depends on pictorial representations and written records. Wood of course represented the most important single material, and was often joined by leather and even wickerwork as a way of affording cover to the personnel. Sometimes iron plates were attached and served as armor for the sides of towers exposed to enemy action. On the whole, however, iron was considered so scarce and expensive as to be employed mainly for the heads of battering rams and also for the nails, rivets, axles, and hinges between moving parts that many of these devices required.

Though the devices described in the previous paragraphs were of course much larger than the weapons carried by individual men, they resembled the weapons in that they, too, were powered by human muscle. It is for this reason that they may be included under the rubric of tools, although admittedly a siege tower several stories high and weighing many tons, such as was employed by commanders from Alexander to King Edward III of England, represented a tool of a rather peculiar type. In the absence of a new energy-source, the price that had to be paid for power was size and unwieldiness. Rams, mantelets, towers and various crane-like devices powered by men and used for lifting troops onto the walls could only be moved with great difficulty, if at all. Hence their deployment often had to be preceded by the construction of massive earthen ramps, a job that might take weeks or months and which the besieged would resist by every means at their disposal.

If the tactical employment of the apparatus comprising a siege train was always problematic, moving it from one town to another was even more so. Some of the devices could travel in a disassembled state in wagons or on the backs of pack animals. Others, however, were so large that they could only be built on the spot, for which purpose it was necessary to have suitable craftsmen, raw materials, and a supply of those parts such as rivets, nails, clamps, etc., that could not be readily manufactured out of local resources. Devices too heavy to be easily moved about were not, of course, useful for field warfare. On the other hand, one suspects that it was precisely for this reason that nomadic peoples such as the Mongols who carried all before them in the open field ran into difficulties when they entered western medieval Europe, an area that was so densely studded with castles that the remainders of over ten thousand are known from France alone.

Although the Bible in the book of Chronicles, Part 2, says that King Uziah of Judea built stone-throwing machines to protect Jerusalem, the contemporary records of other people living in the Mediterranean area do not mention them. It is possible that we are confronted by an anachronism. This assumption is strengthened by the fact that the Greeks did not copy these machines from their eastern neighbors, as they did in the case of so many other devices, but apparently invented them independently. According to the engineer Hero who lived at Alexandria during the second century A.D., the invention was made at Syracuse in Sicily around the year 400 B.C. and may have been connected with the abortive Athenian siege of the town, that had just ended.

Early Greek ballistae are best described simply as oversized cross-bows, although in point of historical fact technological development seems to have proceeded the other way around and derived the smaller weapon from the larger engine. These devices, mounted on wooden stands and cocked by means of a lever or winch, fired heavy arrows to an effective range of perhaps 200 to 300 meters, with some pretense at accuracy, but at a slow rate which normally made them unsuitable for use in field combat. These machines were soon followed by others employing the energy stored in ropes that were twisted into skeins. Cocking was done by a team of men using a pin-and-ratchet mechanism; release was effected by means of a trigger. Aiming could be carried out either by swinging the entire engine around, or—in the case of heavy machines relying upon indirect fire—by perforated washers set at different positions so as to regulate the amount of power employed. Depending on size and the details of construction, either arrows or stones, some weighing as much as sixty pounds, could be thrown to a range of between several dozen and several hundred meters.

Mechanical artillery represented a considerable technological feat, and one which has not been easy to duplicate even today; and it differed from other instruments of war in one critical respect. Since the machines were capable of *storing* energy, the direct link between the power of the shot and that of the human muscles working them was broken. Their performance was, up to a point at any rate, independent of their operators' physical condition and also of whether the crew was brave or cowardly, tired or excited. Their introduction both to siege warfare and the field— where, however, limitations of weight and accuracy and rate of fire always constricted their use—therefore led to the emphasis on technical and professional expertise at the expense of individual heroism. As the derivation of the word "engineer" still reminds us, such expertise also led to the rise of a different type of warrior. "Oh Heracles, the valor of men is at an end," the Spartan king Archidamas is quoted as saying when he encountered the new engines for the first time.

Mechanical artillery reached the peak of its technological development around 200 B.C., when mathematical formulae were devised to relate power with size; it subsequently entered a long period of stagnation. It is even possible that the principles of its construction were forgotten during the early Middle Ages. Be this as it may, in any case, around 1050, both the Christian and the Muslim world had reintroduced the machines into warfare, sometimes on a massive scale running into hundreds of units. Another century and a half, and the trebuchet—a counterweight-operated war engine much more powerful than anything known even to the famous Demetrius Poliorcetes—had joined the ranks of mangonels and catapults and petriers and arbalests (keeping the various types apart constitutes a difficult, and perhaps futile, concern of scholarship) without, however leading to fundamental changes in the nature of siege warfare. This was because mechanical artillery, however well developed, never quite acquired the power to bring down entire walls in the manner subsequently made possible by gunpowder and cannon. Although a lucky hit by a heavy stone might bring down part of a crenelation or machicolation, high trajectory fire was useful mainly as a terror-weapon against the interior of towns and castles. The principal function of flat-trajectory arrows was to drive off the defenders from a section of the wall, thus creating safe areas where escalades could be attempted, towers mounted, and rams and bores put to work. Finally, mechanical artillery could be used for launching incendiaries, live snakes, and dead horses—representing an early form of biological warfare—and the occasional delivery of humans or parts of humans as well.

Although ballistae, catapults, and all the rest are most frequently mentioned in connection with attacks on towns and fortresses, the fact that they were also capable of being employed for defense is often overlooked. Indeed it is far from clear how they were first used. Beginning in the fourth century B.C., the walls of many a Hellenistic town included specially constructed rooms for engines. So, 1500 years later, did those of some medieval castles. Since much the same weapons were used by both sides, a clear technological edge on the side of either the offense or the defense did not emerge. Nor could it have been otherwise, or else the complete dominance of one would necessarily have led to the disappearance of the other. As it was, the development of *enceintes* on the one hand and of siege engines on the other, often seems to have proceeded at the same pace. Such was notoriously the case from 400 to 200 B.C., a period of rapid development for both fortifications and siege techniques; as also in 400–1000 A.D., when there was stagnation, and in some fields probably a decline; and from 1000 to 1300 A.D., when development started afresh, leading to a neck-and-neck race until castles and engines both reached the peak of their development during the first third of the fourteenth century. Capturing a well-built fortress that was also strongly held was never an easy task, nor are there clear signs of its becoming easier during the period considered here.

Since breaching the walls was often difficult, if not impossible, many sieges in both the ancient and medieval worlds ended when one side or another ran out of resources. As will be shown in greater detail later on, during the millenia before the invention of mechanical transport (including also the centuries examined in Part II of this study) simply remaining immobile with a considerable force in front of a besieged town or castle, whose surroundings had been emptied of provisions, represented a considerable military-administrative feat. Often it was as difficult as, or more difficult than, husbanding resources inside, so that sieges degenerated into races as to who, attackers or defenders, could hold out the longest. Even when this did not happen, very often it was factors other than the simple balance between offensive and defensive technologies that decided the issue. Rather, the fall of a fortress was brought about by the discovery of some weak spot such as a water conduit entering a wall or latrines leading out of it. Exploiting such a spot might simply be a question of resourcefulness and daring, or it might involve treachery.

In conclusion, it is important to note the prolonged, uneven, often overlapping and sometimes quite rapid development of fortifications and siege technology during the more than two millenia between 750 B.C. and 1500 A.D. However, these developments should not cause us to lose sight of the fact that the period as a whole forms a single unity. It is clear that field fortification changed little, if at all, during the period in question. Fortified systems covering entire provinces and even countries were sometimes built, but were useful mainly for keeping out nomads who, by virtue of their very style of life, were often unable to develop a powerful siege technology. It is worth bearing in mind, however, that such fortified lines had a great future when *enceintes* finally went out of fashion during the third and fourth ages covered in this book. As to siege warfare itself, in spite of numerous short-term fluctuations that occurred at various times and places, the relative power of siege technology and fortifications remained essentially the same. Given that the strongest fortifications were built everywhere of either stone or brick, and that they were confronted by wooden engines deriving their energy from either human muscle (as in the case of rams, bores, and the like) or else from mechanical contrivances, this may not come as a particular surprise. What is surprising is that so many of these factors remained unaltered well into the age of gunpowder.

CHAPTER 3

The Infrastructure of War

IN THE PERIOD under consideration, as indeed in all others, nonmilitary technologies played a decisive role in shaping warfare in general and strategy in particular. Not weapons and arms alone, but every kind of technique was involved. Nor was the impact onesided. If military capabilities were partly dictated by technology, technology itself grew partly in response to military needs. As always, the two factors interacted, and by so doing pushed development along.

Among the nonmilitary technologies that must be considered in this context, perhaps the most important was writing, which was the first and for a long time almost the only means for storing information and transmitting it accurately from one person to another. Writing from the earliest times has always been closely associated with towns and city life. Where these flourished, literacy was comparatively widespread; where they declined, it tended to disappear. The process, moreover, may also have worked the other way around. If the ability to write served as the foundation for large-scale town life, the decline of the town during the Middle Ages was perhaps aided by the fact that Western Europe was cut off from its Mediterranean sources of papyrus after about 600 A.D.

It is a truism that the large, permanent, centrally directed armies which at various times formed such a prominent feature of the Egyptian, Sumerian, Assyrian, Chinese, Indian, Hellenistic, and Roman Empires, would have been inconceivable without writing.

The invention of writing, and the availability of relatively cheap writing materials, were among the factors which enabled these empires to be established and maintained militarily as well as administratively, politically, and economically. The rulers of the time, well aware of this, took good care to man their chancelleries and staffs with trained scribes, secretaries, and priests.

During the early Middle Ages, literacy tended to be confined almost entirely to ecclesiastical organizations, which consequently also emerged as major technological centers where the most advanced engineering of the period could be found, such as windmills and watermills (and later, the mechanical clock). Without the benefit of widespread writing, early medieval military organizations could not be established along managerial, bureaucratic principles. Instead they had to rely almost entirely on personal ties which, in this period, were all but identical with political ties. The size of armies underwent a drastic decline. Probably no medieval king or prince was able to assemble more than, say, 20,000 men under his banner—and the expression is significant in itself since it illustrates how such simple visual means as pennants and standards came to replace written rosters for the purpose of mobilizing and leading personnel. Furthermore, even these small forces could not normally be sustained for very long, either because feudal law only demanded a certain number of days' service a year, or because of the prevalence of sedition in an army organized on the basis of personal ties, and lacking a centralized economico-administrative basis. Although conditions began to improve from the eleventh century, on the whole these problems continued to bedevil warfare throughout the Middle Ages.

Next in importance to writing, and closely related to it, were the technical means of communication employed by armies, a problem whose critical role in shaping warfare has been neglected by historians until recently. Obviously no army, except a one-man army, can either exist or operate without communications of some sort. It is also a truism that the nature of the means of communication in use will exercise a considerable, perhaps determinant, effect on the behavior of both senders and receivers as well as on the kind of information that may be transmitted. When large bodies of armed men are assembled and expected to act in concert, the part played by communications cannot be overestimated.

Until about 1500 A.D., the role of writing on the battlefield itself was fairly limited, often nonexistent. This posed important problems for tactical communications. In combat, commanders such as Alexander, Hannibal, Julius Caesar, and William the Conqueror did not control their troops by means of written messages. Indeed, during most of the time Alexander and William—though not Hannibal and Caesar—were probably too busy fighting for their own lives to pass along messages of any kind. The normal method of battlefield communication consisted of using messengers traveling either on horseback or on foot. Surprisingly, though, the idea that this task required a specially organized body of men permanently at the commander's disposal did not commend itself to all armies and failed to gain universal acceptance. Messengers were relatively slow and sometimes unreliable. Their principal strength—the ability to answer questions and interpret the messages they carried—could also constitute a source of weakness in so far as it might give rise to errors and misunderstandings. In addition, their progress could be, and frequently was, interrupted by enemy action. Messengers, in short, were usually indispensable, but they could not act as the sole means of communication.

To supplement messengers, armies in combat employed other means, both acoustical and visual. Acoustical signals were given by horns, trumpets, bugles and, in China, gongs, cymbals, and bells. Visual signals included standards (sometimes simply a coat hung upon a pole and waved about), flags, shields polished to act as mirrors, smoke, and fire. As compared to messengers, these means enjoyed the advantage that the transmission of information was almost instantaneous. On the other hand, and even though they were often employed in combination, the contents of the information that could be transmitted was strictly limited, since it could never consist of more than a relative handful of prearranged signals. Also, unless proper arrangements were made, a real risk existed that they would go unheard or unseen amidst the stress and confusion of battle.

When the various acoustical and visuals signals were combined into a properly integrated system, as in the case of the well-trained Chinese and Roman armies, their use permitted flexible tactics and freedom of action for the commander. When this was not the case, however, their limitations were such as to make the exercise of effective tactical command almost impossible. In such a situation one of two solutions was usually adopted. Either the troops were massed into a solid block, or phalanx, and sent hurtling forward into the enemy, or else each man and sub-unit fought more or less on his own. Either way, the commander after he had given the signal for the battle to begin would be left with nothing to do, with the result that he would pick up his shield or mount his horse and join in the fray. Sometimes, too, a compromise solution was adopted. Unable to command the army as a whole but unwilling to relinquish all tactical control, generals put themselves at the head of what they hoped would be the decisive wing, entrusting the other to some experienced subordinate. Fighting at the head of their own troops, they often lost touch with the rest and forgot all about them. Unbeknownst to the commander, a great victory might be won or a disaster suffered, a good example being the battle of Coronea (394 B.C.) where news of a defeat came right in the middle of a ceremony in which the Spartan King Agesilaus was being crowned victor by his men.

Whatever the precise nature of the acoustical and visual means of communication in use, their effective range was obviously limited. This put a constraint on the maximum size that individual tactical units could attain; generally the more mobile the unit, and the larger the space occupied by each man, the smaller the number that could be controlled. *A fortiori,* what applied to individual formations applied to the army as a whole. Forces numbering as many as a million troops are sometimes mentioned in Chinese and Indian sources and, incidentally, by medieval chroniclers as well. However, their historical existence is as doubtful as that of the million and a half men (excluding an equal number of camp followers) who, according to Herodotus, accompanied Xerxes to Thermopylae.

Such semi-legendary instances apart, the limits presented by the tactical communications in use were real enough. There were few if any occasions during the two millenia from 500 B.C. to 1500 A.D. when the maximum size of an army concentrated at any one point and made to do battle exceeded 100,000 men. These forces would be spread out over a front no more than 6 or 7 kilometers wide, a figure that remained almost constant from the time of Antiochus III at Rapha in 217 B.C. to that of Napoleon at Austerlitz in 1805 A.D. Usually the maximum distance from headquarters at which forces could be commanded in battle was limited to 3 or 4 km. Even then, a real danger always existed that the front would collapse into several unrelated parts, a situation very familiar to commanders from Alexander to Gustavus

Adolphus and beyond. At distances larger than these, however, even the semblance of tactical control would end.

Strategic communications, too, had serious limitations. Among the earliest are homing pigeons, which were extensively used by many different civilizations. Although homing pigeons can be fast, they are also weather-dependent and unreliable. This led to another problem affecting their use—incalculability, since the time which it may take a message to arrive cannot be foreseen in advance. Optical telegraphs employing fire or smoke signals in relay could in principle transmit information as fast as, or faster than, pigeons, but their effectiveness was also very dependent on the weather. The messages had to be timed in such a way as to prevent their arrival from passing unnoticed. Another very serious problem was that only limited information could be sent by such means. The solution to the time difficulty had to wait until at least partially reliable clocks were developed; the solution to the problem of limited information was finally solved by the invention of the telescope, which alone permitted different signals to be distinguished from each other at a range of more than, say, 500 meters. Although these constraints did not altogether prevent the use of optical telegraphs in ancient Persia, the Hellenistic kingdoms, and Rome, it was hardly ever possible to limit strategic communications to them alone. Instead, reliance had to be placed on messengers, working either on horseback or (in pre-Columbian America) on foot, either individually or in relay between permanent stations established along the roads.

Inevitably, each of these different systems had its strengths and weaknesses. Individual messengers were comparatively cheap and, having arrived, would be able to answer questions. As they were incapable of traveling continuously, however, they were also slow. Messengers working in relay could journey day and night. They were accordingly able to transmit information much faster, but their reports had to be limited to writing and could not be supplemented orally. The establishment and upkeep of relay systems was extremely expensive, hence confined in the main to the most powerful states. Even so, such states almost invariably elected to put the burden of paying for the service on the shoulders of the local population. These problems notwithstanding, relay services were operated in many places from Aechemenid Persia through the Hellenistic empires all the way to Inca Peru and Samurai Japan. When employed to maximum capacity they were capable of transmitting information at 150 or even 200 kilometers a day, although often enough the objective seems to have been less speed as such than the kind of steady reliability needed for day-to-day administration.

Regarded from the point of view of their employment in war, all the long-distance means of communication discussed had one thing in common: they were either too slow, too unreliable, or else too stationary in space, to permit field armies to be commanded from any place except the field itself. This fact, of course, helped shape strategy. It was also not without important political repercussions. A ruler before 1500 A.D. (in fact, until the invention of the electrical telegraph), who wanted to exercise more than the most general degree of control over the operations of his troops, had to be present in their midst, frequently acting not only as his own commander-in-chief but also as his own theater- and battlefield-commander. Alternatively, he could choose to accompany the army in a nominal, supervisory capacity. This often presented a good solution when he either understood something about military affairs or was wise enough to refrain from interfering; in other cases, however, it could lead to the most unfortunate results. In certain respects, the presence of a ruler in the field was both useful and dangerous. It might serve as an inspiration to the troops, but equally it carried the risk that, if something happened to him, everything would at once be lost.

The technologically-based equation that did not allow an army to be commanded from the capital also worked in reverse. A ruler who elected to accompany his forces often took his principal functionaries along so as to have a sort of ambulant capital at his disposal. Even so, the problem of distance meant that the danger of losing political control was always present. This consideration might well induce the ruler to remain at home, in which case political and military leadership would be separated from each other. In this situation, two solutions were also possible. One was to equip the commander-in-chief with letters of instruction, the other to leave him essentially to his own devices. The first course carried the possibility that, if they were to be at all meaningful, the instructions would bind the commander hand and foot. The second implied the risk of giving rise to a situation similar to the one which, in 57 B.C., enabled Pompey to annex half the Middle East without permission from, or indeed the knowledge of, the Roman Senate.

The technological problems that bedeviled the command of field armies as a whole also applied to each of their parts. Indeed in one sense they did so to an even greater extent, since these parts were not stationary but had to be mobile relative to each other. In practice, it was extremely difficult to achieve proper coordination between forces moving rapidly at a considerable distance from one another. Besides the primitive nature of the available communications, the absence of reliable timekeeping devices helped create this situation. As Polybius makes clear, the most important means for measuring time available to ancient commanders were sundials, the use of which not only required considerable expertise but also depended on the weather. To judge by the memoirs of Anna Comnena, towards the end of the eleventh century A.D. even the highly civilized Byzantine court was still regulating its life according to the cock's crow. Mechanical timekeepers such as water clocks or clepsydrae were familiar to antiquity, China, and the Arabs, though apparently not to Western Europe in the Middle Ages where their use may have been inhibited by the freezing of water in winter. Even where they were known, however, their use for the purpose of large-scale strategic coordination was made difficult by the fact that they were not portable. Other common methods commonly employed for keeping time, such as marked candles and the singing of psalms, had obvious shortcomings. In short, the absence of reliable timing devices made the coordination of forces operating beyond visual range of each other a very difficult, often impossible, undertaking. This remained the case throughout the period under consideration, regardless of developments in other respects.

Apart from communications and reliable timekeeping, another basic requirement of strategic coordination is maps. The idea of making a sketch in order to describe terrain and facilitate travel represents a very old invention. However, since most maps were drawn either on perishable or on precious materials—a fact, incidentally, which suggests that they were intended more for display than for use, let alone field use—very few of them have survived. Among those that did, and which are on a strategic scale, by far the oldest come in the form of Sumerian clay tablets. These appear to show stages on the way from Babylon to the Persian Gulf, but are not maps in the modern sense of the term. They are better described as itineraria, or guidebooks. Indeed it seems that the earliest maps not only originated in itineraria, but were often appended to them much in the way of modern guides for tourists.

The one large-scale map left to us from the ancient world, the famous *tabula peutingeriana* the original of which was probably made in Rome during the fourth century A.D., shows this origin clearly. Drawn on a long, narrow scroll, the *tabula* contains information about how to get from one place to the next, indicating the obstacles and resources a traveler might expect to meet when taking a particular road. Though the purpose for which the *tabula* were produced is not known, they are well-suited to display the moves of an army moving from one province to another. However, the map is spatially incorrect. It completely lacks the panoramic, two-dimensional, quality essential for coordinating large-scale movements by independent bodies of troops over considerable distances—a telling comment on the nature of strategy as practiced, say, before Napoleon.

As compared to most medieval land maps, however, the *tabula* represent a masterful achievement. In the Middle Ages, the few maps that were made were often intended not to give directions for travel but to enable their possessor to obtain an idea, however vague, of what countries other than his own, or the world as a whole, looked like. Hence they—like many of their successors until well into the seventeenth century—fulfilled a role similar to that of present-day photography of the *National Geographic* genre. Like that magazine, they abounded with various kinds of pictures, but unlike it, generally the more monstrous the illustrations the better. Itineraries also continued to be used during the Middle Ages, and their limitations were always the same. Even as late as the second half of the sixteenth century, the map which was supposed to guide Spanish commanders taking armed forces from Northern Italy to the southern Netherlands was extremely crude, amounting to no more than a rough sketch with hardly even a pretense to accuracy as to direction or scale. Moreover, and this is a very important point, even such maps as did exist could not be duplicated without distortion before the advent of printing.

Seen from a modern military perspective, the difficulties associated with maps—and, as often as not, with their absence—were always serious, sometimes farcical. Inevitably they meant that armies operating away from home had to depend on local guides, a fact that could lead to disastrous consequences when treachery was involved, as happened, for example, to the Roman triumvir Crassus on his invasion of Parthia in 55 B.C. As might be expected, the weakness of maps and of communications sometimes made it necessary for armies to agree to do battle at predetermined times and places. On other occasions, it caused them to meet purely by accident. Such, for example, was the origin of the encounter between Romans and Macedonians at Cynoscephalae in 197 B.C., and also between the English and the French at Poitiers in 1356. Froissart, who describes that encounter, also tells us of at least one occasion in which an army of English barons heading for Scotland lost its way and spent a couple of days vainly riding about and searching in the moors.

Closely related to the problem of maps, and exercising an equally far-reaching effect on warfare, is that of roads. Without roads no kind of strategic movement is possible, and the larger the movement the better the quality of the roads has to be. As in the case of extensive lines of fortification, the construction and maintenance of roads is extremely expensive. Therefore, large networks could only be created by the most powerful empires, such as the Persian, Chinese, Inca, and of course the Roman. Although the technical problems of road-building were not always simple—witness Roman tunnels and bridges and viaducts—their construction presented an even greater organizational challenge. Where large-scale organization was weak or absent—as in Greece during the period of city states and in medieval Europe—roads deteriorated or were not built. This was true in spite of the rather obvious fact that the men who erected the Parthenon and those who later built the cathedrals must also have been capable of following Roman techniques of laying horizontal walls into the ground.

The importance of organization to transportation is also brought out by the fact that, when it came to vehicles, the European Middle Ages were notably superior to the Romans, having introduced not only the horseshoe but also the modern shoulder-harness and pivoted front axle to allow four-wheeled wagons to turn. As a result of these inventions, the loads that could be hauled by a given team of horses were probably doubled, and this quite apart from the fact that the Middle Ages may have bred stronger animals. In part, the absence of proper roads may perhaps be explained by the nature of the terrain, which was often soggy and required many bridges. Whatever the reason, their lack meant that the impact on strategy of all other technological advances was destined to remain limited.

The question of logistics, equally important, has not yet been discussed. No army can exist without supplies. Deprived of their 3,000 or so calories a day, troops will cease to be troops long before they actually starve to death. Except for places where water transport was available, the means by which an army operating in the field could carry its supplies were essentially limited to the shoulders of men, the backs of pack animals, and wheeled wagons of all sizes. In practice all these means were employed from the earliest times, sometimes individually but more often in combination. The amount of consumables that they could carry, however, was always strictly limited. A simple calculation shows that the relationship between carrying capacity and consumption was always such as to prevent a force from carrying along provisions to last for more than a very few days. Besides, many kinds of foodstuffs could not be preserved for longer than that in any case.

In short, armies that sought to operate at any distance from their starting point were always dependent on the surrounding countryside for supplies. Exploitation could assume a variety of different forms. Sometimes markets were established in which the troops could buy food from their pay or subsistence money. At other times contractors were employed. Often the means employed included requisitioning, or outright plunder. Whatever the means, the effectiveness with which a given tract of land was used was always primarily a question of foresight and organization. A well-organized, disciplined force whose members knew how to look after themselves without scaring away the local inhabitants might live even in relatively poor districts, while an army that did not possess these attributes could starve in areas that were much richer.

In so far as more food was available in certain areas than in others—generally its amount was directly proportional to the density of population, though whether the area was rural or urban also affected the equation—this form of logistics exercised an important, often critical effect on strategy. Paradoxically, this was even more true with animals than with men. Horses in particular are sensitive in regard to food, which is one reason why they were often replaced, for the purpose of transportation, by mules, donkeys, and oxen—the last being extremely slow, but themselves eatable. Whatever animals were employed, their consumption of fodder was such that carrying along more than a minuscule fraction of the supplies they needed was completely out of the question. This again meant putting constraints on the geographical areas in which armies could operate. What is more, both food and fodder were more readily available at certain times of year than at others. The need for fodder in particular tended to make warfare a seasonal activity. Where the role of war in the affairs of the state was very great, as for example in early Republican Rome, even the official calendar could be governed by considerations pertaining to the stomachs of horses. The first month of the year— Mars, meaning war—was the one in which grass covered the fields and the campaigning season got under way. As if to illustrate the effect of the season on logistics, one factor that decisively favored the operations of the Mongols in the thirteenth century was their horses' unique ability to find food under a cover of snow.

Another very important provision for armies, and one which is seldom mentioned in works on military history, was firewood for cooking. Like food and fodder, firewood was too heavy and bulky by far to be transported by an army. Local supplies had to be found instead, often consisting of the houses and furniture of the inhabitants. Firewood, fodder, and food put together— even excluding water—represented well over 90 percent of all the supplies that were consumed by armies on a current, day-to-day basis. In comparison, the demand for all other kinds of supplies was quite small, even trivial.

The amount of baggage that armies dragged along was often astonishing, and sometimes became a serious obstacle to strategic movement. However, most of that baggage consisted of long-lasting items such as tents, bedding, cooking utensils, tools, and so forth. Edged weapons, of course, did not require a steady supply of ammunition, nor for the most part did they require spares. Where headquarters occupied themselves with such matters, dressing a large army might present a difficult problem. (Often, however, they did not, since the men brought along their own clothes.) However, the rate at which clothing was replaced was usually extremely modest. Even where issued on a massive scale, in terms of bulk and weight no other logistic item could even come close to food, fodder, and firewood. Armies therefore were essentially dependent on the countryside for all of these.

Except where suitable waterways permitted cheap transportation on a large scale, itself an important restraint on strategy, armies going on campaign could seldom be supplied from base. Therefore, most armies before 1500 did not really have strategic bases in the sense made familiar by late eighteenth- and early nineteenth-century writers such as Berenhorst, von Bulow, Jomini, and Clausewitz. Instead, all they possessed were camps—more or less permanent, more or less well-constructed and protected agglomerations of huts and tents that followed the armies' moves. Here the troops slept, ate, looked after their weapons, and spent their leisure time. In addition, camps served as points where the heavy baggage was kept and where supplies were brought from the surrounding countryside.

To the extent that it could not do without all these functions, an army was dependent on its camp. However, this was only true up to a point. From Xenophon's Ten Thousand on there are many historical examples on record to show that, provided morale remained intact, it was quite possible for a force to lose its camp and still survive, even prosper. Even in the extreme case of a force fighting with its front inverted and facing towards the homeland, defeat in battle did not necessarily mean that it was cut off from anything. Rather, given the technological conditions of the time, the true meaning of defeat—apart of course from the direct moral and physical loss suffered—was that an army would no longer be able to dominate the countryside from which it drew its supplies. Sometimes such a situation could lead to surrender, as in the case of the Athenians in front of Syracuse in 413 B.C. More frequently, however, the fact that they had neither bases nor lines of communication properly speaking enabled commanders such as Alexander, Hannibal, or Caesar to operate for years in the midst of enemy country with no communication with the homeland except for an occasional letter and an even more occasional reinforcement. Generally speaking, what applied to ancient armies applied with even greater force to medieval ones. Being usually much smaller, the medieval army's dependence upon fixed bases was if anything even less.

Logistics, transport, roads, and maps; timekeepers, standards, trumpets, and the ability to write—in their totality, these essentially nonmilitary technologies probably did as much to shape warfare, and particularly the strategic dimension of warfare, as did any number of weapons and arms. Their combined effect was that there were no real lines of communication to be cut, hardly any "bases" to be guarded or occupied. Also, the technical problems of orientation, of timekeeping, of communication, did not allow forces operating far apart to be easily coordinated and directed against a common objective. Together, these problems meant that armies for the most part could only do battle by mutual consent, tacit and sometimes even explicit. Once the forces confronted each other, the range at which the weapons themselves became effective—and at which they might therefore inflict physical damage upon each other—was still limited to 200 or 300 meters at the outside.

For all these reasons, battle and war tended to coincide: war properly speaking only began when battle was joined. Otherwise, as one authority puts it in reference to Greek times, campaigns were simply extended walking tours. Furthermore, there was a very real sense in which strategy as understood by Clausewitz— namely, that of employing battles in order to forward the aims of war—did not exist, which of course may explain why the term "strategy," in anything like its modern sense, only entered the English language around 1800. All these aspects of war had more to do with nonmilitary than with military technology. As the marked differences between ancient and medieval times prove, it was nonmilitary and not military technology which largely accounted for both continuities and discontinuities. This is also true in regard to warfare at sea.

CHAPTER 4

Naval Warfare

As IN THE CASE of land-based technology, the origins of ships and shipping are lost in the mists of time. No doubt prehistoric man first took to the water by clinging to a floating log. No doubt at some point of time fire was used to hollow out the log, thus creating a canoe of a type that is still in use by certain primitive tribes. Elsewhere, a different solution was employed. Instead of building a boat out of a log, man took several logs and lashed them together in order to create a raft. A slightly more advanced stage of technological development, that also originated in prehistoric times, is represented by boats for which a light framework was sometimes built of wood or wickerwork, and the framework was then covered with hides. Vessels of this type could be seen in India and Mesopotamia even into the twentieth century. It seems probable that the use of the earliest craft was confined to navigable inland waterways. On the other hand, at least a theoretical possibility exists that in coastal areas where rivers were not available the inhabitants proceeded directly to seafaring. In any case, even though the earliest rafts and boats may on occasion have been used for fighting (as it happens, some of the oldest representations of boats in China show them manned by warriors shooting arrows at each other), in no sense could they be regarded as specialized for war.

In all probability, many different factors led prehistoric man to take to the water, among them being the possibility of making a living by fishing just as others did the same by hunting. Fishing,

51

of course, has remained a viable activity down to our own day, although in the case of most developed societies its economic importance is marginal. The principal reason why such societies continue to take to the water, as their predecessors have done for thousands of years, does not lie in the nature of the resources to be found in that medium—though this may be changing as modern deep sea technology is opening up the bottom for exploitation—but rather in the economics of transport. These in turn have everything to do with the relationship between burden-carrying capacity and the power needed for propulsion. Transport by water has always been very cheap compared to transport by land, and often remains so to this day.

In so far as a trade-off exists between size and mobility, the largest technological undertakings created by men have always been represented by works of civil engineering, such as pyramids, or canals, or aqueducts, or else by fortifications. All of these, needless to say, were able to grow to the dimensions they did solely because of the fact that they were never intended to move from one place to another. Next to them in size are ships, since waterborne vessels do not have to drag their own weight along in the same way that land vehicles do. Type for type, ships in general, and warships in particular, have always been bigger than their land-bound equivalents, often representing by far the largest and most complicated movable machines produced by, and at the disposal of, a given society at a given time and place. This was true in regard to the junks of pre-modern China, the galleys and sailing ships of the ancient Mediterranean, and the cogs of medieval Europe. As even a casual glance at a nuclear-propelled aircraft carrier of 90,000 tons burden will confirm, that still remains true today.

Although here and there ships were also built of other materials—papyrus was used by the ancient Egyptians, and leather covered the Irish boats known as curraghs during the first few centuries A.D.—the principal material employed from time immemorial until recently has been wood. The variety of construction that the many different kinds of wood allows is enormous, but wood does impose a certain upper limit on size. If our modern interpretation of the evidence is correct, this limit of approximately 2,000 tons burden seems to have been already reached by late Hellenistic and Roman times, the vessel commissioned by the Emperor Caligula to transport an obelisk from Alexandria to Rome being but one among several known examples. Equally important, trees of the size and quality needed to build the largest and most powerful naval craft are by no means easily found, a fact that has always played a role in determining which societies could, or could not, develop into active seafarers and naval powers.

Sails and oars are the two principal systems of propulsion that have always been used for waterborne craft. The technology of both was already in existence and well developed (e.g. in the form of a folding mast) by 2500 B.C., as a picture of an Egyptian ship from that period shows. The characteristics of the two systems are, of course, very different from each other. Sails are cheap, not only in themselves but because, given a comparatively small crew, the power with which they may supply a ship is very great; hence the size of sailing vessels is limited only by the materials of which craft are made and by the construction techniques in use. On the other hand, even the best-rigged ships are subject to limitations in regard to the ability to maneuver under different conditions of wind. This problem was compounded by the fact that the modern rudder was only invented towards the end of the period we are considering here. Previously, steering had to be effected by means of a pair of oars, attached to each side of the stern. This was a clumsy arrangement, which was partly responsible for the fact that maneuvering at sea was much less accurate than it has since become.

Oared ships, also known as galleys, do not suffer from this particular constraint. They have good acceleration, are extremely maneuverable, and can make way on windless days. Their principal shortcoming consists of the fact that, to make the best use of the limited power available, they must be kept as small and light as possible. As additional freeboard can only be bought at the expense of increased weight (and also because there are limits to the angle at which oars can enter the water without a critical loss of power) galleys must be kept low in profile and, to that extent, unseaworthy. Also, at about one-eighth of a horsepower per man, the crews that were required by galleys per unit of size and burden were enormous. If only because there was normally no room for these crews to sleep on board, the range and endurance of these craft has always been very limited.

As to the speeds attainable by the two types, opinions differ. The answer depends both on the distance and on the type of rigging employed. Obviously no ship powered by the muscle of men can keep up its maximum speed for very long, and a great differential will accordingly exist between the best performance of an oared craft over a short distance and its average cruising speed. For a sailing ship, the question itself may be meaningless if adverse wind conditions require that the vessel proceed from one point to another, not by a straight line, but along a zigzag course, thus possibly doubling the distance it has to cover. Hence, it is difficult to conclude whether a sailing or oared vessel was generally faster. Nevertheless, it stands to reason that the speeds attainable by the two types were comparable under a fairly wide range of circumstances.

There are three major uses of seapower, and all of them have existed from time immemorial. First where circumstances are suitable, ships may be employed to transport men and material from one point to another, and this may well have been their earliest military use. Second, they may be used in order to fight the enemy's ships, preventing him from proceeding with his transports. Third and last, ships may be used to bring force to bear against the land, as Alexander did against Tyre, and the Roman consul Marcellus against Syracuse. It is evident that these different uses require different types of vessels. Not every craft that is suitable for transport (including military transport) may be used in battle, and ships that are optimized for fighting are not likely to be suitable for transport. The third kind of mission normally involves both transport and fighting. Hence, it often requires craft more specialized than either of the first two.

Ships used for transport generally have to be seaworthy, capacious, and reasonably cheap to work. Always, therefore, these ships have relied predominantly on sail. Warships, on the other hand, must be fast—fast enough to catch up with the transports under at least some kinds of conditions—and sufficiently maneuverable both to strike at the enemy and to avoid his blows. These were requirements that could be much better served by oars, though only at the expense of sacrificing range, endurance, and seaworthiness in heavy weather. Also, galleys with their relatively enormous crews were very expensive to operate, presenting a classic example of the way in which military technological design often sacrificed economy in favor of performance.

Of course, the distinction between the two types, sailing transports and oared warships, is artificial to a considerable extent. In practice, sailing ships not seldom carried oars as a supplementary source of power, whereas galleys had masts and sails which were used for normal cruising and which were folded or discarded when the fleet prepared for action. Coming under attack, sailing ships would have to be capable of fighting back, a fact which influenced their design and which ultimately enabled them to dominate war as they already did commerce. Conversely, galleys often carried messages and relatively small loads, particularly cargoes which were either very valuable in relation to their weight or else, like horses, unable to withstand the sea for long. Incidentally, the fact that galleys were often used in this way offers additional support for the belief that, under some circumstances at least, their speed compared favorably with that of sailing vessels.

Whether consisting of sailing ships or of galleys, the seaworthiness and navigational capabilities of navies during the period under discussion were always problematic. Of course this does not mean that very long voyages were not occasionally made. Even as early as Hellenistic times, the Egyptians are believed to have circumnavigated Africa, and a number of authorities give Egyptians, Carthaginians, Irish, and Vikings credit for anticipating Columbus and discovering America. Although some of these claims appear to have a solid basis in fact, there can be no comparison between these voyages and those of Columbus and Vasco da Gama, since it was the voyages of these two that led to extensive exploration and settlement. For this fact the technical capabilities of Spain and Portugal during the fifteenth century were largely, though of course not exclusively, responsible.

To understand the technological factors which governed maritime strategy and dictated what it could and could not do, it is necessary to consider them both separately and in their interaction. The first one to deserve mention is the limited seaworthiness of most ancient and medieval ships. Where naval vessels were not sufficiently strong to withstand storms, really long voyages were out of the question, which explains why many of the longest ones on record were apparently made by accident when a ship was blown off course and lost its way. Instead, navigation tended to be a seasonal activity. Either it was confined to certain months, as in the Mediterranean and later in the seas bordering on western Europe, or else it was compelled to proceed in certain directions at certain times of the year, as was the case in southeastern Asia with its monsoon winds. Either way, the duration of seaborne military campaigns, and the directions in which they could proceed, were limited. Unless a force was capable of looking after itself logistically, it could not be sustained overseas for any length of time.

Next, even where ships were strongly built, the ability of sailing vessels—the only ones at all capable of really long voyages—to proceed against the wind was strictly limited, though just how limited we do not know. Wishing to proceed from one point to another, a fleet either had to wait for a favorable wind or else make a large detour. Either way, the time it would take to cover a certain distance would be difficult if not impossible to calculate in advance. Unless the vessels of a navy took good care to remain together, long waits were likely to ensue as different divisions sailed in different directions and at different speeds. Alexander proceeding up the shore of the Persian Gulf found out to his cost that the same problems also bedeviled sea-to-land cooperation. This was because an army marching unopposed might reasonably be expected to cover so many miles a day, but a navy was always subject to unforseeable events and could not really be depended upon to appear at the right time and place.

Third, during most of the period under consideration, technological reasons caused the majority of voyages to be limited to following the coast or else to island-hopping, a good example being the route taken by the ship which, according to the New Testament, carried the imprisoned St. Paul to his trial in Rome. Sea-charts down at least to the high Middle Ages were hopelessly inadequate. Modeled on the type which the Greeks called *periplous* (literally "go-arounds"), they were basically the equivalents of the itineraries used on land and, like them, consisted simply of lists of landmarks along the coast. Though the compass apparently made its appearance in China around 1150, another century had to pass before it reached Western Europe, and even then its users, possibly out of fear of being accused of dabbling in black magic, hindered its development by keeping it out of sight. Hence, whenever land was left out of sight, navigation became dependent on astronomical means and dead reckoning. Observing the heavenly bodies was dependent on the weather. Dead reckoning was hampered by the fact that it was only in the sixteenth century that the ship's log, by which speed is measured, was invented. In the absence of good instruments, and no instruments were really good during the period under consideration, both methods are also inaccurate and unreliable. Embarking on a long voyage, one never

56

knew quite where one would end up. Often after a period at sea, a ship or fleet would hit land at a point far removed from its intended destination, whereupon they would carry out a turn and follow the coast. The result, once again, was that the voyage as a whole lasted longer than expected. Furthermore, it was impossible to calculate the time required to complete a given course with any degree of precision.

Fourth, given the absence of telecommunications, ship-to-ship and ship-to-shore messages had to be transmitted by a variety of visual means such as flags, the movements of sails, mirrors, fire and smoke signals, among others. None of these was capable of transmitting anything but a strictly limited, prearranged repertoire of messages. In view of the different types of weather likely to be encountered at sea, none of these methods could be considered really reliable, and all were of course limited to short-range work. Whenever maritime strategy involved journeys over longer distances, messenger ships had to be employed, a system that was not only exceedingly expensive but which, in view of the absence of good maps and the general inability to determine the exact location of fleets, could be unreliable as well.

Finally, the impact of logistics on warfare at sea, as on land, has always been considerable. Here, too, technological factors played an important role in determining what was, and was not, possible. Contrasting sharply with contemporary land armies, fleets could not draw most of their supplies from their environment, but had to carry along sufficient stores and provisions to last them from one landfall to the next. In this respect vessels differed greatly according to their type. Whereas sailing ships were often capable of staying at sea for weeks and even months (though fresh water might represent a problem), oared galleys with their comparatively huge crews could never do the same. Therefore, galleys were mainly limited to inland seas, long voyages far away from land being completely out of the question. Also out of the question was the mounting of prolonged blockades, although occasionally a favorable geographic position might enable a power to cut another's lines of communication, as the Athenians did to Corinth during much of the Peloponnesian war.

As might be expected, the disparate technical characteristics and performance of transports on the one hand, and warships on the other, gave rise to many interesting problems in strategic coordination and cooperation. Since communication at sea was as difficult as on land, and since the problems of determining the location of both friend and foe were if anything even greater, coordination usually depended on concentration. Even so the possibility always existed that a sudden storm might blow a fleet apart and cause contact with individual ships to be lost, an eventuality that Julius Caesar anticipated by issuing his captains with sealed instructions before embarking for Africa. On the other hand, the different seagoing capabilities of warships and transports meant that they might have to proceed to their destination by different routes. The risk of doing so was acceptable because sailing vessels, though presenting an easy target for galleys in narrow waters and when leaving or entering port, were frequently able to match or at least outrun the latter on the high sea.

One way of overcoming some of these problems was to aim at a technical compromise between the characteristics of the various types. This seems to have been the real idea behind the later Hellenistic and Roman galleys, known as cataphracts. What with its deck covering the entire ship, elevated fighting castles, war engines and capacity for carrying large boarding parties, the cataphract—especially as developed by Roman hands—was less specialized for ramming than the classical trireme. Contrary to the trireme, too, its propulsion depended mainly on sails. Oars were used mostly for auxilliary purposes or else for specialized tactical maneuvering. As a result, the burden-carrying capacity of a large cataphract with between six to ten rows of oars was considerable. Exploiting these characteristics, a Roman fleet consisting of such vessels could both carry troops and fight. Since it did away with the distinction between warships and transports, it was homogeneous and easy to coordinate—a most important advantage.

The technical means by which ships could fight each other were comparatively few in number and limited in power. Since wood was the most important material used in the construction of vessels, incendiaries—whether shot from bows in the form of burning arrows or else squirted from tubes in various liquid forms—played an important role. Another frequently-used method was ramming, which demanded great speed, maneuverability and skill on the part of commanders and crews. This was the Athenian navy's speciality during its heyday. War engines such as ballistae and catapults were sometimes mounted on Hellenistic and Roman vessels, and their role in ship-to-ship fighting seems to have increased with time. Last but not least, there was boarding, a method which enabled commanders to fight at sea as they would on land.

Though Greek triremes of the fifth and fourth centuries B.C. already carried a party of marines for boarding, this method was greatly developed by the Romans, whose short sidearms were much more suitable for this purpose than were the long Greek spears. During the third century B.C. the Romans defeated the Carthaginian Navy by introducing the *corvus*, a hinged bridge with a spike at its head which, hung on a mast, could be lowered by means of a pulley in order to seize an enemy ship and provide a passage for boarders. Later the Romans experimented with the shooting of grappling hooks from catapults, an invention attributed to Augustus' companion, Marcus Agrippa. All four methods continued in use throughout the period under consideration, though their relative importance was not fixed but varied from time to time and from place to place.

Some types of warships were not intended for battle at sea, but were employed to bring force to bear against the land. During the period under consideration, amphibious operations were a normal part of warfare. However, Pericles in his speeches made it perfectly clear that the function of seapower was not to carry out landings against armed opposition. On the contrary, it served to outflank the enemy and thus make such landings unnecessary. In the vast majority of cases when troops were carried overseas, they landed on undefended beaches. Alternatively, they made use of ports belonging to allies. An army preparing to descend from the sea was sometimes detected and opposed. However, this was not how things were planned, and frequently the result was that the landing would be abandoned or carried out somewhere else. The mobility of seapower as compared with landbound forces, when combined with the shallow draft of most of the vessels in use, for the most part made the development of specialized landing craft unnecessary. At best, special ramps might be constructed to facilitate the embarkation and debarkation of horses, as the Normans apparently did when they sailed to conquer England in 1066.

Except for invasion, the ability of navies to engage in sea-to-land operations was strictly limited by the range of the weapons in use. However, when it was a question of attacking a town that was located near the water, ships often served as platforms for seige engines and for scaling ladders, a use that is already shown on Assyrian reliefs. Since engines could be heavy and ladders very large, sometimes several ships had to be lashed together to carry them, as during the Roman siege of Syracuse in 214–212 B.C. Elsewhere, special vessels had to be constructed. Some of them, notably the Roman *sambuca* or harp, apparently were rather strange in appearance. All such combinations were difficult to handle and barely seaworthy. As always, given a certain level of technological development, increased power was only to be had at the expense of reduced mobility.

The battle of Actium, fought in 31 B.C., marked the zenith of Roman naval development. Both sides, the supporters of Augustus and those of Antonius, relied principally on fleets of galleys with multiple rows of oars which looked like millipedes. Each carried siege engines, archers, and boarding parties. Afterwards, with no opposition left in the Mediterranean, the size of warships declined. The largest types were replaced by a smaller one, known as Liburnian, and more suitable for patrolling and police work. The Liburnian in turn developed into the *dromon*, meaning "runner." This was a relatively small, uncovered galley, with two or three rows of oars, that served as the principal warship of the Byzantine Empire. The smaller size of ships meant that the demand for strength was less. Roman methods of shaping individual planks and making them interlock with each other (mortise and tenon construction) were, accordingly, abandoned. Instead, there came into use a cheaper system which consisted of first setting up the ribs and then nailing the planks to them. From the fourth century A.D., the triangular lateen sail—possibly spreading from Ceylon and Indonesia, where it had long been known—began to replace the square sail used by the Romans. Around 800 A.D. its use had become general, probably increasing by as much as 20° the ability of vessels to sail into the wind.

Little is known of the Arab navies that began operating in the Mediterranean from the second half of the seventh century. In the absence of reliable sources, we can only assume that they resembled those of the Byzantines, drawing as they did on the same seafaring population (the inhabitants of the Phoenician coastal cities), the same raw materials, and the same ports. Early Arab fleets were able to dominate the eastern Mediterranean. However, after the beginning of the eleventh century, the Byzantine reconquest of Crete and Cyprus seems to have confronted them with great difficulties in obtaining wood which, from now on, had to be imported from as far away as the forests of Northern India. Consequently, the Arabs were unable to maintain the quality of their ships. They began to lag behind the Italian city-states, and later behind the rising powers of Turkey and Spain, none of whom suffered from the same handicap.

Starting around 1300, the size of galleys operating in the Mediterranean once again began to increase, until they reached and then surpassed the dimensions of Greek and Roman craft. By shifting from shell to skeleton construction, builders successfully overcame the tendency of galleys to buckle in the center, and were able to launch ships 45 meters long with a length-to-beam ratio of between 6 and 8 to 1. Though there was no return to multiple banks of oars, each oar was now manned by two or three men. The crew-to-burden ratio of these vessels was low enough to enable them to be used not only for war and the transmission of urgent messages, but also for carrying cargoes of high value, including passengers willing to pay for the added reliability of galleys. Tactics also changed, though perhaps less for technological than for commercial reasons. Late in the Middle Ages the large galley, with its crew numbering in the hundreds, represented a formidable fighting machine. This, and also the fact that the purpose of naval combat often was not so much to sink enemy vessels as to capture them, led to an emphasis on boarding. Boarding was usually preceded by the shooting of stones and arrows from engines and crossbows. For defensive purposes there was Greek fire, a somewhat mysterious admixture of combustibles which was squirted from tubes and ignited upon contact with water. It was said to have been invented by a Syrian Greek around 660 A.D., and was used several times with devastating effect to repulse Arab and Russian attacks on Constantinople. Meanwhile the ram tended to grow progressively shorter, a development which carried an additional benefit by making ships more seaworthy and easier to beach.

Although oared craft were destined to surrender their place to sailing vessels, the process was slow and probably could not have been foreseen before 1500 at the earliest. Throughout the first half of the sixteenth century, both types were competing and formed a normal part of large naval expeditions. As late as 1571, at the great battle of Lepanto, all four fleets present (Ottoman, Spanish, Genoese, and Papal) consisted entirely of galleys. Following the traditional tactics, these were formed into two huge crescents that went at each other with cannon, grappling hooks, and boarding parties that fought it out hand-to-hand. When the Ottoman fleet was defeated and destroyed, the Sultan responded by building another of the same type. Though their utility gradually declined, galleys continued to be regarded as symbols of naval power and were employed by Mediterranean navies, by the French and Spanish in particular, until early in the eighteenth century.

Though an inland sea can certainly be dangerous for navigation, the conditions prevailing in the Mediterranean did enable galleys to perform usefully in war so long as they did not extend their operations into the winter months. The seas surrounding northwestern Europe, however, were dangerous all year round, being characterized by unpredictable winds, occasional violent storms, strong currents, and high tides. As a result, galleys of the Mediterranean type were never able to make much of an impression in these waters. The migratory Germanic tribes, and particularly the Saxons who invaded England, developed open, shell-constructed, clinker-built, rowing boats with a length-to-beam ratio of perhaps 6 to 1. These boats, designed for moving people from one place to another, were originally flat-bottomed. They began to be equipped with keels after about 700 A.D., resulting in greater strength and stability as well as improved sea-going characteristics. The Scandinavians during the eighth century added a mast and a square sail. This made even transoceanic voyages possible, and led to the settlement of Iceland and Greenland. In America, however, previous human settlements existed, and the Vikings, for all that they possessed iron weapons, were unable to make much of an impression on the natives.

The differences between Scandinavian transports and warships were minimal. To the extent that a separate military type can be said to have existed at all, it was characterized by a greater length-to-beam ratio and a mast that could be folded when the ship went into action and oars took over. Their shallow draught and the fact that they were propelled by oars also made these vessels ideal for raiding purposes, since they were capable of sailing up estuaries and rivers. As there was neither a ram nor a deck on which war engines could be mounted, the preferred Scandinavian tactic consisted of using grappling hooks, followed by boarding and hand-to-hand fighting at which they were unequaled.

While the open Scandinavian longships with their dragon heads terrorized Western Europe during the early Middle Ages, the future did not belong to them. Rather, it was the humble hulks and cogs, originating in Celtic traditions and developed by the Germanic peoples into rather tubby transport vessels, which were ultimately destined to triumph over both Scandinavian and Mediterranean types. The earliest hulks and cogs we know about, dating to the sixth and seventh centuries A.D., were much smaller than Roman transports. However, hulks and cogs tended to increase steadily in size until ships of 400 tons, with two or even three decks running the entire length of the ship, were not uncommon around 1050. Unlike the Scandinavian longships, these vessels relied exclusively on sails for propulsion. Unlike them, again, they were designed not for carrying people or waging war but for transporting merchandise, often low-value merchandise that could only justify the cost if carried in bulk. Consequently, as compared with all other types then in use, the tubby cogs with their extremely low length-to-beam ratio required small crews per unit of size. This amounted to no more than one man per every eight or so tons of burden, as opposed to perhaps one per two tons even on the largest galleys.

As cogs grew in size, the old method of steering them—by means of oars attached to both sides of the stern—was no longer adequate. Towards the year 1200 shipbuilders accordingly began to experiment with the rudder. Essentially this was a large flat plank attached directly to the sternposts of a vessel and worked by means of a tiller. The precise stages by which the rudder came to be adopted remain unknown, nor is it certain whether the invention originated in the north or was adapted from Mediterranean or even Chinese models. Be this as it may, by the middle of the fourteenth century the rudder, at first used to supplement steering oars rather than replace them, had fully matured. It did much to improve the handling and sailing characteristics of all ships, but particularly those of the clumsy West European types whose ability to maneuver now for the first time began to approximate that of oared craft under some conditions.

Seen from our special point of view, it is paradoxical that the cogs of the twelfth and thirteenth centuries, known to us by way of pictorial representations, evolved primarily as merchant vessels and were by no means specialized for warfare. On the other hand, given the chaotic political conditions of the times, any merchant vessel had to be capable of defending itself at all times. When it came to that, cogs possessed several important advantages. The fact that they were propelled by sails rather than by oars enabled their decks to be raised high above the water. If this was not considered sufficient, they could also sprout massive fighting castles which increasingly came to constitute an integral part of the hull and which represented an important advantage when it came to fighting at close quarters. The favorable power-to-burden ratio enabled these ships to carry large crews—as many as one man per ton—and these crews were free to fight as they did not have to man the oars. The decks permitted war engines to be mounted, and sometimes warships were covered by wet hides to afford protection against incendiaries.

On the whole, however, the distinction between warships and merchantmen was fuzzy. Consequently, most feudal navies consisted simply of merchantmen which were rented out to the King and suitably modified. Though boarding was preceded by volleys of arrows from bows and crossbows, it remained the most important tactic by far. Naval tactics as such barely existed. Seeking to approximate the conditions of land warfare with which they were familiar, crews sometimes went so far as to link their ships together with chains, as the French did at Sluys in 1340.

Beginning around 1100 or so, cogs as they grew larger and larger were able first to hold their own and then to outfight the Scandinavian longship. As the northern peoples abandoned their ancient tribal organization and increasingly introduced feudal political, economic, and social structures, the longship also went into a decline and was finally replaced by West European types. In the south, the cog took much longer to triumph over its rivals. The Crusaders had relied on vessels supplied to them by the Italian city states. Although 1304 is the date traditionally given for the first entry of the cog into the Mediterranean, northerners and southerners must have been familiar with the other's ships long before then. Having entered the Mediterranean, the single-masted, square-rigged cog soon developed a mizzenmast with a triangular lateen sail attached to it, permitting much closer sailing to the wind. This still did not enable the cog to supplant the galley as a warship, but by the end of the fourteenth century the cog stood at least a fighting chance against the galley when an encounter took place on the open sea.

This account of the technical development of ships and of naval warfare is a gross oversimplification. Actually, the number of different types in use was much greater than can be mentioned

here. Moreover, it must be emphasized that their evolution proceeded not separately but with at least occasional interaction. Roman shipbuilding techniques, and the methods of waging war
that were based on them, cannot have gone unnoticed in Celtic
Gaul and even Germany, the more so since the Romans on at
least three separate occasions invaded Britain and also penetrated
the Baltic during the reign of Tiberius. It is possible that some
knowledge of Roman methods was available to Alfred the Great
when he had a fleet of galleys built in the ninth century, knowledge
that was subsequently lost. In any case, some galleys did operate
in northern waters around 1300, though they never became very
popular. Scandinavian and Byzantine shipbuilding techniques are
usually represented as developing independently from each other,
and on the whole this is true enough. However, they came into
direct contact when the Norsemen invaded the Mediterranean
during the first half of the eleventh century. The first encounter
resulted in a Norse defeat, after which they apparently switched
to galleys. In the Black Sea, the two sides met again, as the Russians,
or else their Swedish masters, employed Scandinavian-type vessels.

Undoubtedly, during the millenia up to 1500 A.D. there were
very great changes and developments in maritime technology and
naval warfare. Yet, certain constant features remained prominent
throughout. Perhaps the most important of these was the rather
limited seaworthiness of the available craft—the elements and
not the enemy claimed first place whenever it came to dividing
the energies of the mariner. Consequently, they were unable to
make really long voyages on anything like a regular or sustained
basis. Limited seaworthiness, the inability to sail close against the
wind, logistic problems, and other difficulties associated with command, control, communication, and orientation made it impossible
to command the sea in a modern, Mahanian sense. It also dictated
that virtually all naval battles, as their names indicate, should
take place over small spaces of water and within sight of land.
In any case, the dominant function of navies was not to fight
each other. Rather, they were used to patrol and police, cover
landings—very seldom undertaken against opposition—and assist
in the operations of land armies.

Where it came to fighting, basically the same tactics remained
in use, though ramming tended to decline in importance as opposed to shooting missiles and boarding. As we saw, the same
sails and rigs that provided the transports with the power to carry

men and equipment often rendered them unsuitable for fighting, making it necessary to rely on oars. Perhaps nothing characterizes the essential unity of the period under consideration so much as the fact that, whatever their precise function and relationship to sails, oars powered by human muscle not only remained in use but, where the two systems came into competition, were actually more useful than sails under many conditions and for most tactical purposes. As the Middle Ages came to an end and the modern age dawned, this tended decreasingly to be the case, which is why, at sea as well as on land, we have chosen to take the period between about 1400 and 1500 as our first great turning point.

CHAPTER 5

Irrational Technology

DURING THE AGE OF TOOLS, as in every subsequent age, the evolution of the weapons and equipment of war was not governed solely by rational considerations pertaining to their technical utility, capabilities, and effectiveness. Rather than being the acme of functionalism, the design and employment of weapons were intertwined with a host of anthropological, psychological, and cultural factors, all of which were in a state of constant interaction with each other. These factors frequently pushed development into strange, seemingly illogical, paths. Moreover, they themselves helped dictate what was considered rational at any given time and place. In spite of the obvious relevance of this problem to an activity as permeated by irrational forces as war, surprisingly little serious scholarly attention has been directed to it.

Among the numerous nonutilitarian factors that have played an important role in the design of weapons and weapon systems, perhaps the most important is aesthetics. The drive to decorate, to create forms that are not merely useful but somehow pleasing to the eye, seems to be innate in human nature, and has always found a particularly important outlet in the technology of war. Thus, the Egyptian Pharaohs spent small fortunes to embellish their chariots. There are, in the *Illiad*, few subjects closer to the poet's heart than the decorative value of the arms carried by the principal heroes from Achilles down. That value was equally evident to the rabbis who, as they compiled the Jewish Talmud in the second and third centuries A.D., seriously debated the question as to whether weapons should be regarded as ornaments and might therefore lawfully be carried on the sabbath (the Hebrew word for weapons, *zain*, means decoration in Arabic, to which Hebrew is closely related). Roman soldiers and medieval knights always put a high value on making their equipment fit for display, often spending heavily in order to obtain emblazoned armor, inlaid weapons, silver shields, gold spurs, and the like. None of this made a direct contribution to effectiveness. If anything, the plumes, crests, and winglike contraptions that were often attached to armor probably interfered with it.

The taste for decorating weapons and equipment reached its apogee during that self-proclaimed age of awakening and reason, the early modern period, from the mid-fifteenth to the late seventeenth century. The design of weapons, ranging from handguns to suits of armor to cannon, was a job to which the best artistic talents from Michelangelo and Bernini downward willingly applied themselves. Very often, this resulted in works of such high quality that they are still being preserved in museums and in the dining rooms of the extremely rich. Fortifications, too, were often built with aesthetic considerations very much in mind. This was true not only in Europe (where late fifteenth century Italy offers any number of cases in point) but in places such as Japan where the design that found favor in the eyes of the nobility consisted of structures seemingly about to take leave of the earth and soar into the heavens. As late as the end of the seventeenth century, the commanders of the Royal French Navy commissioned a well known artist, Puget, to decorate the ships being built for Louis XIV with gold leaf and sculptured wooden figures. When the minister of the treasury, Colbert, objected to the expense involved a dispute broke out that dragged on for years, and finally Puget had to be offered a gratuity on condition that he never set foot in the shipyards again.

Related to the problem of decoration, but nevertheless distinct from it, is that of size. The seemingly universal drive towards larger implements can be explained, at least in part, on purely utilitarian grounds, particularly in war, where the equipment in the hands of both sides is used for a head-on destructive clash. Given a certain level of technological development, bigger often means more powerful. Therefore it is easy to discover tactical considerations behind the persistent, and age-old, tendency of pikes and lances to grow longer, for shields to gain weight, for vehicles and engines of every kind to add size, and for warships of any given type or class to become larger and larger.

Though the drive towards size often rests on rational grounds, there clearly is a point where size can mean not increased but diminished effectiveness, if effectiveness is measured by the ability to do "useful" work. Often in the annals of war that point was reached, and then exceeded, leading to monstrous technological creations which later proved useless. A good example is provided by the huge ships with multiple rows of oars that were the pride of many Hellenistic monarchs. In war they turned out to be useless, frequently ending up as trophies in Roman triumphs. Other examples are late medieval armor which, as legend has it, was so heavy and so cumbersome that knights had to be lifted onto their mounts by a crane, could fight none but other knights, and were all but immobilized when unhorsed. Finally, some of the warships of the early modern period, like the English *Mary Rose* and the Swedish *Vasa*, carried so much ordnance (to say nothing of their extremely expensive decoration) that they became top heavy and sank on their maiden voyages.

Admittedly, all these represent extreme cases. A few, and particularly the last two, may well be explained in terms of the luxuriant growth that often accompanies the appearance of new technology. As a look at any collection of early automobiles suggests, it took people time to realize that passenger cars are best designed with two pivoted wheels in front and two fixed ones in the rear rather than with three, or five, or six, in any odd combination. However, in other instances—the oversized Hellenistic galleys and late medieval armor being good examples—oversized weapons probably indicate the onset of degeneration. Since microelectronics is now making small beautiful, would it be altogether unreasonable to suggest that some of today's largest weapons and weapon systems may perhaps be understood in similar terms?

If the irrational element in man has often caused military technology to assume ostensibly useless forms, in other cases technologies that were useful in themselves were viewed in ways that we would regard as irrational. Consider, for example, the tendency to endow weapons with individual names, a custom which is nowadays reserved mainly for ships but which at one time or another was applied to almost any kind of weapon and equipment. In Vedic India during the second millenium B.C., the composite bows used by the warrior-aristocracy already carried the names of women. In the erotic poems written in their honor, the whispering sounds they made when discharged were compared to the sighs of concubines making love. The largest rams and ballistae and catapults of ancient times were often assigned names, a custom which continued throughout the Middle Ages. The swords that are so lovingly described in the *Chanson de Roland*, like the ones worn in a later period by Japanese Samurai, not only carried names but were actually endowed with a kind of genealogy. Allegedly manufactured by a god or by a man in possession of godlike attributes, these swords were supposed to have a personality of their own, some being "joyous," others "grim," and others still "evil." Certain swords attained considerable fame. They were supposed to confer honor not only on their owners, who treasured them and praised their qualities in poetry, but equally on those who were killed or wounded by them. Such a reputation, of course, was not without its psychological value in battle.

Also falling within the province of disfunctional technology, explicable—if that indeed is the word—only on the basis of irrational drives and urges, is the trend towards complexity that has sometimes made its appearance in history. Particularly during the Italian Renaissance, designers and engineers became first fascinated and then obsessed with the possibilities presented by cylinders and pistons and cranks, and axles and cogwheels and cams and screws and bevel gears. Accordingly, they applied their imaginations to the construction of a very large number of complicated machines, the real purpose of which was apparently not so much to do useful work as to explore the ways in which these devices could be combined. A few of these machines were practical, but the majority were not, including many military inventions. Designs for scythed chariots, crank-propelled tanks, oared submarines, flying machines with flapping wings, and siege engines running about with the aid of sails were committed to paper and, in the hope of obtaining funds, submitted to the powers that be. Here and there efforts were made to turn these designs into reality, though never with any noticeable success. Again, it is dangerous to carry analogies too far. However, one suspects that this kind of technological exuberance did not necessarily die with Leonardo.

Finally, to round off this list of various kinds of irrational technology, it is necessary to take a brief look at a whole range of weapons whose use was somehow considered unfair. Had the design of arms and military equipment been governed by utilitarian considerations alone, and indeed had war itself been nothing but a clash between cold-blooded interests, no such phenomenon could have arisen. In fact, however, every historical period seems to have had its share of unfair weapons. In Western civilization until about 1500 A.D., the most important reason why some weapons were considered unfair was because they enabled their users to kill from a distance and from behind cover. The victim being unable to retaliate, such weapons obscured the vital distinction between war and plain murder. One such weapon was the bow, as illustrated by the story of Paris killing Achilles at Troy. Another was the catapult, which was perceived as a device that would render valor superfluous in war. In the Middle Ages knights held similar attitudes towards these weapons, and this sometimes resulted in the execution and mutilation of captured bowmen. During the Renaissance, and as late as the beginning of the seventeenth century, the contempt in which firearms were held not only was responsible for many atrocities of this kind but also found echoes in the works of such writers as Ariosto, Cervantes, Shakespeare, and Milton. The list of weapons which, from their time to ours, were regarded as cowardly ("dastardly" was a term particularly favored by the nineteenth century), and therefore unfair, is indeed a long one. It includes mines, barbed wire, torpedoes, and the submarine, to mention but a few.

A particularly significant category of unfair weapons, and one which more than any other highlights the irrational nature of the entire issue, is that of weapons considered too terrible (read: too effective) to use. An early example of this is provided by the crossbow, a weapon whose use against Christians was outlawed by the Lateran Council of 1139, though its employment against heathens was permitted and even encouraged. Others are red hot cannon balls, explosives dropped from balloons (which, it was argued, would indiscriminately kill both soldiers and civilians), and of course the famous dumdum bullet which was originally invented by the British on the theory that savages of powerful physique could not be stopped by ordinary small-caliber ammunition. Usually the objection brought against these weapons was that they caused "unnecessary" suffering. In practice, since what constituted "unnecessary" was a little hard to define, quite often weapons were called unfair simply because, under the prevailing circumstances, they were more helpful to the other side than to oneself. Of course, none of the above is to say that there were never any rational-utilitarian considerations behind the decision to adopt, or not to adopt, this or that weapon. However, very often in history, such considerations on their own are insufficient to explain what actually happened.

What makes this question of unfair weapons so fascinating, and at the same time constitutes its real value, is the fact that different periods and cultures were by no means always in agreement as to which weapons were fair and which were not. For example, present-day sensibilities are offended by napalm as a particularly horrible weapon. However, Anna Comnena in the eleventh century considered Greek fire a perfectly respectable instrument of war which, to the extent that it was judged by any criteria apart from effectiveness, did honor to its inventor. The same is true in regard to chemical and bacteriological weapons. Though their use is denounced today, both have a long and honorable history in the form of stinkbombs, smoke used to compel the other side to abandon his mines, and even the rotting carcasses of horses which were sometimes thrown into besieged towns with the aid of trebuchets. Nor would we be altogether justified in regarding these methods simply as evidence of the barbarism of earlier times. Taking an "objective" point of view, it is not clear why the use of high explosive for tearing men apart should be regarded as more humane than burning or asphyxiating them to death.

In short, the question as to why, at certain times and places, some weapons should be more acceptable than others depends on factors other than the characteristics of those weapons themselves. In fact, its causes are to be found deep within a civilization and the attitudes that it takes to military conflict. A good case in point is represented by the sword. It is a peculiarity of Western civilization, already beginning in the days of Greece and Rome, that it looks at war in terms of a duel between two parties, a trial of arms. Accordingly, this civilization has always taken to hand-held edged weapons, even to the point of making the sword into the very symbol of war, an idea which still lingers in linguistic usage. To people who were not Westerners, however, this prejudice in favor of face to face combat has always been regarded as slightly quaint. To the great Chinese military writer Sun Tsu, war was neither a duel nor a sportlike contest. Rather, it represented one way, and a rather undesirable way, of settling disputes between social and political groups. For him it was a question, not of honorably meeting an opponent face to face, but of settling the dispute with the least possible disturbance of cosmic harmony, or *dao*.

As one would expect, a point of view which did not regard war as a duel entailed significant consequences for military technology. Among other things, it meant that a very different status was given to the bow. The West often regarded it as somehow shameful and fit only for use by socially inferior troops, but Persians, Arabs, Indians, Chinese, and Japanese held it in high esteem. To them, it was an honorable weapon in the hands of high-class warriors. Frequently, indeed, they endowed it with a symbolic function equivalent to that of the sword in the West. In its turn, this attitude was not without its tactical repercussions. In marked contrast to the West, the East has always considered the ambush not only perfectly respectable but much the most effective means of waging war. This led to an emphasis on traps of all kinds, from the feigned retreat that was the specialty of the Mongols to the excreta-smeared bamboo stakes that so angered the Americans in Vietnam. When war involved a struggle between civilizations whose patterns of thought differed in this way, the results were often markedly savage. Unable to agree as to what constituted acceptable behavior and what did not, each side took the enemy's actions as a pretext for reprisals.

So far we have assumed that one can distinguish between "utilitarian" and "nonutilitarian" forms of military technology, and that the existence of the latter calls for an explanation. However, given that man in general, but man at war in particular, is anything but a completely rational animal, the existence of irrational technology is hardly surprising in itself. On the other hand, the fact that different things are considered "fair" by different civilizations also raises the possibility that our own beliefs concerning the nature of military rationality may be, if not actually wrong, at any rate culturally-determined. Let us assume, then, that people who lived in earlier periods and produced the kind of disfunctional technology discussed here may have known what they were doing. With that assumption in mind, let us reconsider the evidence.

Looked at from this perspective, weapons too complex to serve a practical purpose are only irrational if we think of them as hardware designed to do work, in this case the work of war. However, the idea that war is akin to work is a peculiarity of the present industrial age. It was certainly not shared by many previous societies to which war and work represented opposites and which, as in the case of the crowds that cheered the onset of World War I, liked it precisely because it promised relief from work. During much of history, in fact, far from regarding war as a violent means for pursuing political ends, people thought of it as part vacation, part game, part a somewhat dangerous form of sport. As a result, the technology designed for it often took on a toylike character, manifested in an obsession with complexity for its own sake. The resemblance of war to a game was, as it happened, particularly pronounced precisely in the age of Leonardo da Vinci when it was conducted—on the authority of Machiavelli—by mercenaries and involved little or no bloodshed. However, a tendency to turn war into a game, and weapons into toys, has manifested itself during periods other than the early Renaissance in Italy.

Similarly, the practice of providing weapons with names. In the prevailing scientific frame of reference, such names cannot serve as a useful purpose. Hence the reason given for maintaining this custom is the need to keep up tradition, which in many cases is tantamount to saying that no good reason exists at all. However, things have not always been this way. The ceremony of assigning a name to a weapon, far from being regarded merely as an opportunity to flatter some dignitary through his wife, was carefully conducted to endow the device with the desirable qualities implied by its name. The names of saints that medieval knights emblazoned on suits of armor were supposed to fill a very real need, namely to invoke their protection, whereas the names of enemies which Roman soldiers inscribed on arrows and on bullets fired from slings were intended to help those missiles find their targets. Though few people believe in saints and in magic any longer, both customs still persist. Both are of some apparent benefit in raising troop morale, this being an indication that, in war, things are not always what they seem.

It is also possible to consider the name-giving custom from another point of view. A passing reference has been made to the likelihood that, during the Carolingian period, the minstrels who spread the reputation enjoyed by certain individually-named swords were not retained in vain, and that this reputation was not without a certain psychological value in battle. If ancient siege engines, like late medieval and early modern cannon, were frequently assigned such names as Demolisher, Terrible, or Madwoman, the reason was similarly a desire to frighten and impress. As medieval chronicles confirm, such attempts were sometimes successful. Wars, to quote Patton, are won by frightening the enemy. An enemy who can be made to run away does not require to be killed, so that this approach is actually more cost-effective than the more bloody one commonly used. Looked at from such a point of view, a custom that many would consider irrational suddenly turns out to be rational after all.

Names apart, devices of every kind can be made to take on a frightening aspect by increasing their size. As any dog-owner knows, the feeling that big equals strong is by no means unique to our species, though whether it is biologically determined or culturally "imprinted" I do not presume to judge. Often in history the object of constructing very large weapons seems to have been the desire to impress and, by so doing, either prevent war from breaking out or obtain a psychological advantage should this nevertheless happen. Good examples are provided by the Hellenistic war galleys with their multiple banks of oars, which seem to have been used mainly to escort ambassadors going on diplomatic missions and to project power. The same purpose, it seems, was served by oversized rams, catapults, siege towers, cannon, and the like. One need only read Josephus' account of the Roman siege of Jodphat in 68 A.D., during which he himself commanded the garrison, to realize that attempts to overawe the defenders by confronting them with enormous weapons were sometimes successful. This does not mean, however, that similar claims sometimes made in favor of present-day weapons, warships in particular, should necessarily be taken at face value.

Though little conscious attention seems to be paid to the question of decoration in today's world, one suspects that its influence persists. For example, the Israeli Air Force before 1967 used to wax lyrical about "the deadly beauty" of its Mirage aircraft. The marked differences in the appearance of American and Soviet warships may owe as much to the influence of architects such as Walter Gropius and Mies van der Rohe in the USA as they do to "functional" considerations. Much as the British Navy at one time allegedly saw cannon as brutes which cracked the paint of warships by firing, so the U.S. Navy today seems to regard weapons and antennae and radar dishes as objects that clutter up the decks of vessels and spoil their otherwise sleek lines.

Historically, the problem of aesthetics has often been considered important. There are many cases on record when decoration not only took up the lion's share in the expense of manufacturing military equipment, but was actually allowed to interfere with effectiveness. Though display for its own sake has always been an important consideration, much of the effort that went into decoration can be explained on utilitarian grounds such as the need to cast spells, ward off spirits, and the like. In other cases the object was to terrify the enemy by confronting him with monstrous devices ranging from dragons to the head of Medusa. That head, which supposedly was capable of turning the onlooker into stone, represented a very effective weapon indeed and was regarded as a present fit for a god.

Apart from large size and outlandish design, there are other ways of making weapons appear frightening. Sometimes noise was used, and sometimes fire. For example, Joinville tells us how the Moslems used to fill pots with combustibles, ignite them, and hurl them into the camp of Louis IX at Damietta, thus terrifying the French into surrender. The firearms that came into use soon after 1300 possessed the immense advantage of combining both noise and fire. This fact which may help answer the oft-debated question as to why they were able to assert themselves against older weapons that were often superior to them in reliability, rate of fire, and even power. Nor is the terrifying effect of fire and noise to be disregarded even today. Albert Speer in his memoirs describes how impressed Hitler was when he was shown a film of the howling, flame-spitting V-2, and how he decided to develop it at the expense of the less spectacular, but cheaper, V-1. Similarly, the military effectiveness of weapons such as the World War II German Stuka dive-bomber is said to have owed something to the fact that it came equipped with a siren and emitted a nerve-wracking scream as it dived.

To conclude, the number and variety of examples we have adduced, as well as the fact that they are by no means limited to "uncivilized" peoples and periods, suggests that it might make sense to try to examine our own weapons and weapons systems in similar terms. There is no reason to think that man in general, and military man in particular, has grown markedly more rational since the end of the Age of Tools 500 or so years ago. If irrational factors often affected the design and use of military hardware up to that time, in all probability they continue to do so today. Politicians who order these arms, analysts who are concerned with assessing their impact on warfare, and soldiers who use them in battle would be well advised to take the irrational factor into account.

Furthermore, when it comes to war and warfare, the distinction between utilitarian and nonutilitarian factors may well be open to question if not actually irrelevant. History shows that our usual concept of rationality is too narrow to enable us to come to grips with the problem of war and the technology that is used in it. We have already emphasized that war is an irrational activity of the first order, if only because no rational consideration in the world can ever induce an individual to lay down his own life. Such being the situation, a strong case can be made that possibly the best use of technology in war consists, not merely of accepting the irrational aspects that it presents, but of deliberately manipulating them to one's own advantage. This is all the more true in an age where deterrence has become the cornerstone of strategy, and when the cost of failing to impress the enemy may well be mutual suicide on a global scale. Under such conditions, designing our arms and equipment with such a purpose in mind would appear to make perfectly good sense.

However, even where the intention is to fight and not merely to deter, the best designs are often those that wreck the enemy's nerve. History in her treasure bag has many object lessons to this effect. A recent example is the attack helicopter which, during the war that Israel fought against Syria in Lebanon, apparently owed some of its effectiveness to its remarkable resemblance to some huge, deadly insect and to the psychological effect that this had on the tank crews of both sides. Since man is quick to learn, obviously a device which does not prove its effectiveness will not be feared for very long. On the other hand, by the time its ineffectiveness is discovered the war may well be over. Hence a case might perhaps be made that, the shorter the conflict, the greater the advantage offered by "psychological" as opposed to "utilitarian" designs. Also, secrecy helps. Should one side successfully conceal the true qualities and performance of the arms at his disposal, their mere novelty may well do as much to decide the issue as any "real" technological superiority.

To take the argument to its logical end, in the light of history, the very distinction between utilitarian and nonutilitarian technology often appears misleading. In civilian life, "sexy" products supposedly sell better. In military life, "sexy" weapons often *are* better, to the extent that they help encourage our own troops and demoralize the enemy. What is irrational in one context may well be rational in the other, and *vice versa*. Even more paradoxically, in war and the technology that is used for it, rationality itself consists partly of coming to terms with the irrational. In warfare wisdom consists not only of resigning oneself to the existence of the irrational factor, but of understanding it and actively utilizing it.

PART II

The Age of Machines, 1500–1830

CHAPTER 6
Field Warfare

DURING THAT AGE OF TOOLS, the predominant source of energy employed in warfare consisted of human or animal muscle applied either by individuals or by small groups. True, this rule admitted some important exceptions. One of the purposes behind the phalanx was precisely to bring the energy of many men to bear by forming them into a block and sending them pressing forward, although in this case it is more appropriate to speak of organization than of technology. The construction of some siege engines, notably the ram, permitted the energy of relatively large teams of men to be harnessed and employed in a coordinated fashion. Catapults and trebuchets exploited the energy stored in springs or heavy weights, but ultimately it was the muscles of men which cocked the spring and lifted the weights.

Though the use of sails for transport on land, including specifically military transport on land, was suggested many times, it always fell victim to insuperable obstacles. At sea, sails were of course used from the earliest times. Still, even in this environment, biological energy remained competitive until at least 1598, when a few oared, armored vessels built by the Koreans successfully drove off an invading Japanese sailing fleet. On the whole, biological energy drove the technology of the period and gave it unity.

After 1500, however, the most important weapons employed derived their energy not from biological sources, but from sources that were inanimate, and specifically chemical. It is in this sense that we may speak of them as machines. Indeed a gun of any size may well be understood simply as an internal-combustion engine acting in one direction instead of two. The significance of the new arms was revolutionary in two ways. First, after a period of evolution, the chemical means in use proved capable of packing much greater power, and hurling much heavier projectiles with much greater force, than the largest catapults and trebuchets. Second, their introduction to the battlefield meant that the ability to kill an opponent was no longer directly related to an individual's physical prowess, but tended to become a question of trained, professional skill. These factors, in combination, were to shape combat during the next few centuries.

The origins of gunpowder, like those of the vast majority of inventions before the Renaissance, are shrouded in mystery. Before its invention and to some extent even after it, gunpowder was not clearly differentiated from other compounds possessing similar qualities and serving broadly similar purposes. One class of such compounds is represented by incendiaries. Some of these incendiaries consisted simply of tow, cloth, or some other suitable organic material that was daubed in a combustible and shot to its target by means of an arrow. Others were flammable liquids contained within earthenware vessels (in China, they were placed in bamboo tubes). They were provided with a fuse and hand-thrown at the enemy, or else shot from mechanical artillery. Finally, there were the liquid combustibles squirted from pumps and used mainly for naval warfare. The materials used for making these incendiaries included pitch, bitumen, sulphur, petroleum, and quicklime, the purpose of the last being to achieve spontaneous ignition upon contact with water. The employment of incendiaries in war—particularly at sea and in siege warfare, where there were wooden structures to burn—has been quite common from the earliest times. Naturally, it took time before the distinction between them and gunpowder, which also involves the use of fire, crystallized in people's minds.

Another class of compounds that are related to gunpowder, and which must have been occasionally confused with the latter, are the materials used for fireworks and rockets. A formula for such a material is given by a Chinese manuscript of the eleventh century. It resembles that of black powder, except for an added oily substance (hydrocarbons). Such a mixture would be comparatively slow to combust, hence it would be more suitable for some fiercely burning form of firework than for an explosive. The Chinese, and apparently the Indians as well, used it as a filling for rockets. Originally the intent of the exercise was to drive away demons. There may have been occasions when the demons assumed human form and were confused with the enemy of the moment, this being another example of a kind of "irrational" technology. If this was indeed the case, and if rockets were sometimes used for military purposes, their effect must have been limited, since their power was not great and their accuracy very doubtful.

We do not know just where, when, and by whom the various incendiaries and combustibles were first combined and refined to create black powder, and used to propel a projectile from a barrel. The Chinese, during the twelfth century, invented primitive grenades in the form of paper or bamboo tubes. These were filled with powder as well as with stones, broken porcelain, and iron bullets, and thrown at the enemy. Each of the three separate constituents that go into making a gun being thus available, what remained to be done was to reverse their use and add a touchhole so as to enable the stones, porcelain, and other materials to be fired from the tube. Here is a classical illustration of the way inventions do not create things *ex novo* but rather wrench existing elements from their framework and combine them in new ways. Doing this represented no mean feat, and one that may have owed something to accident. Certainly the idea had occurred to the Chinese by the middle of the thirteenth century, when primitive bamboo guns were in use, soon to be replaced by guns made of metal (the earliest extant example dates from 1356). At about the same time, primitive guns made their appearance in the Moslem world, and Roger Bacon wrote down what appears to be a cryptogram containing a formula for making gunpowder. As with the near-contemporary discoveries of paper, of the compass, and of block-printing, the way in which all these separate events were related to each other remains unknown. Possibly it was the Mongols who brought gunpowder to Europe during the 1240s, or else its use was disseminated by way of the Arab and Byzantine worlds. Guns, too, may have spread in either of these ways, or else may have been independently invented at different places.

During the millenia before the fourteenth century, the military technologies in use in different parts of the world were not homogeneous but extremely varied and intimately linked with different cultures and life-styles. Though some isolated areas (such as Australia and the Americas and parts of Africa) were already lagging behind, on the whole the most advanced regions maintained a balance so that a clear-cut and long-lasting superiority of one over the rest did not emerge. The development of gunpowder and firearms in Europe introduced a fundamental change in this situation, a fact that justifies our concentration on that continent. Within Europe itself, the new arms brought military homogeneity. During the Middle Ages a quiltwork pattern had prevailed, with military equipment reflecting the social status of the user or else his nationality (e.g., Welsh, Swiss, or Genoese). By the end of the sixteenth century, however, all advanced armies were more or less similarly equipped. This fact later enabled Clausewitz to claim that the importance of numbers "in modern war" was increasing every day, a conclusion which does indeed follow if its premise—broad qualitative equality—is granted.

Concentrating, then, on Europe, with only an occasional glance at the rest of the world, the earliest records of firearms being manufactured and purchased and used in war date from the first third of the fourteenth century. Almost from the beginning these arms fell into two classes: small portable handguns on the one hand, and large crew-operated cannon on the other. The distinction between the two classes has persisted to this day, and forms a convenient basis for discussion. This, however, should not blind us to the fact that there have been and still remain in existence numerous intermediary types.

Handguns were simply metal tubes closed at one end. Originally their length was less than 25 centimetres, and their caliber between 25 and 45 millimeters. These guns, if that is indeed the word for so primitive a device, were held in the left hand and fired by means of a match brought into contact with a touchhole. Repeated firing made them too hot to handle, so that they soon came to be clamped onto wooden boards or stocks resembling a miniature baker's trough and possibly modeled on the latter. The stocks were held under the left arm. Alternatively they would be thrust into the ground, in which case a forked rest might be added to make the contraption as a whole look like a small mortar. Loading consisted of first pouring in the fine powder, then a wad, then the ball, and finally another wad. Since barrels were short, the place of the ball was near the muzzle. Consequently power, range, and accuracy were all very poor.

As is often the case when some new device makes its appearance for the first time, an "accepted idea" concerning its principal components and the way it should look did not yet exist. The breaking down of old patterns, which constitutes the essence of invention, meant that there was plenty of room for experiment, and the inventiveness displayed by the creators of early firearms is indeed astonishing. Before the fifteenth century was out, trials had already been made with elongated projectiles, rifled barrels, and weapons that were loaded not through the muzzle but through the breech (some early examples of crude breechloaders are still on display in the courtyard of Windsor Castle). Repeating guns, known as ribaldquins and consisting of many tubes tied together and mounted on a pushcart, had also been invented and may have seen some limited service in the field. If all these devices were ultimately destined to fall into disuse, or—in the case of rifling— to be used on an extremely limited scale for specialized purposes such as hunting, this was not because the ideas behind them were basically unsound, but rather because manufacturing them with the equipment at hand was difficult or impossible. During the nineteenth century, all of them were revived.

Although the exact stages along which portable firearms developed are often obscure, and the various interrelationships are ill-understood, their general outline is well known. Around 1500, the dominant type was the arquebus or harquebus, meaning "hooked tube." It derived its name from the shape of the butt which was now attached to the stock and which, fitting snugly with the human anatomy, was to characterize all shoulder-arms from that time on. The heavy butt made it possible to lengthen the barrel to between 100 and 130 centimeters. This greatly improved both power and accuracy, even though it entailed the complication of adding a ramrod for loading. The weapon continued to be fired by means of a touchhole which, however, had been moved from its original place at the top of the barrel to its right side. The fuse, instead of being held in the hand, was now attached to a trigger. When the trigger was pulled, the fuse was brought into contact with the touchhole. With the invention of the firelock, the arquebus attained a recognizably modern form. During the next three hundred years the principal improvements involved changes in the method of ignition. The firelock was replaced by the wheel lock and, when the latter proved too expensive and unreliable for general use, by the flintlock also known as snaphance. These lasted well into the nineteenth century.

Apart from the changes that took place in the method of ignition, the evolution of portable firearms may also be understood from another point of view. Given a certain level of development, the power of any technological device is a function of its weight and size. In the case of the arms in question, too, what mattered was finding an acceptable balance between weight and size, a balance which determined tactics, and was in turn determined by them. Early firearms were very small but, in order to add power, increased steadily in size. This development meant that, whereas the sixteenth-century arquebus could still be couched in a soldier's arms while it was fired, the early seventeenth-century musket no longer could. The weapon, weighing 12 to 14 pounds, had to be supported by a forked rest. This impeded mobility and made muskets difficult to use on the offense—an unwelcome development. The bayonet, invented around 1660, would have been useless unless the musket was lightened to the point that the rest could be discarded and the weapon swung in the arms of an average soldier. This was duly done, even at the cost of some loss of power. Not everybody liked the change, and the Marechal de Saxe during the middle of the eighteenth century was calling for the introduction of an amusette, an even heavier musket which would have to be pivoted on a wall or attached to a cart. Thus the different qualities demanded of the weapon clashed and interacted, pushing development along.

Since writing and fighting have traditionally made bad bedfellows, the earliest extant documents from Metz (1324), Florence (1326), and Britain (1327) mentioning cannon are typically concerned with their manufacture and sale rather than with their military use. Like portable firearms, cannon were filled with gunpowder and set off through a touchhole. Unlike portable firearms, they were made not in the form of tubes but, if an early illustration is to be believed, in that of pots resting on a wooden stand and firing heavy bolts. From these modest beginnings, cannon rapidly grew to the point where they could no longer be cast by using available means. New methods of manufacture had to be found. Guns, earlier called tubes, were now constructed in the form of barrels. They were made up of staves that were joined together by hoops. Initially cannon manufactured in this way may have been almost as dangerous to their users as to the enemy, but during the fifteenth century they permitted a remarkable increase in power and size. Late fifteenth-century bombards fired round stones, sometimes almost a meter across and weighing in excess of one ton. The guns themselves were almost too heavy to be moved, and resembled earlier siege engines in that they were sometimes manufactured on the spot, as in the case of the Turkish siege of Constantinople in 1453. Not only did the heavy wooden sleds on which they rested have to be transported separately, but the barrels themselves were sometimes made of two pieces that screwed into each other.

Given the immense weight of early cannon, their main use was for siege warfare. Their effective use in the field depended on a general lightening, which was important not only in itself but because it permitted the barrels to be put on wheels. Two developments made this process feasible. One, during the sixteenth century, was the improved combustion that resulted from replacing fine powder by corned powder, permitting a much heavier punch to be delivered by a ball of a given size. The other was improved casting techniques which allowed barrels to be made of a single piece of iron or bronze. Stone balls gradually disappeared, being replaced by iron projectiles which did not shatter when hitting a wall.

The size of cannon continued to decline. Gustavus Adolphus, although he invented the light "leather gun"—actually a three-pounder cannon with brass barrels and a leather cover, small enough to be manhandled on the battlefield—still relied for siege-work on cumbersome "wall-crackers" firing 48-pound balls. His eighteenth-century successors made do with 24-pounders, though even these were almost impossible to move unless river transport happened to be available. Another development occurred between 1759 and 1780, when further reductions in the weight of cannon enabled Frederick the Great and, after him, the French engineer Gribeauval, to create horse artillery and thus achieve mobility on the battlefield. All these, however, were improvements in detail. In principle, the guns with which Napoleon invaded Italy in 1796 did not differ greatly from those with which Charles VIII had done the same almost exactly 300 years earlier.

As in the case of portable firearms, an astonishing variety of inventions were made during the early days of the cannon; however, development centered on the ammunition, rather than on the guns themselves. The replacement of stone by iron balls has already been mentioned. There was also an intermediary stage in which stone balls were sometimes encased by iron hoops. Before the fourteenth century was out attempts were made to manufacture hollow iron ammunition which was filled with explosives and provided with a fuse. The seventeenth century experimented with "chain ammunition"—two balls linked by means of a chain and fired from a single barrel. (Attempts to fire them simultaneously from two barrels were made but proved much too dangerous since precise coordination was impossible.) The early eighteenth century added grapeshot and canister, both of them methods for shooting large numbers of small balls from a single barrel and both well-suited for antipersonnel work at close quarters. Not all of these inventions survived. The problem of fusing a shell in such a way as to cause it to explode when at the target rather than inside the gun only found a satisfactory solution during the second half of the nineteenth century. Chain shot proved most useful in naval engagements where balls flying in tandem stood a greater chance of cutting through the masts and spars of enemy vessels. Grape, canister, and solid roundshot were in general use. For siege warfare, and at sea, solid ammunition was sometimes brought to a red-hot state and so made to serve as an incendiary.

Throughout the fifteenth century and after, the introduction of the new arms met with furious resistance. The echoes are to be found not only in contemporary military records but also in literary works. The opposition centered around two separate, if related, issues. First, firearms failed to observe a proper distinction between nobleman and commoner. By enabling a commoner to kill a nobleman at the pull of a trigger they tended to take the fun out of war, thereby helping to alter the latter's entire cultural, social, and political foundation. Second, these arms were difficult to load and use while on horseback. Though the pistol and the carbine, both of them consisting essentially of smaller versions of the arquebus, were in use during the sixteenth century at the latest, neither of them really solved the problem. Some cavalry, armed with lances and sabers, was still required, but the majority of the forces were confronted with an unpleasant choice. Either they had to dismount to march and fight on foot, or else military ineffectiveness would be the result. It says something about the social makeup of late medieval and renaissance Europe that, after a prolonged struggle, the infantry was able to reassert itself more strongly than at any time since the early Middle Ages. This was not a foregone conclusion, however, as shown by the case of Egypt, where the ruling class of Mamluks consciously and deliberately preferred to keep their horses even at the price of sacrificing military effectiveness. In 1514–15 this reluctance was one factor that led to their defeat and conquest at the hands of the Ottoman Turks. However, it proved a rational enough decision in so far as it enabled them to retain de facto power until the Napoleonic occupation three hundred years later.

Resistance rooted in social and cultural considerations, of course, was not the only reason why firearms were slow to gain general acceptance. As compared to bows and mechanical artillery, early firearms both small and large performed poorly in regard to reliability, accuracy, rate of fire, and even power. Legend has it that the earliest ones were employed chiefly for psychological effect, their most valuable attribute being the noise that they made. Such may indeed have been the case; however, unless it is also effective in some concrete way, the psychological impact of any new technology will soon wear off. In fact, arguments about the relative effectiveness of the different arms persisted well beyond 1350. Longbows, crossbows, and portable firearms were used side by side throughout the fifteenth century, and indeed the English still employed longbowmen at the battle of Ré in France in 1627. Since, prior to the invention of red-hot cannonballs in the eighteenth century, mechanical artillery presented the only means for firing incendiaries (in the form of burning arrows), it too gave way only very slowly. Some limited use seems to have been made of it as late as the first quarter of the seventeenth century.

As firearms took a long time to equal, let alone surpass, the effectiveness of bows and mechanical artillery, their impact upon warfare was not sudden but gradual. This was all the more true because their rise coincided with the reappearance of other weapons taken over from antiquity, weapons that proved extremely effective in spite of their technological simplicity. During the fourteenth and fifteenth centuries the Swiss revived the pike and the military formation that accompanies it, the phalanx. They used them first against the Habsburgs, then against the Dukes of Burgundy, and finally, as mercenaries, in the service of the Kings of France. To counter the pike, the Spaniards experimented with Roman-style sword-and-buckler men, a solution much admired by Machiavelli who, like many other humanists, was obsessed with anything Roman. Neither the Swiss nor the Spaniards relied on these arms alone. Instead, they were freely mixed with halberds, arbalests, handguns, and even cannon.

It took a long time to discover which of these combinations was superior, the more so since the circumstances of their employment were as varied then as they are today. This very often enabled proponents and opponents to introduce special arguments, claiming that this or that victory or defeat was due not to the intrinsic qualities of the weapons but rather to the way in which they were used or misused by a particular force at a particular place and time. As the sentiments of Machiavelli indicated, then as today the debate was not couched entirely (cynics would say, even mainly) in terms of military effectiveness as such, but included cultural, social, and political considerations, as well as special pleading of every kind.

The fifteenth century having thus been marked by an extraordinary amount of confusion, with each army sticking to its own idiosyncratic combination of weapons and tactics, some semblance of order and uniformity was reestablished in the sixteenth. In particular, the battle of Pavia (1525), where the troops of Francis I of France were routed by those of the Habsburg Emperor, Charles V. A decisive moment came when 1,500 of the Emperor's Spanish arquebusiers threw the French cavalry into utter confusion. Thereafter there could be no question but that the future belonged to firearms. To be effective, armies would have to rely on some combination of pikes, handguns, artillery, and cavalry, although the exact proportions continued to be a matter of informed and uninformed debate. Each of the arms in use had its own advantages and limitations. The real art of the commander consisted less of obtaining a superiority in each weapon separately than of combining them all in such a way as to bring out strengths and obviate weaknesses, in general and also in relation to the specific enemy at hand. The greatest victories that have been won in war do not depend on a simple superiority of technology, but rather on a careful meshing of one side's advantages with the other's weaknesses so as to produce the greatest possible gap between the two.

Difficulties were always involved in combining the various arms, and an infinitely large number of methods were devised to deal with the problem. The pike is an excellent example. Until the middle of the seventeenth century it remained the most frequently-employed single weapon; its dominance was reflected in the phrase "to trail a pike" as a synonym for "to participate in the wars." Pikes were suited for fighting at close quarters, where the combination of a bristling forest of points with the power of large formations made them difficult to resist. Their effectiveness, however, depended absolutely on the men remaining in these formations, since individual pikemen with their eighteen-foot weapons were almost entirely helpless against more agile, more lightly armed opponents of every kind. The tight formations demanded by pikes made it difficult to employ them over broken terrain, particularly when such terrain was reinforced by field fortifications as was the Spanish system in Italy. Also, massed formations of pikemen made ideal targets for firearms, particularly artillery. It was with artillery that the French finally blasted the Swiss phalanx from the battlefield at Marignano in 1515.

Armies equipped exclusively with pikes would be unable to strike at each other except by direct push. Consequently even the Swiss, who made the pike into their national weapon, usually combined it with some missile-throwing weapon such as the crossbow which could be employed for softening up the enemy before the real business of the day was begun. From 1450 on, crossbows were gradually replaced by handguns. Had handguns been really effective, armies would never have come to really close quarters, "push of pike," as the saying went. However, lacking such effectiveness, during most of the period success depended on mixing pikemen with arquebusiers and combining the two in such a way that they offered mutual protection. To this purpose late sixteenth- and early seventeenth-century armies surrounded the pike phalanx with "sleeves" of arquebusiers. The arquebusiers would fire until the last moment, then withdraw either behind the pikemen or inside their formations. As time went on the proportion of pikemen to arquebusiers tended to change, the pikemen declining in number and the arquebusiers increasing. It was only the invention of the bayonet, which combined the advantages of pike and arquebus in a single weapon, that finally enabled the pike to be discarded and a single homogeneous type of infantry to be created.

Phalanxes made up of pikemen and arquebusiers when employed against each other were almost equally fitted for offense and defense, but their comparative immobility made them hopeless against cavalry unless the cavalry chose to attack. The threat of cavalry would compel a phalanx to close ranks, and this of course enabled the enemy artillery to come into its own. Artillery in turn was comparatively immobile, hence on the whole better suited to defense than to offense. Its use would cause the enemy to disperse, so that ideally its employment had to be closely coordinated with the cavalry. For its part, cavalry came equipped with a variety of short firearms and edged weapons. The combination did not prove very satisfactory. Firearms were difficult to load and aim on horseback, and edged weapons insufficiently powerful against unbroken infantry in organized formations. Tactics therefore became a question of opening the battle by using cavalry to force the enemy infantry to form into phalanxes or squares, then employing the artillery to break up those squares, then launching one's own infantry against the weakened enemy, and finally sending in the cavalry a second time to deliver the *coup de grâce*.

This, of course, was the ideal sequence. In practice, the number of variations and deviations were all but infinite. To defend itself against both cavalry and artillery, infantry could take shelter in broken ground or—against artillery alone—simply lie down. Given the short range and slow rate of fire of artillery, a bold charge by mounted troops might lead to the capture of the guns; they could then be turned against their original owners or else spiked, that is, rendered useless by having a nail driven into their touchholes. The cavalry if lucky might hope to catch the infantry when out of formation, in which case the likely outcome was a massacre. In practice, every battle would probably see all of these things happen at once at different places along the front, victory going to the side who retained a reserve and knew when to use it in the midst of all the noise, smoke, and confusion. The variety of circumstances under which battles were fought, and of the terrain over which they were fought, was such that the number of possible combinations was very large, certainly too large to enable weapons to dictate the forms that combat assumed. Nevertheless, over time certain formations and tactics did establish themselves as more effective than others.

One very important sixteenth century tactical innovation, which was both cause and outcome of these technological developments, was drill. Drill had been well known to the Greek, Hellenistic, and Roman armies which had maneuvered and fought in well-coordinated infantry formations, but its role during the high Middle Ages—when forces were made up of mounted knights—was naturally much less. Early firearms, however, positively demanded drill for several interconnected reasons. First, the relative complexity of these weapons allowed much room for error. Unless a soldier was carefully trained in advance, he was likely to double load or else forget to withdraw his ramrod, leading to unfortunate results both to himself and to others. Second, to prevent accidents and achieve the greatest possible firepower it was important that the troops be arrayed very precisely so as not to stand in each other's way. Third, the unreliability and slow rate of fire of these weapons made it imperative that they be employed in coordination, to ensure that at least a fraction of the available barrels would be loaded and ready to fire at any given moment. Fourth, the cooperation of musketeers with pikemen demanded the opening and closing of ranks—sometimes, repeatedly—as well as other complex evolutions. The invention of the bayonet brought some relief by putting an end to the last of these problems; the rest, however, remained just as long as the weapons themselves. The answer to them was drill, the rise of which was, in turn, connected with the introduction of drums during the fifteenth century and of uniforms during the seventeenth.

The first great drillmaster of modern times was Prince Maurice of Nassau, and the first drillbooks were published in the Netherlands early in the seventeenth century. Prescribing motions and evolutions in minute detail, these books soon proliferated into an enormous literature as professionals and amateurs tried their hand, the amateurs acting in conformity with the spirit of an age that regarded war as part of a gentleman's education. Soon competition developed between the authors themselves, with the result that their brainwork is replete with evolutions which were often too complex for practical use, and sometimes completely imaginary. Nevertheless, even though subsequent commentators from Napoleon on have tended to deride the formalism of early modern warfare, and of eighteenth-century warfare in particular, these textbooks reflected a real need. Given the characteristics of the weapons of the age, their use by large formations without drill would have been all but impossible.

Overall, the most important development of the period owed its existence to the gradually increasing reliability and rate of fire of the weapons in use. This in turn was made possible not only by successive improvements in locks but also by the introduction—at the hands of Gustavus Adolphus, it is said—of paper cartridges containing powder, wad, and ball in a single package. Improved arms and ammunition enabled the infantry to spread out on the battlefield and thus bring greater firepower to bear. The number of ranks was reduced, falling from eight or ten in the armies of early seventeenth-century commanders such as Spinola and Maurice of Nassau, to four or five in those of Marlborough and his opponents. During the 1740s, wooden ramrods gave way to ramrods made of iron, leading to a further increase in the rate of fire, and this resulted in the adoption of a formation consisting of three ranks. By the end of the century two ranks were sometimes used, one firing and the other loading. Though by this time a growing proportion of the infantry had come to consist of skirmishers, the principle of employing the bulk of the men in ordered formations still applied. It formed an essential part of the most celebrated military handbook of the age, Baron Jomini's *Précis de l'art de la guerre*.

Whatever the precise number of ranks at any given moment in time, and it was not always the same under all circumstances or in all armies, considerations pertaining to both safety and effectiveness demanded that weapons be used in a precisely coordinated fashion. This required great concentration and a wall-like steadfastness under fire, qualities that took years of training and a ferocious discipline to inculcate. The need for discipline in action was reinforced by the inaccuracy of the weapons in use and the consequent desire of each commander to close with the enemy— "look into the whites of their eyes," as the phrase went—before opening fire. To shorten the range as much as possible, each side held its fire until the last possible moment. There was some advantage in being the last to fire, which contributed to exchanges such as the famous one at Fontenoy (1743), where the English and the French each politely asked the other to please shoot first. A volley delivered at point blank range might easily result in 10 or 15 percent of the troops on the receiving end being killed or wounded. Unless held back by discipline and by sergeant majors with demi-pikes at the ready, the rest would naturally turn and run. Given these circumstances, it is hardly surprising that the best armies of the period were those which were most successful in turning their men into soulless robots goose-stepping forward at exactly 90 paces the minute. This was a field where the French were the first to excel, the name of General Martinet even passing into both the French and English languages. Later the lead was taken by the Prussians whose king Frederick Wilhelm—also known as "the soldier King"—beat and kicked the troops into shape so savagely that, under the command of his son Frederick the Great, they proved themselves second to none on every Central European battlefield.

As the role of firearms grew, that of edged weapons used by the infantry decreased. The first to go was the long two-handed ax or halberd, which had already disappeared almost completely by the beginning of the seventeenth century. It was soon followed by the sword, though both continued to serve ceremonial purposes even into the twentieth century. Since the demise of the pike at the very beginning of the eighteenth century greatly facilitated the handling of infantry, it was regarded by Clausewitz as a major turning point. This left the bayonet, an important weapon against both cavalry and infantry. During the period before 1830 bayonet charges were not infrequent, but their number declined over time. We have the testimony of Napoleon's surgeon general, Larrey, that for every bayonet-wound he treated there were a hundred caused by small arms or artillery fire. Still, with the sword and the halberd, the bayonet was not without its supporters. Unlike other eighteenth-century weapons, it remains in limited service to this day, though its most frequent use may well be as a can-opener.

Given the increasing power of the weapons carried by the infantry, the importance of cavalry naturally tended to decline and indeed the period as a whole may well be regarded from this particular point of view. Cavalry had taken pride of place on medieval battlefields. Early in the eighteenth century, however, it only constituted approximately one-third of the most advanced armies, and during the next hundred years this figure tended to decline until it was down to between one-quarter and one-sixth. The cavalry, whether light or heavy, was armed like the infantry with a combination of firearms and edged weapons, though in its case the relative importance of edged weapons was much greater. Like the infantry, but more slowly, it was led to abandon its body armor. Full suits of armor were replaced by others reaching only to the knees, and the process of shortening went on throughout the seventeenth and eighteenth centuries. By the time of the Battle of Waterloo in 1815 only the cuirassier's helmet and breastplate were left, relics from an earlier age that were carried right into the second half of the nineteenth century.

The unique mobility characteristic of cavalry nevertheless meant that it would continue to play an important role. Cavalry remained essential for screening, reconnaissance, and pursuit, tasks which could not properly be carried out by any other arm. Not infrequently, too, cavalry charges launched at the right moment by such leaders as Gustavus Adolphus, Cromwell, Marlborough, Ziethen, and Murat succeeded in shattering the enemy and deciding the issue of battles. Certainly around 1800 an army without cavalry would be at a grave disadvantage against an opponent who possessed it. On the other hand, it was probably the most dispensable among the three arms.

As the role of cavalry diminished, that of the artillery tended to increase. An early eighteenth-century army with one gun per 400 troops would be considered strong and well-equipped even for siege warfare. By contrast, at Borodino in 1812 the French had one cannon for every 200 men. While in principle not very different from the pieces employed since about 1500, artillery did become considerably more mobile owing both to improved casting techniques—which enabled lighter barrels to withstand greater pressure—and also to changes in organization. As a result, the usefulness of artillery as an offensive weapon progressively grew. Though it relied mostly on direct fire, the effective range of artillery exceeded that of the musket by a factor of 5 or 6 to 1. At the hands of a master such as Napoleon, this fact enabled the guns to be rushed across the battlefield, concentrated in the open right opposite the enemy infantry, and employed to tear great gaping holes in their ranks. These holes could then be exploited first by infantry columns closing with the bayonet and then by heavy cavalry which poured in and hacked at the shattered units on both sides. A well-organized artillery service was indispensable to any army. On the other hand, among the three arms it was the one least able to stand on its own.

Overall, the period between 1500 and 1830 was characterized by continuous and fairly steady technological progress. In contrast to the previous age, this meant that there could be no periodic return to old weapons. In a process that was certainly slow by modern standards, some arms gradually became obsolete and were discarded in favor of others that were newly invented. Consequently, over time it was only the technologically most advanced political entities which could stay in the race, whereas the rest tended to drop out. Though Montesquieu during the first half of the eighteenth century might still hold up the Roman army as an example, the point had now been reached where improved arms would have made it hopeless for a Gustavus Adolphus to try to fight a Napoleon or even a General Mack. The importance of keeping technologically abreast, or if possible ahead, of actual and potential rivals certainly did not go unrecognized by contemporaries. Henry VIII, Johan of Nassau (chief artilleryman to his better-known cousin, Maurice), Gustavus Adolphus, and Maurice of Saxe among others took an active interest in, and experimented with, a variety of new weapons of every kind.

To look at the other side of the equation, however, military technological progress was still so slow that a commander might expect to spend his entire career employing virtually the same instruments. Since not one among all the great captains of the age can really be said to have possessed a decided margin of technological superiority, it is difficult to attribute their victories mainly to technology. Nor can the very varied tactics that these captains often invented and employed be explained on the basis of technological considerations alone. For example, though Spinola and Maurice of Nassau both relied on arquebuses, Maurice pioneered the battalion as a tactical formation, whereas Spinola did not. Likewise, there is no doubt that Frederick the Great's oblique order owed more to his reading about the exploits of the ancient Theban general Epaminondas than to any minute differences that may have existed between the muskets employed by his troops and those of his enemies. So far was Napoleon from possessing any decided margin of technological superiority that on occasion he was not above taking over and incorporating into the *Grande Armée* entire captured enemy arsenals. Where arms and equipment on both sides were approximately the same, as they normally were in encounters between the principal powers, the factor which decided the issue was not technology, but the ability to combine hardware, training, doctrine, and organization into a single decisive whole. This whole had to be perfect, not only in the sense of tailoring the different constituents to match each other, but above all in relation to the specific enemy and circumstances and purpose at hand. So it was during the period 1500–1830; so it has always been, and so it will always be.

CHAPTER 7

Siege Warfare

IF GUNPOWDER revolutionized combat, its effect upon siege operations was equally well recognized by contemporaries. Beginning in the sixteenth century, much ink had already been spilled to analyze the competition between fortress and cannon, a subject which for a time became part of the normal education of a gentleman. Later during the eighteenth century, the scope of the debate was immensely broadened as it came to be realized that the effects of that competition were not limited to the military field but led to far-reaching social, economic, and political changes as well. It was argued, and has been ever since, that the castle was defeated by the gun and that feudalism came crashing down as one of the results. This interpretation is, however, open to question.

The introduction of firearms to Europe dates back to the first quarter of the fourteenth century. The earliest were apparently used against personnel rather than against fortifications, the effect being as much psychological as physical. While the first record of an association between cannon and a castle dates to within thirty years of artillery's first appearance, it may be significant that this record tells us of a cannon that was used not to attack a fortress but to defend it. In 1356, an English garrison in Breteuil, Normandy, was being besieged by a French army under the command of King John II. Employing the usual techniques of the age, the French filled in the moat, crossed it, and then brought a fighting tower, or belfry, to the wall. The defenders at first engaged the assaulting party hand to hand, but then suddenly withdrew to allow some form of fire-engine to be used. The text of Froissart, who is our source for this episode, is not clear. While he seems to mention cannon that threw "heavy bolts," in the same breath he also refers to "jets of fire" which were somehow produced and used to set the tower alight. Whatever his exact meaning, the first recorded use of what may have been artillery in connection with siege warfare ended with a temporary victory for the defense since the French tower caught fire and its remains had to be abandoned in the moat. A few days after this episode, the French king felt threatened from a different quarter and became impatient to end the siege. He offered terms, and Breteuil surrendered.

From this point onward, accounts of cannon being used both to attack fortresses and to defend them multiply rapidly. The *Crònica di Pisa*, written late in the fourteenth century, narrates that the Pisans in 1362 used a bombard weighing almost 1000 kg against the castle of Pietra Buona. However, there is no record of its effect on the wall. In 1357 the Duke of Burgundy employed guns—borrowed, interestingly, from the municipality of Chartres—to capture the castle of Camrolles near that town. Twelve years later the municipality of Arras made provision for protecting the town gates by allocating a cannon to each of them. During the siege warfare that took place between Venetians and Genoese in 1379–80—the war of Chiogga—there was much use of bombards by both sides. As in the case of ballistae and catapults in ancient times, artillery could be made to face both ways and this was actually done almost from the beginning.

The earliest cannon also resembled previous siege engines in another respect. Insufficiently powerful to bring down curtain walls, their main use was to clear the defenders from sections of the wall so as to permit mining, boring, or the approach of siege towers. As time went on, the size and power both of individual cannon and of siege trains gradually increased, however, and this made it possible to develop new tactics. Froissart narrates that, for the Siege of Odkruik in 1377, the Duke of Burgundy marshaled no fewer than 140 cannon. Some of them fired stone projectiles 100 kg in weight, corresponding to a 35-centimeter bore. This appears to be the first case on record when artillery succeeded in making a breach in the fortifications, whereupon the castle surrendered. As compared to earlier stone-throwing engines, the ability of cannon to bring about this result probably depended not so much on their power as in the flatter trajectory that they afforded. This made it possible to aim at specific points on the wall and hit them again and again, thus ultimately bringing about a collapse.

The curtain walls surrounding medieval castles were singularly ill-suited to resist artillery fire. Since they were made tall to withstand an escalade, they presented excellent targets. They were designed to withstand boring and ramming, so they were frequently much thinner on top than at the base. A besieger who knew his business might therefore use his artillery to bring the higher masonry crashing down upon the lower, thus simultaneously creating a graduated passage for an assault. Once an effective method for creating a breach was available, crossing the moat that protected most castles became much easier, since it would tend to be filled in by the ruins of the walls themselves. Finally, since curtain walls were high and narrow on top, guns could only be used in their defense with great difficulty, if at all.

In so warlike an age as the late European Middle Ages, these shortcomings were quickly realized. Attempts were accordingly made to modify existing structures, a process which involved several distinct steps. During the opening years of the fifteenth century, gates were already being protected from the rear by the cutting of broad passages known as boulevards (from *bouleverser*, literally, to bowl over) which offered a free field for the fire of cannon. Next, towers were cut down and filled in with earth so as to create a platform for other cannon which were trained outward. Since the towers of medieval castles were for the most part too cramped to serve this purpose, however, the attempt to provide platforms was soon transferred to the curtain walls themselves. Their height was reduced and they were backed up with massive earthen ramps, an operation sufficiently commonplace to acquire a technical term ("rampiring") of its own. Though rampiring helped castles to withstand an artillery bombardment, it also carried the disadvantage of causing walls to collapse outward once the breach was made, thus facilitating assault and entry. The entire process was makeshift by nature, and is perhaps best understood as an attempt to save the huge social and economic investment represented by castles.

Side by side with these expedients, during the late fourteenth century attempts were already being made to construct new fortifications which would be impervious to cannon. First, it was necessary to build the walls in such a way as to enable them to withstand a bombardment. Second, room had to be provided for the use of artillery by the defenders themselves. In Italy, France, and England, the first response to this dual demand was to lower the walls and thicken them, in some cases to as much as 15–20 meters. Next came the abandonment of towers in favor of round, tublike structures known as roundels and described by Albrecht Duerer and others. The roundel's walls differed from those of the tower in that they no longer stood vertical to the ground, but were inclined inward in order to present glancing surfaces for shot. Not only did their flat tops provide a platform for guns, but it did not take long before the walls came to be equipped with built-in embrasures and vaulted casemates. Pointing their cannon outward from these, gunners attempted to create interlocking fields of fire to avoid dead corners. These innovations notwithstanding, late fifteenth century fortresses resembled their predecessors in that they stood out high above the ground. The idea that tall is strong had entrenched itself from time immemorial, and it naturally took a while to be abandoned.

When Charles VIII invaded Italy in 1494 he brought along an unprecedentedly strong siege train that was the wonder of the age. The most modern fortresses he encountered were of the type described above. As Machiavelli derisively says in *The Prince,* they were brought down "chalk in hand," by which he apparently meant that it was sufficient for a French officer to make a mark on a fortress gate for its garrison to surrender in short order. As so frequently happens in war, however, the success of one side—in this case, the attack—was short-lived. The reaction when it came was strong and effective. In the first decade of the sixteenth century, the Pisans and Venetians had already adopted the device of separating their interior ramparts from the outer walls by a ditch. As a result, when the outer wall collapsed it formed a barrier made of jagged stone unmixed with earth, and this barrier came directly under the muzzles of the cannon stationed on the overlooking ramparts behind. In 1504 it was this system which enabled Pisa, a small and weak town, to withstand a French siege employing the most advanced means then available. The potential of the new method was demonstrated even more dramatically in 1509 when the Empire, France, and the Papal State formed an unholy Alliance whose objective was to dismember Venice. The result was a siege at Padua, a siege which ended with the withdrawal of the attackers, partly because of the strength of the fortifications, and partly because the German nobility refused to dismount and fight on foot.

The so called "Pisan rampart," however, proved to be only a foretaste of things to come. For a time, after 1510, there was much experimentation with fortifications made of earth and wood. In 1555, during the Spanish siege of Santhia in Piedmont, a fort of this kind absorbed several thousand roundshot and emerged intact. Meanwhile, Italian engineers such as Antonio da Sangallo and Michele di Sanmicheli were hard at work looking for a permanent solution. Sometime around 1520—although certain forerunners can be traced as early as the 1470s or 1480s—the so-called "Italian" type of fortification emerged, a revolutionary innovation which had the effect of enormously strengthening the defense.

The new system of fortification consisted of three simple elements. First, the entire structure was now built right into the immensely wide ditch, with the result that it no longer projected much above ground and consequently no longer presented a target to the attacker's artillery. Second, a combination of long, straight walls with squat, wedge shaped towers (bastions) permitted the entire length of the ditch to be raked by the fire of cannon that were either trained through especially-constructed embrasures or else were mounted atop the low, flat walls. Third, it was realized almost from the beginning that the bastions could be made to protect not only the walls but also each other. This demanded that they be placed in symmetrical order, with blunt angles pointing outward in every direction. This created the characteristic star-like shape of fortifications, hundreds of which were to dot the European countryside. Naturally, the new arrangements did not emerge all at once. However, by 1560 every one of the essential elements was to be found in the work of a man like Francesco Paciotto da Urbino, who was responsible for the fortification of Turin.

Over the next three centuries, the new type of fortress spread from Italy into France, England, Germany and, above all, the Low Countries, where a triple line of these structures, situated on the Great Rivers and adapted to local conditions, enabled the Dutch Revolt to survive and triumph. Driven partly by the practical challenge presented by the ever growing power of the offense, but partly also by the natural ingenuity of engineers always on the lookout for new problems to solve, fortifications developed in two principal directions. First, the gradually increasing range of cannon caused fortifications to grow larger and more expensive. Second, they began to sprout outworks, which would make it more difficult for the attacker to bring his artillery within range. Initially these outworks consisted of isolated bastion-like structures so situated as to protect each of the star's points. However, it was not long before attempts were made to incorporate outworks and fortress into a single structure, which then led to the construction of even further outworks. Over time, the process could repeat itself several times.

Thus, by the early seventeenth century, fortresses had become immensely complicated affairs made up of a bewildering array of elements. Bastions and outworks alike were provided with ravelins and redoubts, bonettes and lunettes, tenailles and tenaillons and counterguards, hornworks and crownworks. Approaching them from the outside, the traveler would be met by covered roads and cuvettes and fausse brayes and scarps, not to mention cordons and banquettes and counterscarps. Many of these elements were difficult to keep apart, not only for us but also for contemporaries who, like Uncle Toby in *Tristram Shandy*, sometimes covered the whole lot with ridicule. Though the basic principles were the same everywhere, a very large number of variations developed to suit national tastes as well as the peculiarities of the terrain. Naturally, most military architects were run-of-the-mill and content to follow the immense number of handbooks in circulation. However, here and there celebrated architects such as Paciotto, Coehorn, and Vauban developed their own distinctive styles, adding still further to the confusion while at the same time providing additional models for imitation.

The fact that fortresses developed in this way, of course, is itself an indication that offense, and the technological means on which it rested, did not stand still. Though neither cannon nor their ammunition changed much after 1550, artillery did tend to become more powerful. The greatest progress was made in the organization and systematization of siege warfare. The late sixteenth and early seventeenth centuries saw the emergence of well-defined procedures for investing, besieging, and attacking a fortress. Over time, these procedures tended to harden and to assume something of the character of a ritual dance consisting of precisely regulated moves and countermoves.

Arriving on the location, the first task to be performed by the commander of an attacking army was to surround the town and cut off its approaches. This having been achieved, and attempts to obtain the garrison's surrender having failed, the next step was to reconnoiter the terrain to discover the spot most suitable for the emplacement of siege artillery. The first line of parallel trenches would be opened and the guns, often protected by portable earth-filled wickerwork structures, stationed in place. A steady bombardment would drive the defenders off the section of the walls directly opposite, and so enable the attackers to advance towards the fortress by digging zigzag trenches. At a certain distance, a second parallel trench would be opened. The guns were then dragged forward, and the process repeated. Unless it was interrupted by the defenders, who sometimes dug their own trenches in order to reach the enemy and dislodge him, two or three forward bounds of this kind usually brought the guns within range and permitted the actual process of breaching the walls to begin. Once a breach was made, the place would be entered by assault. Allowing for varying local conditions, a skilled commander such as Vauban could calculate the duration of a siege almost to the day, and so of course could the defenders. Consequently the process of surrendering fortresses with honor developed into a fine art, surrounded by elaborate ceremonies and books of rules.

Although some of the older techniques of siege warfare, such as boring and ramming or the use of towers, had entirely disappeared by the middle of the sixteenth century, others still remained in use. Chief among those was the ancient principle of throwing up a wall, or vallation, to prevent sorties and cut off the garrison from the surrounding countryside. This in turn was sometimes surrounded by a second wall, known as countervallation and aimed at frustrating any attempts at relief. While artillery eventually came to present the most important means for breaching fortifications, mining and countermining continued to be used, and their effectiveness was increased by the use of gunpowder as an explosive. Escalading a fortress was still sometimes possible, whereas at other times attempts were made to gain entry by all kinds of underhanded means. Above all, siege operations continued to be conducted at such close quarters that both sides were often able to exchange taunts, promises, and threats, using arrows (until 1600) to shoot messages, or simply shouting at one another. As has always been the case in war—and never more so than during the confused seventeenth century and the cosmopolitan eighteenth—attackers and defenders freely imitated each other's methods. Partly as a result, the race between them was neck-and-neck and was never really decided in favor of one side or the other.

Seen from a wider point of view, not only the techniques of siege warfare but the concept of the siege itself remained essentially the same. Although the most powerful fortresses no longer stood out high above the surface but were partly hidden in the ground, they continued to consist of *enceintes* designed to repulse assault and keep the attackers out. Conversely, siege warfare still aimed at first cutting the defenders off from the surrounding country and then either breaking into the ring or starving them out. Particularly during the age of religious wars between 1550 and 1650, fortresses kept their traditional function as places of refuge. Since the effective range of cannon still did not exceed 1200 meters or so, each fortress represented a stronghold in its own right and there could be no question of building them close enough to each other to offer mutual support by fire. Here and there entire belts of fortresses were constructed to cover all possible approaches into a country; they did not, however, link up into continuous barriers of the kind that have become so familiar since World War I. Since fortresses were very numerous, the role that they played in strategy was if anything greater than it had been even in the Middle Ages. During the period from 1560 to 1700 in particular, warfare consisted less of battles in the open field than of an endless succession of sieges. One early eighteenth-century authority even calculated that there were three sieges for each battle, not counting cases in which fortresses were besieged unsuccessfully.

Thus, the common view that the advent of cannon changed the balance between the attackers and the fortified defense is simply not supported by the evidence. In truth, the two progressed very much together. Often, the very same engineers who built the most powerful fortresses were also responsible for devising the most sophisticated methods for attacking them, the great Vauban being an outstanding if by no means unusual example of this. Since the length of sieges varied enormously, it would be all but impossible to prove that fortresses were becoming easier or more difficult to capture. The supposed advantage of the attackers over the defense cannot have been very apparent to Charles the Bold of Burgundy, who besieged the town of Neuss for a whole year (1475–76) before finally being obliged to withdraw.

Riga in 1700 held out for seven months, Milazzo in 1718–19 for just as long. At the other extreme, ruses and bribes sometimes enabled towns such as Mons (1691) and Huy (1705) to be taken within a matter of days. Most sieges probably fell into the 40–60 day category. To quote Vauban, a resistance lasting 48 days could be regarded as respectable.

In the absence of detailed statistics, the growth in the power of the offensive cannot be proved. Rather, the most important effect of artillery upon siege warfare seems to have lain in a different sphere, namely the greatly enhanced scale on which fortresses had to be built and siege operations conducted. Since cannon, by the middle of the fifteenth century, had outstripped the largest siege engines in point of both power and range, the *enceintes* built to withstand them had to be that much larger and possess far thicker walls. Such structures in turn called for garrisons numbering in the thousands, sometimes more, and also for much increased quantities of stores and ammunition of every kind. Conversely, attacking a first class fortress was by no means a simple operation logistically. To do so it was necessary to concentrate a large force at a single spot and keep it fed over a period of weeks, if not months. Taking the minimum figures of 1.5 kg per day per man and 15 kg per day per horse, and employing the estimate of a contemporary expert, Puysegur, of two horses for every three men, the *daily* requirement for feeding an army of 50,000 troops would amount to approximately 475 tons. Though the quantity of powder, ammunition, and engineering materials needed for a siege only amounted to a fraction of this, in absolute terms it too could be very large.

Thus, the principal effect of the advent of artillery and the concomitant advances in fortification was to make both the attack and the defense of fortresses very much more complicated and expensive. Gone were the days when every prince, baron, or monastery could surround themselves with thick walls which, if never altogether impregnable, were at least able to force a considerable delay on an attacker. Gone, too, were the days when the most important arms, or at least some fairly effective arms, could be made by the village blacksmith. Instead, military technological progress created a situation where warfare in general, and fortress warfare in particular, came to demand a combination of financial muscle, bureaucratic organization, and technical expertise. All of these were to be found less in the feudal countryside than in the bourgeois-capitalist town economy which, spreading from south to north and from west to east, played an ever-increasing role.

In their opposition to the nobility both of Church and State, the burghers of the towns found useful allies in the monarchies. The monarchs were the only ones who could afford to build and maintain cannon. Consequently, their power grew and grew until it became absolute. Ultimately the net effect of these developments was a great increase in the minimum size necessary to make political units militarily viable. Instead of being a pastime for individual lords who relied on their vassals, or else an expedient used by towns which called out the citizen-body, the conduct of warfare tended to become centralized in the hands of kings and later in those of national states.

While the trend towards larger political units capable of sustaining the new scale of war in all its forms was both marked and steady, it was by no means simple or linear. The period from about 1450 to 1650 was as unsteady politically and marked by as many wars as any during the Middle Ages. So many peasant uprisings and national revolts and religious conflicts and civil wars were taking place that very often even contemporaries were unable to discover who was fighting whom, let alone what for. Though sieges were frequent, small-scale guerrilla warfare was endemic in the countryside between the fortresses. Often it was all but indistinguishable from simple brigandry. In the hands of military contractors such as the seventeenth-century commander Wallenstein, war itself for a time was turned into a form of self-sustaining capitalist enterprise which promised riches and even principalities to the most successful practitioners. Whether this situation reflected the dominance of offense over defense, or the other way around, is difficult to say. In any case, military technology was but a single factor among the many that were involved. War is too complex a tapestry to be dominated by a single thread, however thick and however brilliant.

A new equilibrium was established during the second half of the seventeenth century. With armies becoming increasingly professional, the role of irregular warfare declined, though it never disappeared altogether. Fortresses and siege operations continued to be vital constituents of war. Though the scale of both had greatly increased and was still increasing, few if any new principles were added, so that even as late as 1832 the French army during the siege of Antwerp was found reading Vauban and employing the traditional methods. Long before this time, the borders of the most important states had come to be protected by double and sometimes triple belts of these structures. Partly as a result, the complete conquest and subjugation of one country by the other was generally regarded as no longer practicable. A new political order, based on an acknowledged, if dynamic, balance of power, was created and maintained itself. Entire countries were turned into quasi-fortresses, protected as they were by brick strongholds covering the best approaches, and held together by roads and later by railroads. Thus a clear separation between "front" and "rear" was created, acting as one of the factors behind the development of the modern distinction between combatants and noncombatants. This, in turn, lasted until the invention of aircraft. By enabling armed forces to overfly national borders and penetrate into the enemy's soft interior, aircraft led to the breakdown of hitherto prevailing international law, a breakdown with which we are still trying to contend.

Within each state separately, artillery not only helped royal power assert itself against all competitors but actually turned into its symbol. Cannon fired salutes when princes were born, decorated their palaces while they reigned, and increasingly figured in their funerals when they died. Louis XIV even caused his guns to be emblazoned with the words *ultima ratio regis,* which was an accurate if cynical description of their function. While kings played with real cannon, lesser mortals often did the same with custom-made smaller versions or, failing this, had models placed on the mantelpiece. Such martial displays notwithstanding, warfare continued to be dominated as much by humdrum nonmilitary technology as by spectacular fortresses and cannon. Ultimately, it was developments in nonmilitary technology that accounted for the revolution in strategy usually associated with the name of Napoleon Bonaparte.

CHAPTER 8

The Infrastructure of War

THE IMPACT OF GUNPOWDER on warfare made itself felt in the field of tactics above all. Its effect on organization, logistics, intelligence, command and control, and on strategy itself, was much less, and for the most part indirect. To understand the technological reality underlying the evolution of warfare in these fields, it is necessary to turn mainly to nonmilitary technology.

The invention of gunpowder is commonly regarded as a revolutionary event in world history, and indeed this has been the prevailing interpretation since Francis Bacon early in the seventeenth century described it as such. Since warfare for millenia had in fact been all but identical with combat, it is easy to understand how such a point of view came about; we suggest, however, that it has now become out-of-date and therefore something of an obstacle to true comprehension. Once the old-fashioned identification of warfare with combat is abolished, a very different perspective emerges. Battle is seen as one of the principal means employed by war, but not its end-all.

We have seen how organization constituted perhaps the weakest single link in medieval warfare, and how this weakness rested at least in part on technological factors such as the absence of cheap writing material and the subsequent decline of literacy. The fact that armies were organized on the basis of personal ties rather than on bureaucratic principles undoubtedly does much to explain the chaotic nature of warfare—and of much else besides—during the early Middle Ages before the year 1000. From that point onward, however, there was evident an unmistakable reversal of the trend. As town life, commerce, and a cash economy slowly expanded, military-feudal service was replaced more and more by money-payment, known as *scutagium* or shield money, which could be used to obtain mercenaries. This in turn implied a growing use of written records, receipts, rosters, etc. The proliferation of written documentation was greatly helped by the arrival of paper from the east, an event which seems to have occurred at almost the same time as the introduction of gunpowder, which may indeed have been related to it. Paper in turn opened the way towards the experiments with movable type and printing which were finally crowned with success in 1453. Between 1500 and 1850, though the techniques of printing did not develop very much, its productivity rose three or fourfold. The spread of printing was critical to the rise of military bureaucracies and of modern armed forces. Equally important was the invention in Italy of double-entry bookkeeping and the replacement of Roman by Arabic numerals. Arabic numerals in turn led to the discovery of logarithms by William Napier, and of the decimal system for recording fractions by Simon Stevin. Significantly, Stevin was one of the outstanding military engineers of his age. He wrote a handbook on artillery and served as tutor to the Prince of Orange.

Though we cannot attribute the explosive growth that occurred in the size of armies to these inventions and discoveries alone, this growth would certainly not have been possible without them; as is so often the case, technological developments formed a necessary cause but not a sufficient one. During the second half of the sixteenth century, the Spanish, French, and Austrian monarchies were each able to mobilize upwards of 100,000 men at home and abroad. At the height of the Thirty Years War, Gustavus Adolphus in Germany is said to have had a total of 200,000 men under his command. At one time during the War of the Spanish Succession, France had approximately 400,000 men under arms, while the armies of Habsburg Austria were not much smaller. Though methods of enlistment and conditions of service varied considerably from one country to the next, virtually all of these men were paid soldiers. Though most of these troops might be sent home when the war came to its end, all armies now contained a hard and constantly growing core of long-serving regulars. The most powerful eighteenth-century states were easily capable of maintaining 100,000 or so men under arms at all times. These men had to be administered, paid, fed, clothed, armed, housed, and cared for by the establishment of pensions, hospitals, orphanages, and the like. These problems were compounded by the fact that during most of each year the forces were not concentrated at a single place but scattered in garrison towns, thus presenting the central military administration with the problem of maintaining uniformity. This was a task at which they were on the whole successful, and one which surely could not even have been attempted had the technical equipment at hand been limited to that available during the Middle Ages.

As an improved technological infrastructure permitted the size of armed forces to grow, the number of troops that could be concentrated at any single point and made to do battle also tended to increase. Towards the middle of the seventeenth century a battle with 30,000 to 40,000 men taking part on each side would be considered very large, but within a hundred years such battles had become commonplace. Some engagements were much larger, as when 90,000 Frenchmen fought 110,000 Allies (British, Dutch, and Germans) at Malplaquet in 1709, or when a total of 130,000 troops clashed at Fontenoy in 1743. Towards the very end of this period, the *levée en masse,* or national mobilization, was adopted in France and was soon imitated by other countries. Though its introduction was not primarily a question of technology, it did require a suitable technological base to make it possible. The *levée en masse* enabled Napoleon to keep under arms upwards of a million men at one time, with his opponents following closely. As a result, battles in which both sides together numbered 150,000 became commonplace; the largest ones could involve 250,000 (Wagram, 1809; Borodino, 1812) or even 460,000 (Leipzig, 1813). By that time the sheer force of numbers had begun to transform the entire basis of strategy.

As printing and improved administrative techniques developed to the point that they permitted such forces to be mobilized and maintained, strategic control and staff work were also gradually transformed. Though they liked to pose in military garb and often assumed nominal command during important events, most rulers during this period no longer took the field, let alone fought with weapon in hand. Instead, they spent the war years safely ensconced in their palaces, many of which bore appropriate names such as Karlsruhe (Charles' Rest) or Sans Souci (Free of Care). From there, they sought to control operations through the machinery provided by the newly established ministries of war, relying on the gradually evolving royal mail systems for communication. War being a sporadic activity, these systems were originally established on a temporary basis. It was only in the eighteenth century that they began to compete with the older and better established commercial networks. Even as late as 1815, news of Napoleon's defeat at Waterloo first reached London via a private homing-pigeon service operated by the House of Rothschild.

Though communication networks were far more comprehensive and systematic than anything known to the Middle Ages, the technological means at hand did not allow the speed with which messages were transmitted to be increased by much. Though there may have been some improvement in roads—which, during the eighteenth century, for the first time began to approach the quality of the old Roman roads—carriages were still carriages, and horses, horses. Consequently, commanders who were waging war at a distance of perhaps several hundred kilometers from their capital were bound hand and foot by detailed letters of instruction. Most politico-military information probably traveled at from 60 to 90 kilometers a day, so that the French commander in Germany during the Seven Years War would have to wait two weeks to get an answer to any letter he sent to Versailles. Thus the peculiarly hesitant, slow, and convoluted nature of military operations between the age of Condé in the middle of the seventeenth century, and that of the Duke of Brunswick a hundred years later, is in part explained. As Schlieffen put it very well, these commanders were not really authorized to make war at all. Rather, it was their task to occupy a province, or besiege a town, after which they were to pause and wait for further instructions. Thus, the universal employment of written messages to control strategy worked as a brake on operations, by no means the last time a technology or technique acted in this way.

During this period, administration and staff work were clearly separated from each other for the first time. Not only did eighteenth-century armies very often carry around their own portable printing presses which were used for disseminating information, but some staff work came to be done with the aid of standardized printed forms. Perhaps the earliest of these were the various documents needed to keep track of the enlistment, pay, transfers, promotion, and discharge of personnel, as well as the entire apparatus of military law and military justice. Approximating staff work proper more closely, there were the *ordres de battaille, états de situation,* enemy reports, and so forth, all of which tended to assume a more regular and formal character. Without printing, eighteenth-century armies would not have been able to exist. Also essential were the desks, chairs, filing cabinets, and similar equipment, that they carried along on a campaign.

Though printing and writing helped shape staff work, on the battlefield itself their role continued to be very limited—a fact that in the eyes of some people comprised one of the attractions of a military career. Sometimes a written or printed general order was issued before the beginning of an engagement. Once the fighting was under way, however, command and control were exercised mainly by oral means, combined with all the traditional acoustical and visual methods of communication. Whether it was a general or the ruler himself who was in charge, commanders gradually ceased to fight in person, though this does not mean that they were always out of harm's way. The normal position of the commander increasingly tended to become a hill situated some way to the rear and overlooking the field, and this position might be changed once or twice during the engagement.

Though the invention of the telescope helped commanders to retain some form of control over fronts that were now often 5 or 6 km long, the early modern period saw no further technological advances in the fields of tactical intelligence, command, control, and communication. Some organizational improvements did take place towards the end of the seventeenth century, when specialized and fully militarized groups of guides and ADCs and adjutant generals were created and employed on a variety of tasks. Where these groups were institutionalized and properly organized and trained, they could carry vast military benefits. However, perfection in this regard only came during the nineteenth century, and even Napoleon was not yet above entrusting the most important messages to miscellaneous locally-recruited personnel.

Just as the technology of communication was all but stagnant, progress in the field of transport was also slow, a factor which continued to impose serious limitations on the movements of armies. The most advanced energy sources of the time were represented by the windmill and the waterwheel. During the high Middle Ages both had come into widespread use, but both were altogether unsuitable for employment in the field. Although there were some marginal improvements in the form of better carriages, armies going on campaign were still dependent on the shoulders of men and the straining muscles of animals except where water transport was available. Though the proportion of cavalry was everywhere on the decline, horses were needed to drag the artillery and its ammunition, as well as the truly astounding amounts of baggage which eighteenth-century armies considered necessary for survival. As a result, horses were not only altogether indispensable but extremely numerous. The poor roads and the dependence on horses continued to put severe constraints on the seasons in which armies could operate and the places where they could go. Only a few states, such as France or Prussia, were sufficiently well-organized to set up fodder-magazines, which enabled them to spring a surprise—the term, of course, is significant—on an opponent by opening a campaign earlier than had been expected.

What applied to horses also applied to the men. Only a small fraction of the needs of an army could be supplied from base. In the absence of refrigeration, most foodstuffs had to be gathered on the spot in repetitive, frequently well-organized operations every four days or so. Consequently the need for food constituted a very serious obstacle to operational and strategic mobility. The problem of local supply was rendered even more difficult since the armies of the period were made up, to quote the Duke of Wellington, of "the scum of the earth, enlisted for drink." So bad was the problem of desertion that the troops could not be permitted to forage on their own, but had to do so *en bloc* and under guard. The French revolutionary armies were, at least during the early years, less afflicted by this problem, and Napoleon seems to have been the first commander to set up a properly organized military requisitioning service. As a result, his troops were able to march somewhat faster and farther than most others, a most important advantage that goes some way to explain their success.

European commanders during the Middle Ages had been accustomed to plan their operations without maps of any sort, large-scale strategic maps being seldom required for the type of campaign in which they engaged. We simply have no idea how wide-ranging conquerors such as Tamerlaine and Ghengis Khan managed in this respect. The maps issued to Spanish commanders during the second half of the sixteenth century were, as previously noted, nothing more than rough hand-drawn sketches. The first maps bearing a "modern" character, in the sense of attempting to give a true two-dimensional representation of an entire province, were apparently produced in Lombardy towards the end of the fifteenth century. With the advent of the printing press the world finally had a technical instrument that permitted maps to be reproduced accurately; therefore the impact of printing on cartography was if anything even greater than its contribution to military administration.

Also, the creation of a cartographic infrastructure for strategy was helped by a revival of interest in town planning that took place during the Renaissance. The planned construction of whole urban complexes, which had been familiar to the ancient world, required the rediscovery and introduction of surveying instruments and techniques, and it did not take long before both were applied to military purposes as well. Triangulation was invented by the Dutchman Snellius around 1617, and first used by him to determine the exact distance between the towns of Alkmaar and Bergen-op-Zoom. Seventeenth- and eighteenth-century maps were, accordingly, fully capable of showing the relative location of towns, roads, rivers, and natural obstacles of every kind. They also gave distances, which were often marked not only in miles but also in hours of travel, an interesting reminder of the itineraries from which they originated. On the other hand, they were still not provided with contour lines, and therefore unable to present terrain in plastic form.

These maps represented reasonably good instruments of strategy, but often they did not go far enough. Particularly at the beginning of the period, maps still retained a traditional decorative function—the same quality that nowadays causes many of them to be treasured as works of art. This frequently was allowed to interfere with accuracy and usefulness. One late sixteenth- or early seventeenth-century map represents the Low Countries in the form of a stylized lion, tail and all. Scale also presented a problem, since during the eighteenth century there were fifteen different kinds of mile in use in Germany alone.

In addition, surveying over small distances is much easier than over long ones, with the result that most of the available maps covered specific towns and regions rather than entire countries. The first attempt to map such a country by means of triangulation rather than by guesswork was made by Giovanni Maraldi and Jacques Cassini during the 1740s. The country they surveyed was France, and their work was only completed on the eve of the Revolution. Even after triangulation had come into use, coverage both of individual states and of Europe as a whole tended to be spotty. Comprehensive sets of standardized maps drawn to a single scale were much sought after, difficult to obtain and, when obtained, jealously guarded. When F. W. Schettan's topographical atlas of Prussia and her neighbors was completed in 1780, it immediately disappeared into the state archives.

Finally, the reproduction of maps remained a slow and expensive process. Even when maps of a certain region were available, the number of copies might not be sufficient. For example, when Frederick the Great invaded Silesia in 1740 he was compelled to rely on captured Austrian maps. Sixty years later Napoleon's marshals often marched into the unknown, entirely dependent for orientation on locally-recruited companies of guides and on their own self-confidence. Another indication of the relative scarcity of reliable and up-to-date military-geographical information was the fact that sketching constituted an important art. It continued to be taught to officers right down to the end of the nineteenth century, when photography finally took over.

The collection of the type of statistical information that is vital for the planning and conduct of war made some progress between 1500 and 1830. In France, which led the way, such personalities as Sully, minister of war to Henry IV, Colbert, minister of finance to Louis XIV, and Fénelon, tutor to Louis XV, preoccupied themselves with the problem. The registration by the Church of all births and burials had been made mandatory in 1597, but it was only after 1736 that the information assembled by such means had to be recorded in duplicate with one copy surrendered to the representatives of the government. Even so, progress was slow. Correctly assuming that a census was nothing but a prelude to new taxation, the population down to the very end of the eighteenth century habitually resisted an actual count, with the result that demographic statistics even of small countries could vary by as much as 50 percent. When Necker, minister of finance to Louis XVI, wanted to know the number of France's citizens as a means towards estimating the crown's revenues, he was reduced to averaging the number of births during the period 1767–72 and multiplying the result by 25.5, or 24.75, or whatever other guesstimate was available on their proportion in the general population. A proper statistical office charged with the preparation

Until 1500 A.D., almost all weapons were hand-held. This picture from ninth-century Spain shows the most common ones: sword, spear, lance, bow, and, for protection, helmet, shirt of mail, and various kinds of shields. *Pierpont Morgan Library, New York*

Ancient siege weapons are illustrated in this relief from an Assyrian king's palace in the eighth century B.C. Note bows, special curved shields, and scaling ladders. *The British Museum, Jerusalem*

Roman maps, such as the *Tabula Peutingeriana,* shown here, were well suited to help a traveller move from one province to the next. However, they completely lacked the two-dimensional quality necessary for coordinating the movements of forces over large spaces. The section reproduced here has Asia Minor on top, Palestine on bottom, the Mediterranean with Rhodos in between. *Austrian National Library, Vienna*

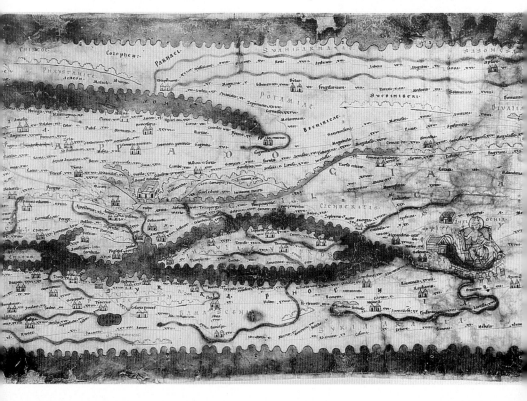

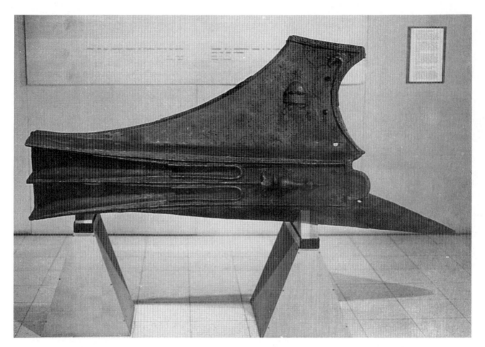

The principal weapon of the ancient Greek galley was the ram. This unique sample, cast in bronze and weighing just under half a ton, was found by divers off the coast at Atlith, Israel, in 1983. Note that it is decorated with a trident, even though it would be under water when the ship was afloat. *National Maritime Museum, Haifa*

Weapons, often designed on aesthetic as well as utilitarian principles, were sometimes so heavily decorated that they became all but unusable. This pornographic pistol, made in the first half of the seventeenth century, is of unknown French or English origin. *H. Pollock,* Ancient Weapons *(1926)*

Siege warfare during the early modern period was a complex operation dominated by artillery. This contemporary representation of the siege of Althona, near Hamburg, in 1691, shows moat, bastions, siege artillery, mantelets, and zig-zag trenches. *National Army Museum, London*

Animal-drawn carriages formed the backbone of military logistics from the earliest times until the nineteenth century and beyond. This drawing shows Wellington's Army on the march in Spain, complete with baggage and women. *National Army Museum, London*

The most important weapons used in the field during the period 1500-1830 A.D. were muskets, cannon, and, in the hands of cavalry, cold steel. Here is an artist's impression of the French cavalry's charge against a British infantry square at the battle of Waterloo in 1815. *National Army Museum, London*

Naval tactics before about 1700 consisted of a wild *melee* of ship against ship. A contemporary French engraving of the naval battle of Agosta in 1676, shows the battle between the French and Dutch fleets. Note broadsides delivered at extremely close range. *U.S. Navy Photo*

The first British steam-powered ironclad, HMS *Warrior*, was launched in 1861, but followed the traditional concept of what a warship should look like. Later, the rigging disappeared, and the numerous cannon along the broadsides were replaced by far fewer ones in revolving turrets. *Imperial War Museum, London*

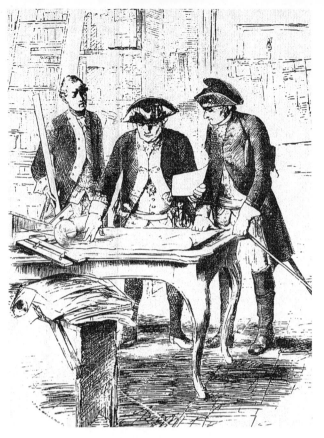

Professionalism reached the technical branches before it affected the other services. A nineteenth-century picture depicts Prussian engineers at work during the age of Frederick the Great. *F. Kugler,* Geschichte Friederichs des Grossen *(1842)*

The invention of invention caused war to extend its reach from the battlefield into the workshops and from there into the research laboratories. A Royal Ordnance Factory at Woolwich, London, pictured here, is manufacturing machine guns, around 1900. *National Army Museum, London*

of regular statistical reports was established by the Revolution, which entrusted it to a great scientist, Lavoisier. It was from this office that the remaining countries took their cue, mostly between 1810 and 1830.

Though the technical development of mechanical timekeepers during the period is comparatively well-documented, almost nothing has been done to investigate the extent to which they were used and how they affected general habits of thought, let alone military habits of thought. The earliest devices of this kind made their appearance in Europe almost simultaneously with gunpowder. Like firearms, timepieces represented machines properly speaking and indeed were destined to serve as models of a cosmos which, from the time of Newton, came to be understood as a gigantic machine with God acting as the spring. During the first two or three centuries, mechanical clocks were too cumbersome and unreliable for field service, with the result that military timekeeping remained essentially unchanged. Good portable clocks and watches that were at least half-way accurate were available for sale from the beginning of the seventeenth century, and the best late-eighteenth-century watches were almost as good as the average modern watch before the age of quartz.

Technical characteristics, however, are meaningless in themselves. As commander-in-chief of the Continental Army, George Washington did not see fit to note the hour at which he sent or received letters, and indeed throughout his military correspondence there are surprisingly few references to the clock. The marshals and generals of the *Grande Armée* were certainly rich enough to afford watches, yet in message upon angry message the Emperor himself had to remind them of the need to put not only the hour of dispatch but also the date and place on the letterhead. Napoleon himself frequently formulated his orders in terms of the clock ("General A's division will leave at such and such an hour, followed at half an hour's interval by the one commanded by B") but on other occasions ordered battles to start *au point du jour* ("at the crack of dawn"). Then, too, there is the fact that before the advent of railways and telegraphs, the clocks of different places were not necessarily synchronized but often showed local time. Throughout the period under consideration, and indeed down to the very end of the nineteenth century, this meant that the hour in province Y might well differ from that in province Z, making nationwide strategic coordination that much more difficult, or else indicating—which is perhaps the more likely explanation—that such coordination was rarely practiced.

Another sphere in which technological developments were minimal was that of military intelligence. From time immemorial, armies had been dependent on books, diplomats, and travelers for long-range strategic information about the enemy and the environment. Tactical information was obtained by means of personal observation, or else with the aid of scouts, prisoners, deserters, local inhabitants, and spies. The latter were typically soldiers, dressed up in a variety of disguises—for example, that of a farmhand. The spies would then go to the enemy camp accompanying a bona fide visitor, such as a peasant out to sell his wares. The peasant's loyalty was in turn guaranteed by taking his wife hostage. All information, except for that originating in a commander's personal observation, traveled at a speed similar to the movement of the forces themselves. In this they differed sharply from modern forces, who have technical means capable of transmitting intelligence at the speed of light. On the other hand, communication between a commander and his sources of information was normally direct. Since intelligence departments only made their appearance toward the end of the eighteenth century, a multiplicity of organizational echelons did not interpose themselves between a commander and his sources of information, so little time was wasted.

To draw the threads of the argument together, the armies of the eighteenth and early nineteenth centuries were numerically much stronger than their predecessors. Such size would not of course have been possible except for the much-improved administrative techniques that had gradually become available since the Renaissance. At the same time, however, the technical means of transmitting information, on which command, control, communication, and intelligence depended, had not undergone any corresponding improvement. To cope with this dilemma, armies distinguished between the tactical and the strategic levels. On the tactical level, a solution was sought and found in terms of careful organization—it was from the sixteenth century onward that companies, battalions and regiments made their appearance—and in the imposition of a ferocious discipline such as enabled Frederick the Great to say that soldiers ought to fear their officers more than they fear the enemy.

On the strategic level, generals being notoriously more difficult to discipline than privates, an answer proved less easy to discover. Beginning around 1760, however, the French in Germany took the lead in experiments aimed at dividing armies into self-contained, permanent *strategic* units. Such units had not been seen in Europe since the fall of the Roman Empire or—considering that the legion was pre-eminently an administrative organization—ever. Each such unit was made up of a properly balanced combination of all arms, and each was provided with its own headquarters and system of communications to make independent operations possible for a limited time. First the division, and then the corps, appeared on the scene, and with them the first general staffs to coordinate the movements of the army as a whole.

Thus, the combination of large numbers with weak communications technology compelled commanders to search for new organizational forms, which in turn would not have been possible without corresponding changes in doctrine and training. Once all these elements had been put in place and thoroughly assimilated, the effect on strategy was revolutionary, indeed explosive. For the first time in history, armies on campaign stopped marching about in single massive blocks, or else in detachments that spent most of their time waiting for each other. Increasingly out-of-date was the age-old contrast between those detachments and an army's main forces. More and more often armies were made to actually *consist* of their detachments. As the term *corps d'armée* already implies, the individual corps each constituted a miniature army, complete in every part. They moved along on their own, often at 24 or even 48 hours' distance from central headquarters.

Operating with their forces dispersed on such a scale, commanders found that the number of strategic combinations open to them had increased tremendously. Instead of simply facing each other's main forces head on and either offering battle or declining it, generals could now assign each army corps a different task forming part of an overall plan. Thus one corps could be used to mount a diversion and distract the enemy's attention; a second, to outflank him on one side, while a third outflanked him on the other; a fourth, to prevent reinforcements from arriving on the scene; and a fifth, to form a general reserve. The real trick, of course, consisted not only of coordinating the corps in their different roles, but also of altering those roles at a moment's notice in accordance with the latest intelligence. While none of this was fundamentally new, previously it could be done only on a tactical scale, say at a maximum distance of 5–10 kilometers. Under Napoleon, maneuvers taking up 25, 50, or even 100 kilometers of space became routine.

At the same time, the set-piece battle entered a decline. One reason was that commanders were unable to exercise continuous strategic control over their much-enlarged and widely dispersed forces; another was that engagements could get under way much faster, since each corps deployed on its own rather than all together. Since the corps operated independently and away from each other, a clear center of gravity was often lacking, and it became much more difficult for intelligence to determine the enemy's true intentions. Consequently the percentage of encounter battles tended to grow after 1790. More and more often hostile corps on detached missions blundered into each other without any orders from, or indeed without the knowledge of, central headquarters. Under such circumstances, even the best plans laid down by the commander-in-chief were no longer enough. Instead, and supposing everything else to be equal, the side whose generals displayed the greatest enterprise and marched towards the sound of the guns possessed an advantage and tended to win the contest. Thus, closing the gap between numbers and the technical means available to coordinate them on campaign demanded both a supreme brain at the top and flexibility at the bottom. During much of the Napoleonic period this combination was available to the *Grande Armée* and enabled it to overrun most of Europe. Towards the end, however, a certain decline on both sides of the equation seems to have taken place, and this played an important role in enabling France's enemies to catch up.

Yet a third important effect of the new organization—and hence indirectly of technological factors—upon strategy was the decline of siege warfare. Though existing literature tends to exaggerate the importance of gunpowder, the properly designed and defended *enceinte* was able to hold its own for centuries in the teeth of the worst that firearms and artillery could do. Towards the very end of the eighteenth century, this situation changed. Though the relationship between the technical capabilities of fortifications and cannon had not undergone any fundamental shift, the entire question was being rendered increasingly irrelevant. This was because, given their newly acquired size and the way in which they now operated, armies under most circumstances became capable of overcoming fortresses simply by masking and bypassing them.

As Napoleon's career vividly illustrates, and as he himself remarked on one occasion, sieges of the traditional type became not so much easier to mount as for the most part superfluous. Though they did not entirely disappear, they declined in relative number, as did the role that they played in strategy.

Although each of the above developments separately may be regarded as revolutionary, together their impact was even greater than the sum of their parts. Not only the conduct of strategy, but its very meaning was changed. Well into the eighteenth century, battle and warfare were all but identical. This was because, paradoxically, in another sense they were entirely separate, war apart from battle being almost indistinguishable from a somewhat violent form of tourism accompanied by large-scale robbery. Not long after the end of the Seven Years War, however, campaigning at last began to take on a more pronounced military character. To paraphrase one of Napoleon's most celebrated boasts, the soldier's legs became an instrument for making war rather than simply a means for bringing them to the place where battle would take place. In the future, at any given moment during a campaign, one part or another of an army would be likely to be engaged in actual fighting. Fighting was thus continuous, instead of being limited to isolated encounters with a clear beginning and an equally clear end. The great battles of the Napoleonic period—Austerlitz, Jena, Wagram, Borodino, and Waterloo—were destined to be among the last of their kind. Increasingly during the nineteenth century, battles were to last for days and then for weeks or months. They did not take place at or near individual places, but spread until they covered entire regions, countries and even continents. Compared with any previous period that one selects, this was a revolutionary development indeed, and one which is truly paradigmatic in that, much as it owed to technological factors, it cannot be explained in terms of hardware alone.

CHAPTER 9

Command of the Sea

THE DEVELOPMENT of land warfare to 1500 or so has been presented in terms of tactics on the one hand and everything else on the other. Although many different factors were involved and helped change the way things were done both on the battlefield and in war as a whole, the thrust of the argument has been that, since the effect of gunpowder was restricted mainly to the battlefield, overall there was more continuity in the conduct of war than is often believed to have been the case. When we look at the evolution of naval technology during the early modern period, however, an entirely different situation presents itself. This is because, at sea, it was not just the weapons in use but the ships and the ways of sailing them that underwent a decisive transformation. In many respects the year 1500 or thereabouts marks a more important watershed in naval warfare than it did on land.

Around the year 1300, if not before, northern types of ships had reached a degree of development that enabled them to invade the Mediterranean and maintain themselves there. Dutchmen, Englishmen, Frenchmen, and Germans going to the Levant were therefore no longer entirely dependent on Italian vessels and crews as they had been during the Crusades. The very fact that they were able to establish themselves in an area which had previously formed an Italian preserve indicates that, technologically speaking, they had drawn level with the locals. As different techniques met, the result was the creation of hybrid types. This interaction worked in both directions. The northerners took over the lateen sail. The southerners returned to the square sail which they had apparently abandoned almost a millenium earlier.

It was not long before both northern cogs and southern galleys began to be equipped with two or even three masts instead of one. This made it possible to carry both kinds of sail, combining power with maneuverability. By 1500 another sail, known as the spritsail, was attached to a mast jutting forward from the bows of sailing ships. By providing leverage against the rudder—which by now had become standard on all ships and was built right into the sternpost—the spritsail enabled vessels to sail as close as 80 degrees to the wind and also to pull away from a lee shore— a most important tactical capability which had hitherto been possessed exclusively by galleys. During the sixteenth century, rigging underwent further improvements as the various mainsails were made divisible, thus affording better control and better survivability in storms. It would be difficult if not impossible to say just when the combined thrust of these evolutionary developments was strong enough to justify talk of a true technological revolution, but such a revolution certainly did take place, with perhaps the most far-reaching results in the whole of history.

The first home of the full-rigged ship was, it seems, in the Basque country of northern Spain, symbolically located midway between western Europe and the Mediterranean, both of which had contributed elements to its development. From there the carracks—originally an Arabic word meaning simply "ship"—and caravels spread out in all directions. Most of these vessels were between 200- and 400-tons burden, though a few were much bigger and may indeed, for the first time since the classical age, have pushed against the limit of what is possible in wooden craft. Even the smaller ships, however, were much more sturdy and seaworthy than any of their predecessors. If only because these qualities meant that navigation need no longer be confined to the summer months, far longer voyages could be made from the fifteenth century on. Except in so far as they needed to take in fresh food and water, something which their boats could do almost anywhere, the endurance of ships during the period we are now entering was almost unlimited. Before the end of the fifteenth century this endurance permitted America to be discovered and the East Indies to be reached by sea. In 1527, the globe itself was circumnavigated for the first time by one of Magellan's ships in a journey lasting three years, and thus illustrative of the kind of endurance involved. The outstanding novelty of these voyages did not consist so much in the sheer physical feats that they represented, however admirable those might be; rather, what gave them their epoch-making significance was the fact that they could be repeated and indeed soon became quite common.

The growing seaworthiness and endurance of ships during this period also interacted with another factor. As compared to their predecessors, including the medieval cog, full-rigged ships required little manpower to operate. Around the year 1500 the figure stood at perhaps one crew member per 10–15 tons of burden, and the ratio improved steadily thereafter. The advantage that this presented could be put to use in several ways. It contributed to the endurance of ships and their range, but it also meant that much heavier loads—or, alternatively, larger complements of fighting men—could be carried on board and put ashore when necessary. The principal distinguishing feature of the new vessels was the favorable energy-per-man ratio provided by their sails and rigging. The manner in which this ratio could be exploited for military purposes concerns us here.

The newly-found range and endurance of sailing ships would have been of little use had the instruments of navigation still been confined to those of the high Middle Ages. We shall not delve deeply into the history of this difficult and highly technical subject; suffice it to recall a few landmarks. Possibly originating in China, a primitive compass in the form of a pointer suspended by a thread, or else floating freely in a bowl, seems to have been in use in the Mediterranean from the late thirteenth century on. Not long after 1300 this was apparently replaced by a needle swinging freely on a dry pivot, which in turn was mounted in the center of a wind rose (sometimes provided with degrees), thus giving rise to the first modern compass. While the sources are scanty and difficult to understand, it seems that most of these technical innovations were first adopted in the Mediterranean, particularly in Italy, which from 1300 until at least 1500 or 1550 constituted Europe's scientifically and commercially most advanced region. By contrast, through most of the fifteenth century, pilots in the Northern and Baltic Seas continued to rely mainly on traditional astronomical measurements and soundings, facts which in themselves suggest that they were not ready for, or else not interested in, really long voyages beyond the shallow coastal waters of these areas.

If the science of navigation was originally developed in Italy, Spain, and Portugal, by the early seventeenth century primacy had passed to the Dutch and then to the English. In 1598, William Gilbert was able to offer proof of the earth itself being a magnet. Shortly thereafter Dutch skippers, acting upon the Stadtholder's personal orders, were found systematically registering and reporting the deviations of the compass at whatever points their voyages took them. Early in the eighteenth century the traditional cross staff, itself a substitute for the older astrolabe, was replaced by the quadrant. Incorporating a mirror as well as a small telescope, this instrument for the first time enabled an observer to see sun and horizon simultaneously, which meant that the angle between them could be measured regardless of the ship's movements. In 1757 the first sextant was developed out of the quadrant by extending the latter's arc from 90 to 120 degrees. With that the problem of determining latitude at sea finally found a satisfactory solution, and one that was not to be improved upon until the advent of inertial- and radio-controlled navigation in the twentieth century.

Finding longitude remained more difficult. Speaking of the location of the blessed country, Rafael Nonsenso in More's *Utopia* promised to give it exactly, "latitude and all"; from this we can appreciate the difficulty of determining longitude at sea. The normal method of sailing from one point to another was to proceed to the correct latitude, then to turn east or west until land was sighted. Though Christiaan Huygens in 1657 published a book describing how the newly invented pendulum clock could be used to determine longitude, the machine he built was not portable. Towards the end of the century, the invention of the spring balance permitted clocks to go to sea, but early versions did not compensate for differences in temperature and hence were insufficiently accurate. When Thomas Cook went on his first voyage in 1768 he still carried no chronometer. Instead he relied on the services of a Greenwich Observatory astronomer who determined longitude by complicated lunar calculations. The problem of constructing a clock which would be accurate, portable, and weather-resistant was finally solved by John Harrison, whose instrument was first tried by Cook on his second voyage of 1772.

Much earlier than this, during the fifteenth century, the compass had already been combined with the newly invented portolan chart. Deriving from the *periplous*, medieval portolans (or portolanos) at first consisted of a set of written sailing directions which listed courses, anchorages, and ports. After 1400, however, a rough sketch showing the coast and giving the location of the ports began to be appended to the text, and this type of chart gradually took over the generic name minus the o. Beginning not long after 1400, portolans came to be marked with so-called loxodromes. These were lines emanating from the wind rose and giving a set of courses. The navigator had to decide which of the loxodromes ran parallel to the course he needed to take from his point of departure to his destination. This gave him the heading he needed to steer. By the year 1400, if driven off course, he was equipped with a set of tables which allowed him to break his sailing down into two perpendicular directions and then calculate his position.

Like the instruments used for navigation, the art of making maritime maps was originally dominated by Italians, Spaniards, and Portuguese. Later, Antwerp and then Amsterdam became centers for the making and publishing of navigational charts, the names of Mercator (who gave his name to a whole class of maps using a projection with parallels and meridians at right angles), Ortelius, Waghenaer (whose name was also destined to become generic), and the publishing firms of Blaue and Elsevier becoming particularly well-known.

Armed with full-rigged ships and reliable instruments of navigation, European sailors, merchantmen, and soldiers were able to embark on an adventure of epic proportions, one which transformed Western Europe from a small peninsula of Asia into the mistress of the world. As the so-called "Columbian" epoch dawned, entire new continents were opened for conquest, trade, and settlement. As economic life expanded to take advantage of the new opportunities, navigation was transformed. Exploding beyond the traditional confines of inland seas and coastal waters, it began to surround the globe with an intricate network of trade routes. As time went on and the cost of shipping declined, the types of commodities that traveled by these routes tended to expand. Originally limited mainly to bullion, spices, and slaves, by the eighteenth century they included coffee, tea, sugar, tobacco, dyestuffs, hides, raw cotton, some textiles, porcelain, rare woods, weapons, and many other items. Intra-European trade was economically even more important than these colonial products. Such humble but vital items as grain, salt, dried fish, furs, wool, iron, and timber were now traded by sea. By the sixteenth century some states were no longer able to feed themselves from their own agriculture, and their number increased steadily throughout the period.

Whenever valuable merchandise is carried from one destination to another there will be attempts to divert it by force. The same ships that plied trade routes could also be used to prey upon them, and indeed in the absence of a satisfactory juridical system the boundary between commerce and war was seldom very clear. States, kings, and private persons—often it would be impossible to say who acted in what capacity—pooled their resources and organized expeditions that some would describe as peaceful trade, some as legitimate military activity, and others as piracy pure and simple. After about 1700, increasing political centralization at home caused privateering to decline and then disappear. However, *la guerre de course*, or commerce-raiding, continued to be waged very much on the old principles. Technologically, the factor which made this form of war possible was the tremendous mismatch between the growing endurance, range, and general navigational capabilities of ships on the one hand and the available means of strategic command, control, and communication on the other. To transmit messages beyond visual range, fleets and navies still remained entirely dependent on dispatch boats. However fast these could sail, their speed was not much greater than that of the fleets themselves, and was subject to the same vagaries of wind and weather. The only way to reassemble a fleet which had been blown apart by a storm was to have the captains make for some prearranged port and wait for the last one to arrive. Throughout the classic age of sailing ships, the peculiar combination of these technological capabilities and weaknesses made commerce-raiding an attractive proposition, whether it was carried out by private individuals or at the orders of some central government.

To protect themselves against roving enemies, the Portuguese and the Spaniards—whose ships at first carried the most valuable cargoes—soon came to realize the value of grouping them in convoys and providing those convoys with armed escorts. By the second half of the sixteenth century, accordingly, treasure-laden vessels in particular began to be protected in this way, despite the tremendous economic and administrative inefficiencies involved. To deal with these convoys and their escorts, the first battle fleets properly speaking were organized during the early decades of the seventeenth century. The wars between Spain and the Netherlands, and subsequently those between the Netherlands and England, were principally waged with each side attempting to cover his own convoys while disrupting and, if possible, capturing those of the enemy. Occasionally convoy-warfare could yield spectacular results, as when the Dutch admiral Piet Heyn captured part of the Spanish Silver Fleet in 1628. Usually, however, defeat at sea merely meant that the economic life of a country would be slowly throttled. Of course, all countries were not equally vulnerable to the interruption of their trade. To some it spelled comparatively rapid death, to others it presented little more than a nuisance, whereas others still were almost completely immune to this form of war and have remained so to the present day.

As merchantmen became increasingly differentiated from warships, the battle fleets themselves came to be regarded as the proper target to be attacked, since once they were disposed of the rest would constitute easy prey. Battle fleets sometimes chased each other across entire oceans, as during the celebrated train of events in 1805 which led to the Battle of Trafalgar. Nevertheless the majority of encounters between them took place not on the high seas but in coastal waters as one fleet intercepted another either leaving port or preparing to enter it. A fleet actually inside a protected harbor was generally safe. On the other hand, ships caught inside an unprotected anchorage would be trapped and almost completely helpless, as happened to the French on the Nile in 1798. Once a naval battle was won the victor would enjoy command of the sea of a type very different from anything that could be achieved by earlier vessels with their various technological limitations. As the victor's convoys sailed in safety, those of the loser would be swept from the seas. Yet, command of the sea, while it could thus become more complete than in earlier times, was seldom absolute. Given the problems of command and control, individual merchantmen and raiders were often able to get through.

To completely choke off a country's maritime commerce, and to prevent any threat to one's own merchantmen, it was necessary to resort to blockade. The extraordinary endurance of the ships of the age, combined with the short range both of their own weapons and of shore-based ones, made them well-suited to this purpose. Provided enough ships were available, blockading a country was principally a question of organization. It was necessary to maintain the ships, replenish them, and keep the crews in good trim. Only the last could in any sense be said to constitute a technological problem, but it was one which played an extremely important role in naval warfare during the classic age of sail. The miserable quality of the food and drink issued to the men, their cramped and damp quarters, and the absence of waterproof clothing, is well known. Throughout this period, probably more men died at sea of these causes than were ever killed in battle. The situation began to improve only towards the end of the eighteenth century when a Scottish naval surgeon, James Lind, finally found and introduced a reliable cure for scurvy. It says something about living conditions aboard, however, that Nelson's men were expected to do their duty barefooted, and that even at the beginning of the twentieth century the crews of British warships were still not issued cutlery for the table.

To quote a famous dictum of Clausewitz, what cash-payment is to business, fighting is to war. However beautiful the strategic combinations made possible by the ships, they were only valuable if they could be translated into the hard language of tactics and weapons. In the previous period, by and large, there was no clear-cut distinction between transports and warships. In regions where galleys were used, they were employed mainly for military purposes. Early modern sailing vessels, however, still had not undergone a process of specialization.

Beginning approximately in 1340, there are records of artillery being carried aboard ships of both types. Like their counterparts on land, the earliest seaborne cannon were probably cast of bronze and rather small in size. Apparently their principal use was against personnel, which meant that high mountings represented an advantage. As time went on and cannon tended to become bigger and heavier, however, such mountings presented a problem, since the weight of metal would elevate a vessel's center of gravity and thus result in dangerous instability. From about 1430 on, guns were therefore placed on the centerdecks of sailing ships and made to fire through ports cut in the hull. Such ports were easier to cut in Mediterranean hulls, which were made of planks placed parallel to each other, than in northern hulls with their overlapping planks. This fact gave the Mediterranean ships a technological advantage, whereas the northern nations had to learn how to build hulls of sufficient strength, and were temporarily compelled to import Italian shipbuilders. By 1470 or 1480, however, this stage had been passed and the shipwrights of Horn in the Netherlands, or Luebeck in Germany, could match anything built in Venice or Genoa.

After the introduction of artillery at sea, the days of the galley were numbered, even though the process by which they were finally superseded proved to be long and uneven. It was not that the owners of these craft were reluctant to adopt cannon, but the weight of metal that they could carry was extremely limited. Every ton added meant a decrease in speed under oars. Furthermore, the bigger guns in use from 1400 on had a strong recoil. This recoil had to be absorbed by the structure of the ship, and because the galley had to be kept light, it proved to be a disadvantage. Ton for ton, sailing men-of-war could carry more, and bigger, cannon than could galleys. This did not matter much so long as guns remained relatively scarce, but scarcity is a function of price, and after 1500 the price of artillery began to go down quite sharply. In particular, the English during the reign of Henry VIII successfully experimented with making barrels out of iron. Iron guns were considered to be of lesser quality than bronze ones, but they cost only one third as much. Despite repeated royal prohibitions, they soon turned into an export article. During the second half of the sixteenth century, countries such as France, the Netherlands, Sweden, and even Russia (using imported Dutch personnel in the first of many attempts to overcome its technological inferiority) started their own iron-cannon foundries. In the long run, numbers combined with low prices overcame technological excellence as such. There may be a moral here.

A large galley around 1600 could carry perhaps 6 or 7 cannon, mounted in the bow and pointing forward. In contrast, even a quite small sailing ship could carry 40, and the time was soon to come when some sailing men-of-war were able to mount 100 cannon and more. Though galleys still enjoyed some advantages, notably in narrow waters and in their ability to offer support to amphibious operations requiring high maneuverability, these facts decided the issue against them. The favored tactic of galleys had always been boarding and ramming, but a situation now arose in which a vessel approaching another would be blown out of the water long before it could do either of these things. More and more, battles at sea came to consist of artillery duels. Given that accurate shooting was even more difficult to achieve at sea than on land (where irregular bores and ill-fitting ammunition caused rules of thumb to be employed in preference to the most advanced scientific knowledge), and also because ships were well protected by stout wooden armor, these were invariably conducted at very short range, "yard arm to yard arm," as the saying went. A battle between individual vessels might last for hours. Sometimes it ended when one side finally sank the other, but on other occasions the cannonade would be halted short of this and a boarding party sent in. The slow pace of operations gave the loser plenty of time to contemplate his situation, and frequently he would strike his colors before the final butchery could get under way.

After 1660 or so, merchantmen and men-of-war were no longer the same. Merchantmen remained tubby and discarded most of their guns; men-of-war grew longer and mounted as many as 120 cannon. To engage in an artillery duel, ships had to turn their broadsides upon each other. Initially this was done by each captain individually, but it did not take contemporaries long to realize that coordinated action would lead to better results. The "line ahead" now took the place of the "line abreast," which had been characteristic of oared vessels. Increasingly after 1660, the Dutch and the English led the way and began to experiment with detailed procedures for tactical command and control. Fighting instructions, their number running into the scores and sometimes into the hundreds, were codified into weighty tomes carrying the official seal of admiralties. By day, transmission was by means of colored flags being run up and down masts. At night, colored lights served the same purpose in a more limited way. As on land, tactics became a question of engaging in precise maneuvering aimed at catching the enemy at a disadvantage. Once the two lines were parallel to each other, what mattered was to prevent friendly ships from obstructing each other's field of fire, and to correctly distribute the targets among them.

Eighteenth-century naval tactics are often represented as a stereotyped, minutely regulated affair in which all the initiative lay with the admirals whereas individual captains and ships were reduced almost to the position of puppets on a string. There is much truth in this view, but it does not represent the whole truth. Though a "typical" system of tactics did exist and was broadly dictated by the nature of the technology in use, within that system a great deal of room was left for variation, originality, and even idiosyncrasy. In particular, the two most important navies of the period—the English and the French—were notoriously different in the approaches they took. Being offensively minded, the English usually chose to enter battle with the wind at their backs (technically this is known as taking the weather gage), which enabled them to bear down on the enemy. By contrast, the French usually had the wind blowing in their faces, i.e. they took the lee gage. This meant that they were not able to initiate an action against the enemy's will, but could always escape if necessary. Under such conditions, those English guns which were directed towards the enemy would point downward towards the enemy's hulls. Facing the wind, French cannon were pointed upwards towards the other side's masts and rigging. These differences were accentuated by the fact that, whereas the English relied on artillery and drilled their guncrews to a high degree of efficiency, the French were in the habit of putting marines on their masts and raking the enemy's decks with small-arms bullets, one of which was to kill Nelson at Trafalgar. English superiority in gunnery, and possibly better seamanship overall, meant that they were usually able to emerge as victors, despite the fact that many of their ships were smaller, slower, and less well-designed.

Though warships during the Columbian period were perfectly suited for fighting each other, their capability for waging amphibious warfare was strictly limited. This was not because ships were unable to carry armaments as heavy as, or heavier than, anything available on land. Rather, the limiting factors were the smaller amount of ammunition they could afford to expend, the extreme inaccuracy of their fire, and the much greater vulnerability of their wooden hulls as compared to the stone, or brick, that they faced. Repeated treaties in which the English tried to prevent the French from fortifying the Channel ports, and equally repeated French violations of these treaties, represent one indication that ships were normally no match for up-to-date fortresses. Where a shore was properly defended it could be held, and the attempt to prove the contrary was made only on rare occasions.

As early as 1200 B.C., the "peoples of the sea" tried to conquer the Egyptian New Kingdom and were repelled. In the Mediterranean and Western Europe, successive attempts to occupy islands such as Sicily and England enjoyed success. China's Mongol rulers on one occasion (1281) mounted an invasion of Japan but failed in the face of a "heavenly wind," or *Tai-fun*. However, all such operations were limited in range. Usually a voyage ending on an enemy coast was limited to a range of perhaps 200 km. Here and there much longer voyages ended in the settlement of new countries, but they could be successful only when they led to uninhabited areas. Elsewhere, not only Europe but every other part of the world was immune to long-range military invasion by sea, the reason being not the technological superiority of one but the primitiveness of all.

During the period after 1500, this situation changed. European ships were now at last perfectly capable of reaching distant continents, and of doing so on a sustained basis. Wherever they went, opposition by sea was negligible. It was only in the Far East, in China, that the European sailors met with a naval technology at all equal to their own. But while the largest Chinese war-junks were as big as their Western opponents, even they showed important weaknesses in seaworthiness and, above all, the quality of the ordnance that they carried. Once they had rounded the Cape and arrived in eastern waters, European vessels normally experienced little difficulty in destroying native fleets and, in consequence, taking over and dominating maritime trade routes. Nor was it long before trading stations and factories and even towns were established.

As British operations during the War of 1812 so vividly demonstrated, where shores were undefended and reasonably accessible a battlefleet escorting transports could put troops ashore almost at will. Once ashore, European weapons were normally superior; even where this was not the case, however, European discipline and European drill would carry the day against much larger native forces, as was the case of the English in India. Still, however great their superiority on the open sea and on the coast, European penetrations of the hinterland for the most part remained shallow and far between. That this was a question of technology, and not of political factors, is proved by the fact that it was true almost everywhere, whether the lands in question formed part of a well-organized empire such as China, or were inhabited merely by primitive tribes. When it came to occupying entire countries in Africa and Asia, and to a lesser extent in the Americas too, it was not so much weapons that presented success, but the lack of effective land transport, of communications, and of cures for various exotic diseases that formed the crucial missing links. Generally, these only became available in the nineteenth century.

CHAPTER 10

The Rise of Professionalism

FROM THE DAWN of recorded history, military organization has assumed many different forms. All of these were ultimately rooted in political, social, and economic structures, but all of them were also partly the product of the technology in use. Little can be learned from archeological evidence about early armed forces. To argue backward from the military organization of primitive tribes which still exist or which existed until recently, however, one can conclude that the first war-making societies probably did not recognize the distinction between civilians and soldiers, let alone professional soldiers. With them it would be more correct to speak of warriors, who were simply adult members of the tribe. Very often the only way to gain recognition as an adult was to assume the role of a warrior, sometimes symbolically but often enough literally by killing an enemy, as among some North-American Indian tribes. As is indicated by the Greek word *stratos,* which means host, under such conditions armies—in the sense of specialized war-making organizations standing apart from society as a whole—did not exist. Rather, it would be more correct to say that, when hostilities threatened or broke out, the entire tribe was put on a war footing and fought on the basis of the same organization as governed its day-to-day life.

Naturally, tribal organizations could only survive so long as the military technology in use met a very specific set of requirements. It had to be cheap, or else it would be beyond the reach of every member of the tribe. It had to be simple to make, or else the difficulty of its manufacture would give rise to a specialized class of artisans which might then be able to translate its skills into economic and political power. Either the weapons had to be very simple to use or else they could not be specialized for war; where these conditions were not met, their use would presuppose specialized military training and hence the rise of a warrior class sufficiently well-off economically to be able to take time out for that training. As a result of all these requirements, the weapons employed by tribal societies for war were normally much the same as those employed for games, sport, hunting, and certain types of magical-religious ceremonies. Indeed, those activities themselves were often not clearly differentiated from each other and from war.

We do not know just where and when weapons first reached a stage of development in which they could no longer easily be purchased, or manufactured, or used, by every male member of the tribe. Probably the change did not occur quickly in all places at once. In any case, tribal organization was not compatible with settled life, or perhaps things developed the other way around and it was technological advances which caused the nomadic way of life to be abandoned. The earliest urban civilizations known to us, those of Egypt, Sumer, India, and China, had already reached a stage of development where weapons were not available to the whole population but concentrated in the hands of certain groups.

The organization of these military groups varied greatly from time to time and from place to place. Sometimes, as in the Greek *polis* and Republican Rome, the system was tymocratic or money-based. A census was held and the citizens were divided into classes according to the amount of property that they owned. Those above a certain minimum were obliged to acquire the arms appropriate to their class, spend a certain amount of time training with them, and fight when necessary. At other times and places, political and economic power was concentrated in the hands of a central government which issued arms—manufactured either in its own shops or by contractors—and hired troops. In some cases the forces at the government's disposal might be permanent, in which case it is possible to speak of standing armies. In others they were raised only in emergencies, so that the term mercenaries would be more appropriate.

In many cases different types of military organization existed

138

side by side, not merely at different places but within the same civilization, society, and state. Indeed one might argue that the period before 1500 A.D. was characterized precisely by the fact that even quite primitive tribal structures that were centered around the bow remained not only viable but perfectly competitive, as the establishment of the vast Mongol Empire during the thirteenth century shows. The various forms did not necessarily exist in isolation but often gave rise to combinations. The nature of these combinations was not based on the weapons and technology in use, but was most certainly affected by them.

To focus on military professionalism, in one sense it represents a very ancient system indeed. By the time of Christ, if not long before, standing armies had already been maintained by governments in the Far and Middle East, and also in the Mediterranean area. These armies consisted of men who looked on war as their trade and expected regular payment for their services. A good example is the Roman Imperial Army, which survived in recognizable form for several centuries. During the first century B.C., between the time of Marius and that of Augustus, its personnel was transformed into regulars who regarded war as their trade and who soldiered as a living. Not only did these troops develop a strong corporate identity and *esprit de corps,* but advancement within the army was at least partly by merit. Nevertheless, Roman professionalism was so different from that in our time that the very use of the term may be misleading. Whereas today it is the officers above all who consider themselves military professionals and are so regarded by society at large, in Imperial Rome the situation was just the opposite. There, professionalism was limited to the rank and file and to the centurions, the latter corresponding approximately to the present day NCO. Above the rank of *primipilus,* or senior legionary NCO, appointments did not go by professional merit but were restricted to members of certain well-defined socio-economic classes, the *equites* and senators. To them the suggestion that they soldiered for a living would have come as an insult, even if (or particularly when) it was true. Under the Roman army system it was thus the base which contained the expertise, whereas the top consisted, in principle at any rate, of amateurs and political appointees. This is not quite what we would expect in a professional force today.

Feudalism, the foundation of numerous societies during ancient and medieval times, was another very important form of military organization. As a military system, feudalism arose where weapons were not concentrated in the hands of a central government, but were nevertheless so expensive or else so difficult to make and employ that their use was confined to a narrow, normally hereditary, class. The nature of the weapons themselves varied very greatly. In some places it was the chariot, in others the horse-and-composite-bow combination, in others still the horse combined with expensive iron armor that formed the military-technological basis of a warrior aristocracy. As a look at many times and places— India during the second millenium B.C., Homeric Greece, Mamluk Egypt, medieval Europe, and Samurai Japan—shows, feudalism as a form of military organization was compatible with any of these weapons. There can be no question of strict technological determinism here. Indeed, all but identical weapons were often used by troops whose military system of organization did not follow feudal principles. These considerations notwithstanding, feudal military organization, like any other, clearly does rest upon certain technological foundations. Take those foundations away, and feudalism itself will crumble into dust, though only someone untouched by the least historical sense would expect the process to be simple, or smooth, or painless.

Where feudalism reigns, the establishment of a military organization properly speaking poses special problems. Feudal warriors derive their status in life largely from their ownership of certain expensive weapons which are difficult to use and require much training. Hence, they are apt to regard themselves as the equals of all other warriors equipped in the same manner. Armies made up of such warriors will tend to be impermanent, organizationally unarticulated, and difficult to discipline. Furthermore, they are likely to attempt to turn war itself into a ritual, designed less with "utilitarian" considerations in mind than to preserve their own special status against outsiders. In such societies war itself will often be regarded as the exclusive domain of a single class. People who do not belong may be forbidden to carry weapons altogether, as was the case in Japan under Tokugawa rule. Also, fights between them and the aristocracy (and among themselves) will not count as war but merely as police work, hunting, sport, or entertainment.

Such being the nature of feudalism in general, and of European feudalism during the Middle Ages in particular, its incompatibility with military professionalism will be readily understood. Though kings and great lords frequently did maintain permanent bodies of retainers, these were bound to them by personal ties—either as relatives or as servants—and could not be described as professional soldiers. To feudal knights, on the other hand, war represented not so much a profession as a vocation. They practiced it not in order to earn a salary, but because it was the manifest destiny of the class to which they belonged. Though the training of knights began from the moment they could stay in the saddle, the goal and outcome of this training was less professional expertise as presently understood than an entire way of life. Since there were no permanent units, they could not serve as the basis of a corporate identity, nor did *esprit de corps* arise except on an ad hoc basis. There were no officers in our sense of the word, or perhaps it would be closer to the truth to say that the forces consisted exclusively of them. An ordered system of ranks and promotions did not exist. Selection for command was by socio-political status, so that commanders tended to be simply better-sired men than their followers.

Against this rather unpromising background, the rise of military professionalism in early modern Europe was the outcome of many factors, some of them technological and others not. They included the growing power of kings and of centralized states, the tendency to substitute wages or salaries for feudal service, and, from the fifteenth century on, the persistent attempts of great lords to develop the retainers of their households into the nuclei of standing armies. Among the numerous technological factors involved, perhaps the most important were the invention of paper, printing, and related techniques for the storage and dissemination of information. These innovations helped increase the size of armed forces and improve their administration. Ultimately, they also permitted a revolution in military education.

War has always been, and in some ways still remains, a practical affair above all. Therefore, the need for theory was slow to gain recognition, and indeed is by no means universally accepted even today. In many different societies, and at many different times and places, the training received by warriors remained rudimentary for centuries after the instruction of other experts—doctors, lawyers, or priests—had been formalized and entrusted to specialized schools. Specialists in violence—the anachronism is deliberate—were not educated as other professionals were. Though virtually all societies that engaged in armed conflict recognized the need to acclimatize novices to war, and often appointed specialized personnel to supervise the process, in virtually every historical army this acclimatization was limited to instruction in the basics, i.e., physical hardening and weapons drill. Beyond this, specialized training for the higher posts did not exist. Preparation for them, to the extent that it was considered necessary at all, depended primarily on serving a kind of practical apprenticeship either in the units themselves or on what passed for staffs. The scarcity and cost of textbooks was one of the factors that contributed to this situation. Though textbooks did of course exist, and though some are even known to have been written (and sometimes read) by commanders of every epoch, before 1500 their circulation had been too small to permit the education of the majority of officers to be based on them.

During the early modern period, this state of affairs no longer applied. Books on military affairs were by no means the last to come off the printing presses. By the end of the sixteenth century it was possible to read, either in the original or in translation or both, modern editions of Thucydides, Xenophon, Polybius, Caesar, Livius, Onasander, Polynaeus, Frontinus, and Vegetius, as well as printed versions of the Byzantine military classics which were brought to the West after the fall of Constantinople in 1453. Simultaneously there arose a vast military and naval literature written in the modern European languages, initially Italian but later also German, French, Dutch, Spanish, English, and Swedish. Side by side with books, military periodicals gradually appeared. By the late eighteenth century, these were well on their way to turning into specialized vehicles for expressing views and exchanging ideas on war. Beginning with siege warfare, the most technical subject of all, the idea began to catch on that war was not merely a practical pursuit but also rested on a substantial theoretical basis. This theoretical basis became the concern of professionals, or perhaps it would be closer to the truth to say that a professional was increasingly defined not simply as one who cut throats for a living but as somebody who had studied and mastered the theoretical foundations. It would be ridiculous as well as unhistorical to attribute these developments solely to technological factors. Still, for military book-knowledge to be possible and to count for something there must be books, and whether there are books in sufficient numbers and priced sufficiently low depends as much on technology as on anything else.

While printing was contributing to the rise of military professionalism in this way, other technologies were pressing in the same direction. In the fourteenth century, the free companies appeared. These were bands of skilled warriors who rented themselves out to the highest bidder. Often they specialized in some particular weapon, notably the crossbow, which while not regarded as fit for a gentleman nevertheless required some skill to operate. Since these characteristics applied equally well to the first firearms, it was only natural that the troops who used them should be organized in a similar manner. This was all the more true because firearms, particularly cannon, were difficult to make and to use. Often the same personnel was employed on both tasks, and indeed artillerymen very soon came to constitute a kind of international guild with their own patron saint and jealously guarded professional secrets. As time went on and prejudices against the use of the new arms diminished, this personnel tended to be integrated into the structure of armies, thereby becoming regulars like any others. Indeed a turning point was reached when, during the third decade of the sixteenth century, the use of firearms in the attack or defense of fortresses came to be regarded as an honorable and even commendable form of war for which one could be awarded the highest decorations. The net result of the successive technological inventions was to increase the demand for skill. Though skill is not the same as professionalism, where the technology in question was too complex and too expensive to be owned by individuals, professionalism inevitably grew out of increased skills.

The role played by ordnance, particularly heavy ordnance, in promoting military professionalism is brought out in yet another way. Guns required powder and ammunition, classes of supplies that could neither be gathered in the fields nor plucked from trees. Consequently, nothing was more natural than to make artillerymen responsible for supply, maintenance, and transport. Hand-in-hand with transport went engineering, particularly fortification and the construction of pontoons for crossing rivers. From these activities, engineers—the very word stems from the medieval war engine, hence is of military origin—spread into related activities such as building roads and constructing bridges. All these were skilled activities. Not infrequently they demanded very considerable mathematical knowledge, which could only be acquired from the mouth of experts instructing people who themselves wanted to become experts. No wonder, therefore, that it was precisely the artillery and the engineering branches of armed forces which were among the first to acquire a professional outlook. During the period under consideration, the importance of these branches grew and grew. As it did so, their outlook, based on knowledge and skill, clashed head-on with the traditional aristocratic approach which was rooted in breeding, honor, and social status. What was more, war itself was brought down from the high pedestal on which it had been put by feudal civilization. Increasingly, as technology and professionalization advanced, war tended to shed its supposedly ennobling characteristics and turn into a mere tool of policy, regrettable but sometimes necessary.

As one would suspect, the same factors that tied military technology to the rise of professionalism also applied to nonmilitary technology as used in war. Often, indeed, the two were inseparable, and frequently the same personnel were involved. Throughout the sixteenth and seventeenth centuries, the same men—one cannot find a title sufficiently wide to embrace all the various skills that they possessed or claimed to possess—who built windmills and lathes and pumps and waterwheels also erected fortifications and designed engines of war. An interesting, if little-known, case in point is that of Antoine Andreossy, who for many years served as Napoleon's chief of artillery and as such was responsible not only for the guns themselves but also for the various activities outlined in the previous paragraph. Andreossy, a professional engineer himself, was descended from a family of such engineers. Among them was an Andreossy who, during the reign of Louis XIV, had served as de facto constructor-in-chief of the Canal du Midi, which was the largest single engineering project undertaken in Europe since the fall of the Roman Empire.

If increasingly complex technology helped military professionalism develop on land, *a fortiori* this was true at sea. As Plato pointed out in *The Republic,* since technology is vital at sea not only for efficient work but for sheer survival, a captain's knowledge and competence count for everything. In fifteenth-century Venice, naval officers along with clerks and, for some reason, barbers, were among the most literate groups in the population. Later, those vast, complicated, wind-driven machines, the eighteenth-century men-of-war, required tremendous amounts of skill and science to operate, let alone to fight successfully. Naval warfare now covered much of the globe and frequently involved very extensive voyages. These could not be carried out except on the basis of professionally-acquired mathematical and navigational techniques. To cope with these demands, naval officers became distinguished from civilian sailors and acquired an identity of their own. The French and British navies in particular served as nurseries for an intellectual elite of a new type. Among the members of this elite, it was expert knowledge that counted. As time went on and different technologies leapfrogged each other in their successive advances, shifts occurred in the relative status of the technicians aboard. Until the middle of the seventeenth century it was the gunners who commanded the highest wages, but subsequently primacy shifted to the deck officers whose task was to sail the ship while coordinating and integrating the work of everybody else.

With complex technology demanding high skills, and at the same time helping make available textbooks to teach those skills, military training was gradually turned into a formal affair comprising courses and examinations. The first modern military schools were established in sixteenth-century Spain and taught the art of gunnery. Later the seventeenth and eighteenth centuries witnessed the founding of cadet schools and officer schools and, after 1763, military academies for staff officers. Even a brief list of these schools would include the Écoles Militaires at Paris, Mézières, and St. Petersburg; the equivalent institutions at Berlin, Munich, Wiener Neustadt, and Woolwich, all of which specialized in the production of junior officers; the naval colleges of Dartmouth, Toulon, Le Havre, and Brest; and junior academies such as at Potsdam and Brienne le Château, the latter primarily a school for artillery specialists where Napoleon received his initial training. Towards the very end of the period we are dealing with here, two of the most celebrated institutions offering military instruction opened their doors, the Berlin Kriegsakademie and West Point. Of these, the Kriegsakademie owed everything to the desire to raise professional standards, whereas West Point was an engineering school first and foremost, and to some extent has retained that character down to the present day.

During the early modern age the growth of technology in general, and of military technology in particular, acted as a spur to the rise of military professionalism, though it did not constitute its sole cause. The process was neither smooth nor easy. One need only recall the reluctance of Louis XIV to make Vauban, a commoner whose military-professional credentials were as good as those of any other man, into a *maréchal de France* to realize how far this was from being the case. Throughout the eighteenth century, and much of the nineteenth, the most important armed forces failed to adopt a system under which officers and commanders would be appointed and dismissed solely by their professional merit. Everywhere, social standing and seniority continued to play a large role, though a case might be made to show that the seniority system itself tended to foster a corporate identity and hence a professional outlook among the officer corps. During the early years of the Revolution in France, and in most countries during the Restoration that followed, appointments went not to professionals but to men considered politically reliable by those in power, a system which has by no means disappeared even in the most advanced twentieth-century armies. Naturally, different countries have at different times adopted different attitudes towards professionalism, some regarding it with favor, others opposing it, others still resigning themselves to it.

In the long run, the technologically generated thrust towards military professionalism proved irresistible. Gathering momentum, it turned into one of the cardinal phenomena of warfare not only during the period before 1830 but also in the one succeeding it. The process by which the officer corps of the most advanced countries adapted itself to the new situation worked simultaneously from the bottom up and from the top down. At one end of the scale, officers who were technical specialists—like those responsible for army ordnance, or in charge of the army's health—demanded, and gradually obtained, status and privileges similar to those of the rest, a good example being the rivalry between "sailors" and "engine men" that divided the British Navy during the second half of the nineteenth century. At the other end, high-ranking commanders from the age of Moltke on were gradually transformed from fighters into military experts whose precise function is perhaps best called the management of violence. Regardless of the position that they took in the hierarchy, more and more officers found themselves unable to function except on the basis of specialized education and expert training in such fields as engineering and business administration. This trend culminated in the second half of the twentieth century when, in West and East alike, perhaps the majority of commanders actually became almost identical with engineers and managers.

The historical development of the rank and file has been somewhat different. Medieval armies had neither file nor rank in our sense of these terms. Sixteenth- and early seventeenth-century common soldiers were mercenaries who served for the duration and, though often quite well trained, possessed an outlook that made them all but indistinguishable from a horde of ruffians. The growing importance of firearms, however, made strict discipline absolutely necessary. Beginning around the time of Gustavus Adolphus and Cromwell, one army after another came to consist of personnel who, since they served for long periods and were regularly paid, could be subjected to strict control. Eighteenth-century soldiers were, in one sense, professionals. Though their skills were not exactly admired by society at large, they did serve for a living (even if the choice of a living was often forced) and on a long-term basis which made thorough training possible. Towards the end of the period there appeared clear signs that the NCO corps of various countries were developing professional attitudes in the modern sense of the word.

With the French Revolution, the drive towards professionalism among the rank and file was interrupted, and some would say reversed. The reason was the institution of the *levée-en-masse* in 1793, a development which every other country was soon compelled to follow. During the next century and a half, and in spite of post-1815 attempts to put the clock back, other ranks even in the best armies—often, particularly in the best armies—neither could be described as professional soldiers nor regarded themselves as such. A hard core of NCOs, who nevertheless did not normally expect to spend a lifetime in the service, was surrounded by a popular militia, made up of short term conscripts who received intensive training and were then transferred into the various classes of reserves. Mobilization, itself made possible by a series of important technological innovations, enabled these nonprofessional warriors to be recalled to the colors at a moment's notice.

Thus, the move toward professionalism in the rank and file was delayed by the introduction of short-term universal conscription. Its goal was precisely to enable countries to wage war *without* turning all their manpower into professionals, and in this they were successful for a while. However, after 1945 a variety of ideological, political, social, and economic factors joined forces against conscription. When these were combined with the pressures brought to bear by a highly sophisticated military technology, the outcome was inevitable. In country after country, short-term service came to be regarded as incompatible with the long period of training required by many modern weapons and military equipment. The conscript army was either abandoned altogether or replaced by a mixed-force structure. A typical example is the German Bundeswehr, 40 percent of which consists of conscripts doing rather simple jobs, and 60 percent of regulars performing the "real" work requiring training and skill.

However, even the armed forces of countries such as the Soviet Union and Israel, which for various reasons held on to the idea of a nation in arms, saw themselves compelled to man such technical services as the navy and air force with a much higher percentage of professionals. The rationale is that professionals are the only people capable of dealing with the complexities involved. At the very least, a professional force will prevent the waste involved in using the extremely expensive machines used by these services for continuous retraining. Elsewhere, the idea that professionalism is the key to warfare has gained hold to such an extent that common soldiers in the U.S. Army are currently graded as specialists rather than privates, corporals, etc. The military in many less-developed countries have been forced to take the same road, even though the technology at their disposal is often much less sophisticated. To be taken at all seriously, it is necessary to adopt at least the semblance of "professional" norms.

Just because a more or less consistent trend towards greater military professionalism has existed for about five centuries, and because this trend was closely linked to the advance of war technology, it does not necessarily follow that the two will continue to march in step indefinitely. In particular, two factors appear noteworthy. First, it has recently been suggested that the latest technological developments diminish rather than increase the demand for military-professional skills on the part of the rank and file. They do this by automating some functions previously reserved for humans, and by transferring much of the work previously involved in repair and maintenance to civilian specialists. Second, since much modern military equipment is simple to use, at present the highest training may be required not for those who drive tanks or operate guns, but for those who specialize in close-in fighting on foot.

Finally, a skill-oriented professional attitude, like anything else, has its price, particularly when it is pursued for its own sake and regardless of everything else. It may undermine the kind of authority and loyalty that are vital to the functioning of any armed force. Given that war remains the province of hardship and fear, of suffering and pain and death, it is dangerous to overemphasize the mastering of technological skills as opposed to maintaining the eternal qualities of the warrior. The combination of professionalism and technology may also result in narrow-minded specialization more suited to a debating society than to an organization whose task it is to cope with, and indeed live in, the dangerous and uncertain environment of war. The price of professionalism may exceed its benefits, and this quite regardless of the nature and quality of the technology at our disposal. Judging by the inability of the Americans to win in Vietnam, and of the Soviets and Israelis to overcome irregular forces in Afghanistan and Lebanon, could it be that this point has already been reached?

PART III

The Age of Systems, 1830–1945

CHAPTER 11

Mobilization Warfare

UNTIL ABOUT 1830, warfare was very largely an affair of using individual tools and machines. Some of these tools and machines were team-operated, and a few of the largest even required the coordinated action of hundreds of men; however, they were not integrated into complexes, or systems. Whatever their source of primary energy, each of them worked essentially on its own. The type of coordination that did exist affected not the technical means but rather the men who operated them, who were subject to a common discipline and worked in response to common signals. However, the technological implements themselves could not be said to be integrated. Each of them—be it a sword, or a chariot, or a ship, or a gun—was perfectly capable of performing its function separately, and to a large extent that was precisely what they did.

The Napoleonic corps, the Roman legion, and the Hellenistic phalanx are best categorized as organizations. Organization required the coordinated action of many men working in concert. Though it used hardware, and though its structure was partly determined by that hardware, ultimately neither the phalanx nor the legion nor the division can be said to have consisted of hardware. Regarded from this point of view, the entire period until 1830 was characterized by an absence of coordinated technologies. After 1830, for the first time, not only men but technological devices as well were integrated into systems.

In previous chapters, we mentioned long-distance communication systems which, from early times, were sometimes used in order to link together provinces and countries and which were absolutely indispensable for the conduct of strategy. The most important consisted of horsemen working in relay on the one hand and optical telegraphs, or semaphores, on the other. The limitations of these means set certain maximum limits to the size that political entities could attain and also to the effectiveness with which they could mobilize their resources for war. Given the almost endless variety of circumstances, not only of terrain and climate but also of internal structure and cohesion, it would be absurd to try to fix those limits with any precision. They did exist, however, and the history of politics and of warfare cannot be understood without reference to this factor.

The use of optical telegraphs, for example, was fairly widespread during antiquity, particularly along the Roman *limes* in Britain, Central Europe, and the Middle East. Though capable of transmitting messages quickly and effectively, the most important factor governing the construction and employment of such systems has always been the fact that the naked human eye is incapable of making out different signals over more than a comparatively short distance. Regardless of whether it was fire, smoke, or mechanical means such as flags that were employed in making the signals, either the information to be transmitted had to be prearranged and limited in content, or else the stations had to be sited very close together. This made their construction and maintenance over anything but short distances prohibitively expensive. Add the need for excellent organization, and it becomes clear why no such systems were apparently constructed in Europe following the fall of the Roman Empire.

Around 1610, the telescope was invented by Hans Lippershey at Middelburg, the Netherlands. Its tactical importance was realized almost immediately, but so was the fact that, by extending the power of human vision, it was capable of granting optical telegraphs a new lease on life. By the 1650s, a proposal to this effect was put forward by the great English scientist, Robert Hooke, and by the end of the eighteenth century the idea of erecting a semaphore system was being seriously discussed. Various schemes for its construction were submitted to the royal government of France, but it was the National Assembly that finally acted, assigning the project to Carnot in his capacity as minister of war. The first line of the Chappé telegraph, known after its originator, Claude Chappé, was constructed in 1794. Its primary purpose was military, and its usefulness in this field is brought out by the fact that the first message that it carried informed the government in Paris that its forces had retaken the town of Le Quesnoy from the invading allies.

The Chappé system consisted essentially of a series of towers, each one so situated as to be visible from the ones adjacent to it on both sides. Atop each tower a single large movable beam was mounted, with a shorter beam, also pivoted and movable, attached to each of its ends. Ropes attached to the legs of the beams, which were illuminated at night, permitted them to be moved about in space and set into 192 different positions. These positions could be made to represent individual letters, words, or whole phrases. Messages could be transmitted either in clear or in code. Normally each station was manned by two men, one to read incoming messages and write them down, and the other to transmit. Depending on the terrain, the distance between stations averaged between 8 and 10 km. However, when visibility permitted, the director of a line could order intermediary stations to shut down, thus increasing the speed of transmission. Obviously, the speed at which messages could be transmitted over the system depended on the weather as well as on the length of the messages themselves. Assuming the weather to be reasonable and the message to consist of only a few hundred characters, the telegraph was capable of passing on information at 400 km a day, a performance not attainable even by the best organized mounted-relay systems.

What made the Chappé telegraph into a revolutionary development was the fact that it constituted a real technological system. If it was to work at all—and especially if optimal performance was to be achieved—the operation of each one of several dozen stations forming a line had to be coordinated very precisely with that of all the rest. Without a strong and very visible directing hand, the system would not operate, since the elimination or malfunctioning of even a single station could paralyze the entire line. It was necessary to lay down detailed procedures for initiating signals, terminating them, and verifying them, for closing down and opening entire lines as well as individual stations, for establishing orders of priority and assuring adherence to those orders, and so on. The function of management became even more complicated when a line branched into two, as was the case at Strasbourg, or when it was a question of coordinating the traffic being sent and received on various lines running in different directions, which was the task of central headquarters at Paris. To put it anachronistically but quite accurately, the distinguishing feature that made the telegraph into a system was not just the simple hardware employed—every one of its elements separately, and possibly even all of them together, had probably been in existence since Roman times if not earlier—but rather its absolute dependence on the quality of the software employed. It was in this that the epoch-making significance of the invention lay.

Given the great expense involved in the construction and operation of optical telegraphs, it is hardly surprising that their primary use was military. In France, the country of origin, employment in the system was turned into a sinecure for soldiers invalided from the *Grande Armée*. It is on record that, in 1809, it was the semaphore which first informed Napoleon that the Austrians had invaded Bavaria and thus opened the campaign that ended at Aspern and Wagram. In Britain a system similar to the Chappé telegraph was built around 1800 and used to connect the Admiralty in London with the principal ports. The Russians, never far behind when it comes to the military exploitation of new technologies invented by others, constructed a line between St. Petersburg and the naval base of Kronstadt, and another between St. Petersburg and Warsaw. Even as late as the 1830s, a line was being constructed to link Berlin with Trier, the objective being to serve warning in case of a French invasion of the Rhineland, which at that time constituted a Prussian province with no territorial connection to the rest of the country.

Although electricity had been known to man since classical antiquity, the idea of using it for long-distance communication is much more recent. For millenia electricity was regarded as an esoteric phenomenon, a matter of mere curiosity left to scientists or cranks. By the middle of the eighteenth century, however, the combined efforts of these men had led to the invention of friction machines for generating static electricity, and of the Leiden Jar for storing it. In 1753, an anonymous author writing in *The Scots' Magazine* suggested that these means be used for the construction of an electro-optical telegraph. During the fifty years that followed, numerous attempts were in fact made to build such a device. The future, however, lay in another direction.

The development of the electromagnetic telegraph involved sending electricity over wires and detecting it at the other end by means of a magnetized needle. Though experiments took place in France, Russia, and England—it was in England, incidentally, that the first operational system was built—in the end the name most commonly associated with the new device came to be that of an American, Samuel Morse. Morse's original contributions were essentially two. First, he provided relay stations along the wires and thereby made possible a great increase in the range over which information could be transmitted. Second, he devised the dot-and-dash code named after him, a very great improvement, considering that earlier proposals had suggested that signals be detected by administering an electric shock to the operator.

From the very first, in every country that adopted them, one of the principal uses to which electric telegraphs were put was to help manage the railways. Indeed the two technologies not only developed simultaneously but often did so at the hands of the same people. Space prevents us from describing the transformation of horse-drawn trolleys, riding wooden tracks and serving principally in order to move the product of mines and collieries to waiting barges, into steam-driven, steel-made trains running over integrated rail networks. The hardware involved has been portrayed a thousand times, and its inventors made into the subject of innumerable admiring biographies. What has largely escaped the attention of most investigators, however, is the extent to which the railway, like the telegraph but on a vastly greater scale, presented a system and depended on a system-approach for its operation.

Unlike carriages, which hitherto had been used in order to carry passengers and freight, trains could neither stop to let each other pass nor temporarily leave the track. Therefore, even in the case of the simplest single-track railway, it was necessary to know exactly when the line was vacant and when it was in use. To permit traffic to run in both directions over a single line provided with sidings, one had to know just when which points would be reached by what trains. Trains had to travel at fixed speeds and according to fixed timetables. The spread of railways helped put an end to local times, and led to the synchronization of clocks, first on a national and then on a global basis. A system of signals had to be developed, operatives had to be trained to recognize them, and their employment had to be coordinated. When it was a question of operating not just a single line but an entire rail network, with many kinds of trains running at different speeds in many directions and stopping at innumerable stations, the task of management became formidable. It could not even begin to be accomplished without the telegraph, whose wires were strung out along every railway track of any importance and soon started multiplying prodigiously.

If the Chappé telegraph had been conceived and built primarily with military objectives in mind, the same was not true in regard to either the electrical telegraph or the railway, both of which owed their development mainly to civilians. Once they were in existence, however, the military significance of these devices soon came to be appreciated. Writing in the 1830s, the German economist Friedrich List proved remarkably prescient in sketching the advantages that railways would bring to the army possessing them. During the 1840s large-scale experiments in the transport of troops and their supplies by rail took place in many countries, including England, France, Germany, and Russia. Since it was not as yet clear what railways could and could not do, not all these experiments were successful, and some ended up in a mess. There was also considerable opposition to the railways themselves, the Prussian generals in particular recalling Frederick the Great's dictum that more and better roads would only facilitate invasion. In any event, the first recorded military use of the railway took place under somewhat unusual circumstances in 1848. When the Prussian monarchy moved in troops to suppress a liberal uprising in Baden, the rebels commandeered a train to retreat from Rastadt to the Swiss border. One of those who escaped in this way happened to be Friedrich Engels.

During the 1850s, primacy in the military use of the railways was firmly in the hands of the French. They not only constructed a field line to supply their troops besieging Sebastopol in the Crimean War, but were able to move a quarter of a million men into Italy during the War of 1859, thus giving the first large-scale demonstration of the railway's military potential. By comparison, the Prussian efforts were puny. In 1852, their mobilization against Austria was badly organized and ended in humiliation at Olmütz. In 1859, an attempt to deploy an army on the Rhine fared scarcely any better. However, under the leadership of Prince Regent Wilhelm I (later to become German Emperor) and Helmut von Moltke the elder, chief of the general staff, the Prussians proved willing and able to learn. An expert on railways, Count von Wartensleben, was added to the establishment of the staff.

Von Moltke himself sat on the state committee for railways and thus took a hand in shaping Prussia's civilian railway network. Plans were drawn up in painstaking detail and rehearsed and revised many times. The effort paid off: though the forces involved were relatively small, the Prussian and Austrian mobilization and deployment on the Danish frontier in 1864 proceeded without incident.

The real demonstration of the power of the new technological instrument for war and conquest, however, was to be given in 1866 and 1870–71. While the world held its breath, Prussian mobilization and deployment during the wars against Austria and France proceeded with a clockwork precision that could barely be imagined until then. Hundreds of thousands of men were called up, formed into regiments, the regiments formed into divisions, the divisions into corps. Each unit was then issued with arms, merged with its supporting services, marched to designated stations where they were awaited by specially designated trains, and transported to the border where unloading proceeded with the same relentless efficiency. In both cases, so superior were the Prussians in utilizing telegraphs and rails that the outcome of the conflict was decided almost before the first shot was fired. This was due less to superiority in hardware—if anything, it was the French who had more and better rails and rolling stock—than to infinitely superior coordination and use.

After 1870, there was no looking back. The importance of the new technologies had been demonstrated as convincingly as could be, and every general staff hastened to add a railway department to its structure. Since service in these departments required extensive mathematical knowledge, they attracted the *crème de la crème*. Their social prestige and influence rose in proportion. The officers in charge were military technicians pure and simple. For the first time, they not only commanded specialized units and offered advice, but actually took over the conduct of war. As one would expect, nontechnical considerations were ignored in a relentless drive for maximum efficiency. Since it was believed that the side that could mobilize and concentrate troops the fastest would inevitably win the day, every important power sank years of work and uncounted sums of money into perfecting its railway system. To achieve optimum performance, these systems had to be very tightly coupled. Every step had to be calculated and rehearsed long in advance, with the personnel fully instructed and waiting only for the arrival of the relevant telegrams which, in their turn, were lying ready and waiting only for the date to be inserted. Under such conditions, a defect at any one point would reverberate all through the system. For example, the failure of a train to complete its unloading on time would block the arrival of the next train, and so on down the line.

More ominously still, by a series of almost imperceptible steps the various national systems came to be integrated not only within themselves but also with each other. To prevent a surprise attack in which the defending side would be caught with his reserves still unmobilized and undeployed, continuous surveillance and round-the-clock watches were instituted. Commanders-in-chief were warned never to be far away from the end of a telegraph or telephone line, and the day was to come when presidents went to bed with earphones clamped to their heads. All this was done in the name of exercising better control, but in reality the outcome was just the reverse. A situation arose in which, if country A took the first step towards mobilization, countries B and C and D were compelled to follow suit. This would drive country A to take the next step, and so on in a sequence of moves so closely tied to each other as to be almost automatic. Thus the systems approach, considered absolutely indispensable for efficiency, was not without its dangers. In 1914, with the would-be commanders standing helplessly by, it played a major role in dragging the world into the largest war in history to that point.

In the hands of men like Schlieffen, Ludendorff, and Groener, the noble art of mobilizing a country's army and deploying it on the frontier reached a pitch of perfection that has not been surpassed since. Nor, apart from short-term fluctuations, was the need for a systems approach obviated by the technological innovations that followed. The introduction of radio after 1900 offered a means of communication which, since it was free of wires, was capable in principle of reaching from any point to any other regardless of movement, distance, and intervening terrain. However, over time its very success caused the number of users and the amount of information transmitted to grow to the point where, on pain of mutual interference and absolute chaos, it was necessary to integrate the various broadcasting and receiving sets into inconceivably complex systems. The same fate overtook the motor vehicle. Initially, columns of these vehicles seemed to offer greater flexibility than the railroads, owing to their ability to go wherever there are roads, and this promise was indeed realized up to a point. As their numbers grew, however, it was gradually realized that motor vehicles too could only be employed if they were integrated, not just with each other but also with the vast logistic tails that supplied them with fuel, spare parts, and maintenance and repair services.

In short, the technological revolution that opened with the telegraph and the railway very largely turned war itself into a question of managing complex systems. Time after time some new tactic or technological device seemed to offer a way out, but in each case the end result was more integration, not less. Integration permitted greater and greater forces to be mobilized, husbanded, focused, and finally hurled at the enemy. To this extent, it is understandable that victory in World War II did not go to the side whose soldiers fought the hardest, or that came up with the most brilliant operational schemes. Rather, those belligerents gained the upper hand whose administrators, scientists, and managers developed the means by which to set up gigantic technological systems and run them as efficiently as possible.

The use of systems also permitted, if it did not demand, a vast increase in the scale on which war was waged. By 1914, telegraphs and railways for the first time had made the military populations of entire countries and continents both readily accessible and easily deployable. Total mobilization for war was turned into a practicable proposition. Consequently, armies came to be counted in millions, not in miserly hundreds of thousands as had been the case during the nineteenth century. Not only the absolute numbers, but the percentage of the population that could be mobilized increased. Thanks largely to advances in the technologies of administration, communication, transportation, and public health, countries such as France and Germany became capable of putting up to 10 percent of their populations into uniform, and of keeping them there almost indefinitely. When the war was stationary, and sometimes even when it was not, the armies made up of these men resembled nothing so much as cities, albeit somewhat dilapidated ones. To the astonishment of many a visitor, these cities took upon themselves the gargantuan task of supplying the men with food and drink, clothing and tools, transportation and medication, in short everything from boot repair to spiritual care. Virtually every service that, in civilian life, was available from government departments or private business was duplicated in the army.

As an outcome of these developments, modern total war became a terrible reality. The concept dates to the period after 1919, and is here employed to describe a form of military conflict in which not only armed forces but entire populations are involved. True, situations akin to total war had existed in earlier times. Where society and the military are identical, as in many tribal societies, war is total almost by definition. Rome during the Second Punic War had engaged on a conflict that was as total as anything witnessed during the twentieth century. However, earlier total war was limited to political entities small in both population and size. Rome during late Republican and Imperial times was no longer able to wage total war, nor were most of its early modern successors. Historically speaking, large states have always been incapable of mobilizing all their resources, even if they knew what those resources were. Though the French National Assembly after 1793 was able to create unprecedentedly large armies, a combination of administrative inefficiency and relative technological backwardness still prevented total mobilization. Under such circumstances, the famous declaration concerning the "permanent requisitioning" of all Frenchmen (and Frenchwomen) was little more than a rhetorical exercise.

As the Industrial Revolution got under way and spread during the nineteenth century, the ability of a nation to mobilize was revolutionized. Already in 1861–65 both belligerents in North America employed railways and telegraphs to mobilize resources on a continental scale, dwarfing all past conflicts. When World War I broke out, the instruments needed to repeat the performance on an even larger scale were ready and waiting. This fact, however, was not immediately understood by politicians and commanders. In England, Lloyd George in August 1914 declared that business would continue as usual, and when Lord Kitchener declared that the war would last for at least two years and started putting Britain's entire male population into khaki, his colleagues in the cabinet thought he had gone mad. Elsewhere the situation was as bad or worse. In Germany, where the prestige of the military was higher than anywhere else, the General Staff regarded economic matters as beneath its dignity. To the extent that such matters were considered at all, the principal concern was war-

caused unemployment. On their side, German government officials refused to purchase grain from neutral countries, their rationale being that they as mere civilians had nothing to do with
war, the conduct of which was exclusively a matter for the armed
forces.

Slowly, the truth dawned. Though there was much resistance
to be overcome, by 1916 the most important countries had carried
the trend towards total mobilization close to its logical conclusion.
Since technology had turned war into a question of economic
and industrial mobilization, governments set up new departments
to coordinate everything from raw materials to wages, and from
transport to the number of calories to be ingested daily by each
citizen. Far from giving rise to unemployment, the war effort
resulted in an insatiable demand for labor that could only be
met by calling up men, women, and children to serve in fields,
factories, and offices. In their most extreme form, these efforts
were aimed at turning entire nations into social systems, finely
geared and attuned to the creation of the greatest possible military
power. Clearly there was more to this than technological developments alone, but clearly nothing of the kind could have been
carried out without the aid of the telegraph, the railway, the rotary
press, and a thousand other devices. The net result of all these
developments was that technology permitted large states to exploit
the economies of scale in order to wage war as efficiently as, or
more efficiently than, small ones. In the future, even more than
the past, what counted would be the big battalions—and, behind
them, the big Gross National Product.

Once the politicians and commanders decided to mobilize their
male populations, in one sense they overshot the mark. In 1914,
and to a lesser extent in 1939, the instinctive reaction of the
military to the unexpected prolongation of hostilities was to put
everything and everybody into uniform. As the war dragged on,
it became increasingly clear that this was a mistake. The same
technology that made military mobilization possible also demanded that it remain incomplete. It was not enough for machines
to be deployed on the battlefield. For them to do useful service,
it was first necessary to have them designed, developed, produced,
and supplied with fuel and spare parts. War itself extended its
tentacles deep to the rear, spreading from the trenches into the
fields, the mines, and the factories. Not content with the mobilization of those, it reached further into the design bureaus and,

ultimately, into peaceful university laboratories where the most esoteric work was done and the potentially most powerful weapons were developed.

As war expanded in this way, both the meaning of strategy and its scope underwent a subtle, and at first imperceptible, change. Instead of being merely a question of concentrating the maximum force at the decisive point at the front, as Jomini and Clausewitz had taught, strategy now acquired the added dimension of an exercise in correctly distributing one's total resources, both human and material, between the fighting front and the rear. Instead of being concerned with waging military operations, it became occupied with the overall coordination and integration of a country's military effort. To cope with the new reality, a new term—grand strategy—was coined by the theoreticians and sometimes applied by those in charge. For a variety of reasons, both ideological and structural, grand strategy was a field where Germany lagged behind the Western Allies during both World Wars, and for this, of course, she paid the ultimate penalty of defeat.

Total war did not arise all at once, nor was its appearance welcomed by all concerned. Men such as Lloyd George in Britain, Clemenceau in France, and Ludendorff in Germany were brought to power by it and throve on it. Others scarcely noted its existence, as was the case of Foch when he brought out the fifth (unrevised, except for a new preface) edition of his *Conduite de la Guerre* in 1918. During the period between the wars, public opinion with few exceptions was quite reluctant to come to grips with the new phenomenon, preferring to bury its head in the sand. While here and there attempts were made to understand the implications of total war, much of the most advanced military thinking of the age consisted precisely of attempts to put the genie back into the bottle from which, unfortunately, it had escaped. Hans von Seeckt, Charles de Gaulle, John Fuller, and Basil Liddell Hart all tried to devise a variety of means, including technological means, to this end. Though tanks and fighter-bombers won spectacular victories in 1939–42, in the end the attempt ended in failure, as perhaps it was bound to do. A handful of Panzer divisions, however brilliant their tactical and operational handling, did not prove capable of meeting the mobilized power of entire continents. Though it took time to do so, and though at certain moments it was touch-and-go, the systems approach by permitting unprecedently massive forces to be created and deployed ultimately dominated the Second World War as it had the First.

By the time it did so, however, war had been transformed out of all recognition and was no longer war in the traditional sense. In the West, the idea that war is an instrument of politics, rather than an agonistic contest or a violent struggle between individuals, had not been quick to assert itself. In essence it dates back no farther than the sixteenth century, when it was first voiced by Machiavelli and Jean Bodin. Early in the nineteenth century it received its classical formulation at the hands of Clausewitz who said that war is a continuation of politics with an admixture of other means. Through most of the years before 1914, this idea was widely accepted. Though politicians and generals were often at loggerheads over the limits of each other's rights, almost everybody agreed that war was but one instrument of national policy, and not necessarily the most important instrument at that.

The idea of war as an instrument of politics, however, proved incompatible with the harsh facts of total war. Already towards the very end of the nineteenth century, the first dissenting voice was heard in a book by a German General, von der Goltz, entitled *The Nation in Arms*. Precisely because it disputed the primacy of politics over war, this work was widely acclaimed. More significantly still, what began as an extremist writer's militarist dream was destined to be transformed into horrible reality during World War I. Though the war opened with the usual political aims of national aggrandizement, it very soon escaped political control. So far from serving as an instrument of politics, that war and its successor all but swallowed politics, so that what was good for the war was considered good for the nation.

This applied both internally and externally. Internally, adherence to the systems approach dictated by the dominant technologies led to a conscious attempt to abolish politics. In many countries, and not just in the totalitarian states, the declared aim was to replace politics by organization, avowedly just for the duration of the war but sometimes with the not-so-secret intention of setting up a permanent, efficiency-serving, military dictatorship. Externally, war—far from being but one form of political intercourse between states—expanded to the point where intercourse other than the most brutal forms of force all but disappeared. When Hitler declared a war of annihilation and invaded the Soviet Union in 1941, the German Foreign Office was left with little to do.

When the Allied leaders made Unconditional Surrender their declared goal in 1943 they thereby came close to abdicating their function as politicians. As Ludendorff had written in 1936, under the conditions of modern total war Clausewitz's dictum had to be stood on its head. Instead of war being the continuation of politics, in a very real sense politics became a mere appendage of war.

To draw the threads of the argument together, from early in the nineteenth century technology underwent a fundamental change. This change affected first the infrastructure of war and then, increasingly, its conduct as well. Each of the newly invented machines separately was much more powerful than its predecessors. Though that was important, above all it was the fact that they could only be produced and used in integrated systems which brought about the new situation. As more and more individual tools and machines surrendered to the drive for efficiency and were integrated into systems, success in both peace and war tended to depend more and more on the ability to understand these systems, cope with them, and manage them.

Though the systems approach originally manifested itself in the telegraph and the railway, it did not stop at these and other technological devices. As it invaded other aspects of life, nothing was more logical than that attempts should be made to turn entire societies into systems, with war serving as the principal though by no means the sole driving force. None of these attempts was completely successful, while some—notably the Technocratic Movement in the United States—ended as ludicrous failures. They did, however, go far enough to turn modern war into something new, unprecedented, and monstrous. From being the servant of policy, war came to be all but identified with it. From being a finely honed rapier, it turned into a juggernaut that crushed everything in its path. In the end, however, the same relentless drive towards technological efficiency and power that helped produce total war was also responsible for its demise. On 6 August 1945, a fine summer day, a thousand suns shone when the first nuclear device was dropped. With the deployment of its own supreme product, total war practically abolished itself, and the history of mankind took a new turn.

CHAPTER 12

Land Warfare

DISCUSSING LAND WARFARE, we saw how strategy was transformed by the French revolutionary armies and especially those of Napoleon. This development was not primarily the outcome of technological innovation. On the contrary, training, organization, and doctrine—all of them anchored in the newly established democratic regime and in the *levée-en-masse*—were employed to overcome the technological limitations that had previously confined strategy in a straitjacket. Except for somewhat better maps, roads, and the Chappé telegraph, neither Napoleon's conquests nor his subsequent defeat can be explained in terms of technological factors. The *Grande Armée* and its opponents possessed very similar arsenals, and given the somewhat cosmopolitan character of war in this period it is not surprising that all armies freely imitated whatever small technical advances were made by the rest. Personally, Napoleon did not always react favorably toward new technology. Though he took the initiative in attempts to develop the first canned foods, he began his career by disbanding the royal balloon corps and ended it by rejecting the submarine offered to him by Robert Fulton.

For over two and a half centuries after 1550, the pace of military-technological innovation on land was very slow, often so slow as to be almost imperceptible to contemporaries. Such a state of affairs was scarcely conducive to reflection on the subject. Writing in the 1820s, Clausewitz only devoted a passing glance to the question of armament, and then only to belittle its importance.

Since he died aged fifty one, it is anybody's guess whether his eyes would have been opened by the technological revolution that was just around the corner, or whether he would have followed the example of Jomini and become ossified in his own system. Be this as it may, the year 1830 marked an important watershed. Coming from various directions, there sprang forth a number of near-simultaneous inventions that were destined to alter the entire character of war.

We have seen how the rise of the telegraph and the railway contributed to the elevation of war itself to an entirely new level; it remains, therefore, to trace their impact on strategy and operations. From this point of view, their most important characteristics were their immobility and inflexibility. Telegraph stations, like railheads, are not easily moved from one place to another. Both are a part of systems, and are accordingly vulnerable to disruption, not only by the enemy but also—in the absence of proper instruction and discipline—by one's own troops. Neither instrument can be constructed in a hurry, and where this is done performance is almost certain to suffer. Once the lines are laid or strung on poles, the speed of electricity in transmitting information over any distance is of course absolutely unmatched. However, the same is not true of the railroads which required large-scale, highly specialized facilities for loading and unloading. Railroads therefore can be remarkably inefficient when it comes to transporting large forces over distances smaller than 100 km. Further, railroads were confined to certain types of terrain but could not be made to operate successfully in others. Obviously both the railroad and the telegraph were much more useful for national strategy in its widest sense than for campaigning proper; more for conducting a one-sided engineering exercise, as during mobilization and deployment, than for active operations in the field when the enemy was close at hand and capable of disrupting the works.

A considerable period of time had to pass before these facts of life were fully appreciated, or perhaps one should anticipate and say that, in the end, they tended to aid the side which appreciated them first. If one's own side was to strike first, mobilization and deployment had to be accelerated by means of the new technological instruments. It was necessary to have not only an efficient organization but also, above all, the railroads themselves complete with rolling stock and all the ancillary equipment. Under such circumstances, it is scant wonder that strategy itself came to be increasingly governed by the configuration of the railway network. Though theoretically the option existed of shaping the railways to match one's strategy, this was such an expensive undertaking that, in practice, no great state embarked on it on more than a marginal scale. During the wars of 1861–65, 1866, 1870, and to a lesser extent 1914, both sides for the most part deployed their troops not where they would do the greatest good but wherever the railways and unloading stations happened to be situated. Fear of cavalry raids prevented the disentraining of troops close behind the frontiers; instead, armies willy-nilly started their march into battle from stations well to the rear.

If the deployment of armies numbering several hundreds of thousands of men was to be accomplished within a reasonable time, every available line had to be used. Assuming that the process got under way at the same moment on both sides, and everything else being equal, the side with the largest number of railways would win the race. Initially, however, railway lines were neither very numerous nor closely grouped together. These facts militated against the traditional precepts of strategy, which posited that everything depended on concentrating the greatest number of troops at a single spot. More by accident than by design, offensive strategy as practiced in the age of the railway turned into a question of so arranging and coordinating the march from the unloading stations into battle that each of a number of widely separated forces would arrive on a pre-selected battlefield at the same moment, if possible crushing the enemy between them. Defensive strategy consisted of using rails on internal lines to prevent this from taking place and, if possible, beating the enemy in detail.

The strategy of external lines, as it was to be dubbed by critics writing mostly with the benefit of hindsight, was also required by another factor. By the second half of the nineteenth century, thanks to technological and other developments, field armies numbering a quarter of a million men and more had become commonplace. Their sheer size, as well as the vast supply trains on which they depended, meant that concentrating them at a single spot for any purpose other than fighting a great battle became, in von Moltke's words, a calamity in its own right. Where traditionally the wings of an army had been situated perhaps 5 to 6 km apart, Napoleon had increased this to between 25 and 75 km; when larger distances were involved, as during the Russian campaign of 1812, even he tended to lose control. By the 1860s, however, strategic dispersion over fronts several hundred kilometers wide became the rule. Exercising control over such distances was only practicable with the aid of the telegraph. It also presupposed an efficient general staff, of the type first developed by the French Revolutionary armies and later perfected by the Prussians.

Though the telegraph permitted forces to be controlled even when they were hundreds and thousands of kilometers apart, as happened in the United States, its use for tactical purposes was not initially very important. Wires were slow and difficult to lay in the field. Transmission procedures were cumbersome, partly because it was necessary to prevent tapping of the lines, which was already practiced in both the American Civil War and the Prusso-Austrian War. Moreover, the capacity of the apparatus was too low to permit effective two-way communication. For all these reasons, but particularly the last-named, the telegraph was not really very suitable for transmitting detailed orders to subordinate commanders who were facing the enemy in the field and therefore required a rapid-reaction capability. Instead, its most effective use was for passing on the kind of general directives, or *Weisungen,* which were employed by von Moltke to command his armies. Where this fact was understood, the telegraph was capable of making a decisive contribution towards victory. Where it was not, as in the case of the Austrian campaign in Italy in 1859, the telegraph easily lent itself to the exercise of command by remote control with all its attendant evils. In time, the factors working in favor of dispersion made operations far from headquarters the norm on both the strategic and the operational level; control tended to end where the wires did. During the wars of the middle of the nineteenth century this was usually the site of army headquarters. Below this, corps, division, and regimental commanders were condemned to fight largely on their own, sometimes successfully and sometimes not.

As telegraphs and railways together helped transform strategy, weapons also underwent dramatic changes. Developments included the invention of the percussion cap, of the cylindro-conical bullet, of rifled barrels, of breech-loading mechanisms, of metal cartridges, of magazine-fed small arms, of machine guns, of smokeless powder, and of TNT-filled explosive shells fused with clockwork timing mechanisms. But it was the invention of the recoil system that, from 1897, revolutionized artillery and made the French 75-millimeter piece into a model for everybody else to imitate. Few of the ideas behind these inventions were really new. Some of them—notably rifling, the principle of which had been long understood—had even been incorporated into previous weapons and used on a limited scale. However, for the most part, breech-loading mechanisms before Dreyse, like machine guns before Maxim, proved too expensive or too unreliable or too cumbersome for general use. Their development and introduction during the nineteenth century cannot be understood outside the context of the Industrial Revolution, which provided not only new materials (steel) for the new weapons but also the energy, machine tools, and techniques for working those materials.

Throughout the nineteenth century, these and other technological developments leapfrogged each other. Sometimes one type of weapon progressed faster, sometimes another. Never at any moment was it clear which device would be successful and which one end up as a failure. Hence their combined impact was impossible to foresee, an aspect of technological dynamism that contemporaries were quick to comment on and complain about. Ultimately the net effect of the progress in weapons technology was to increase enormously the volume of fire that could be delivered, the range at which it could be delivered, and the accuracy with which this could be done. The combination of all three factors meant that, square meter by square meter, the battlefield became a more deadly place than ever before. Metal in the form of bullets from quick-firing rifles and machine guns, as well as fragments from artillery shells, came hurtling through the air in quantities that would previously have appeared absolutely incredible. In the words of a book that acquired great fame after 1919, warfare entered a new medium and increasingly took place in a storm of steel.

Faced with the potential of the new weapons, tactical reactions took many different forms. During the 1850s, and again (although much less excusably) during the first years of the present century, there was much grandiloquent talk about the need to strengthen the spirit of the troops, as if sheer willpower could render men bulletproof. The French in taking this line at Solferino in 1859 seemed to enjoy some success. When the Austrians tried to duplicate the performance against the Prussian needle gun in 1866, however, the result was nothing but repeated defeats at Nachod, at Skalitz, at Soor, and at Schweinschadel. As Engels was to write, on the whole the troops proved themselves to be more sensible than their commanders. For them, the instinctive thing to do in the face of the terrific firepower directed at them was to crouch or lie down behind cover. The tactical significance of this was that, perhaps for the first time since the invention of organized warfare, infantry no longer fought standing erect on their feet and organized in formation. This was a truly revolutionary change, the impact of which would take several decades to work out.

The idea that, in the field, low was safe and tall was dead was first translated into practical terms during the American Civil War. It was then that the hastily assembled, half-trained, citizen levies on both sides came to rely heavily on improvised field fortifications. As the war drew to its end, entire belts of such fortifications were sometimes constructed in front of Richmond and other cities. In Europe, thanks partly to the effective use made of the railways, the Prussian campaigns against Austria and France assumed a mobile character and did not witness much use of field fortifications. However, during the Russo-Turkish War of 1878, the Boer War of 1899–1901, and of course the Russo-Japanese War of 1904–5, such fortifications really came into their own. Well before 1914, abundant evidence was available to show that, in the next war, the spade would play as big a role as the rifle, but this was understood only by a handful of observers. If one was to admit that the future of war lay underground, it followed that the conflict would be neither brief nor pleasant. Such conclusions were not likely to commend themselves to a generation brought up on *la guèrra fresca e gioiósa*, and on the ideas of Theodore Roosevelt, Rudyard Kipling, and Friedrich von Bernhardi.

If entrenchment presented one way of dealing with the firepower of the new weapons, camouflage was another. It may be argued that camouflage aimed at preserving secrecy and achieving surprise has always existed; nevertheless, in the last years of the nineteenth century it gained a new lease on life. After millenia in which war had been regarded as a colorful spectacle, indeed often presented as the most colorful spectacle of all, drabness quite suddenly became the order of the day. Gaudy, multicolored uniforms then went out of favor, despite much resistance from conservatives. The new uniforms had colors known by such names as horizon blue, earth brown, field gray, and olive green, all of which were as likely as not to be stained by greasy-grease. Headgear also became less decorative and more functional, plumed and crescented and spiked hats gradually giving way to steel helmets—

derived from those long worn by miners and thus symbolic of the transformation of war from an aristocratic pastime into industrial-type work—and peaked caps. Weapons themselves, instead of being brightly polished as hitherto, were given a coat of dull paint which in turn was only the first step on the way to reducing their "signature." Of course, none of this should mislead the reader into thinking that military display is no longer important. Though uniforms in most countries are no longer made of red and blue and yellow fabric, spotted camouflage clothing ("tiger suits") and jumpshoes can serve just as well when it comes to showing off. Commanders may have surrendered their fancy dress in favor of combat fatigues, but they have taken their revenge by flying helicopters and surrounding themselves with motorcycles, the more powerful the better. Nor, it is necessary to add, should these things be thought of solely as childish vanities. Every good army in history has been proud of its dress and equipment, and this is as true today as it was before the introduction of modern technology.

The third way in which armies responded to growing firepower was dispersion. Dispersion can be represented in terms of the number of soldiers per square meter. In the ancient Greek phalanx, which as the name implies fought in a single block, this ratio stood at 1:1. By the eighteenth century it had decreased to perhaps 1:10 for armies as a whole, though in each individual line the troops continued to stand almost shoulder to shoulder, forming a human wall. It still stood at 1:25 during the American Civil War, which was the last one to be fought largely with muzzle-loading weapons. From this point on, the figure declined very rapidly. It was around 1:250 in World War I, several times that in World War II, and has continued to decline since then. Dispersion being the order of the day, the old-time military formations, which for millenia had constituted the very core of tactics, disappeared. Abandoning such groupings as Roman wedges, Spanish *Tercios,* Swedish crosses, and Napoleonic columns, from the time of the American Civil War entire armies began to fight in long, thin skirmishing lines. As time went on, these lines tended to become more ragged and less cohesive. It was not long before the troops, instead of advancing steadily in the open, took to leapfrogging from one covered spot to the next. This gradually caused the battlefield to assume an eerie, empty look. It also meant that, notwithstanding the growing lethality of modern weapons, the percentage of casualties suffered by entire armies per day of fighting generally underwent a sharp decline.

As in the case of entrenchment, the trend towards dispersion did not represent a planned development. On the contrary, in most armies it was bitterly opposed by headquarters, especially higher headquarters, who resented the loss of control and did everything in their power to counter the growth of chaos on the battlefield. To this end they made use of the rapidly developing telegraph as well as the telephone, which made its debut in the field around 1900. Control-by-wire was pushed progressively forward and downward until corps, divisions, regiments, and even battalions were hooked into the network. From then on, if an officer was to be on call by his superiors he had to be within reach of a signaling detachment or telephone booth. Under such circumstances it is scant surprise that warfare tended to bog down and become stationary. Commanders took up their posts wherever the wire ended, usually in convenient country houses and not seldom many kilometers behind the front. As the gap between officers and their men grew, personal leadership became all but impossible to exercise. Here and there, as during the great British offensive on the Somme in 1916, officers down to battalion level were actually forbidden to accompany their units from fear they be beyond the reach of their superiors.

If the offensive power of the infantry declined under the fire-power brought to bear by the new weapons, that of the cavalry suffered even more. From the days of Cromwell during the English Revolution to those of Ziethen and the *alte Dessauer* in the Seven Years War, cavalry charging with cold steel had held its own on the battlefield, and several important Napoleonic battles were even decided by this means. However, at Waterloo the French cavalry failed. As the nineteenth century wore on and the mounted arm found itself confronted by increasingly deadly weapons, its functions more and more came to be restricted to reconnaissance, to covering the flanks, and raiding at times and places where the enemy was not present in strength. Cavalry could also be employed as mounted infantry and used to enhance strategic mobility. Where war was waged by amateurs, as it was on both sides in the United States in 1861–65 and on the side of the Boers in South Africa in 1899–1901, cavalry often continued to do sterling service in all these roles.

In Europe, aristocratic cavalry officers—long accustomed to regard themselves as the cream of the army—did not easily resign themselves to the new age. The charge of the light brigade at Balaclava, an affair so stupid (or heroic, depending on one's point of view) as to appear almost unbelievable, has entered history. So have several similar episodes during the Franco-Prussian War, when the cavalry of both sides tried to charge as if needle guns and *chassepots* and *mitrailleuses* and breech-loading artillery did not exist. Though not every one of these attempts ended in failure, all had to be paid for in horrendous casualties. This did not prevent the jingling, jangling cavalry of all belligerents from picking up its lances and riding to war again in 1914. Mounted troops performed usefully both in Palestine and on the Eastern Front, and later also during the Russian Civil War and the Russo-Polish War. However, this was only made possible by the fact that modern technology in these theaters was relatively thin on the ground. Though cavalry still had its supporters who went on prattling about the nobility of the horse and the magnetism of the charge, by 1920 its days on the battlefield were clearly over.

Though the importance of the horse as a fighting platform declined after Napoleon, down to the end of World War I its role in tactical and operational transport was as great as, or greater than, ever before. Convoys of horse-drawn wagons were used to connect the railheads with the front, but during the last decades before 1914 their task became increasingly difficult. This was because, as compared to their predecessors, repeating rifles and machine guns and quick-firing artillery required vastly greater quantities of ammunition. During a campaign lasting five months in 1870–71 the average Prussian cannon had fired just under 200 rounds. In 1914, armies suddenly discovered that the 1000 round per barrel reserve with which most of them went to war would suffice for no more than six to eight weeks. By 1918, during the great German and Allied offensives on the Western Front, there were batteries which fired as many as 450 rounds per day. In the same period, consumption of infantry ammunition by the German Army had risen to 300,000,000 rounds a month. Transporting just this ammunition represented a formidable task, let alone transporting the numerous specialized spare parts required by modern precision-engineered military equipment. Untold kilometers of field railways were laid, and vast columns of horse-drawn vehicles were organized, but these did not suffice to offset the growing immobility of armed forces and their inability to operate far away from the railheads. Motor vehicles brought some relief, but generally they were neither available in sufficient numbers nor free from logistic problems of their own.

By 1916, the year which in some ways represents the onset of modern technological war, these developments had reached their logical conclusion. On both sides, the armies had thoroughly entrenched themselves. Though food and fodder—particularly the latter—continued to be the most bulky single items consumed by armies in the field, two-thirds of a typical division's daily supplies now consisted of ammunition, spare parts, fuel, and engineering materials. Bringing all of this forward to the troops was a hard enough task; moving it again after it had been unloaded and put into storage was an almost impossible one. Consequently, wherever the technology-to-space ratio was high, the fronts froze. Even where the troops, by employing new technology or novel tactics, succeeded in breaking through the opposing positions— as happened with increasing regularity during the last year of the war—the logistic system was hopelessly unable to follow and would bring them to a halt after a few days' advance.

Time after time, the outcome of offensives was the creation of a salient or cauldron in the front. Into these cauldrons both sides would direct incredibly intensive firepower, facing those unfortunate enough to be caught inside with a tolerable imitation of conditions hitherto thought to prevail only in hell. The resemblance was strengthened still further by the ubiquitous presence of mines, of barbed wire—a late nineteenth-century American invention originally used to herd cattle on the prairie—and of ground churned up to such an extent that some of it has remained uncultivable to the present day. To make the analogy complete, noxious and asphyxiating gases, released from cylinders or else from bursting artillery shells, frequently hovered over the battlefield. Employed under the right circumstances, and in combination with conventional shrapnel-firing artillery, gas was a very effective weapon since the same dugouts that offered protection from the shells were the first to be filled by the heavier-than-air noxious fumes. As a side benefit, not only did gas kill and incapacitate soldiers, but it also frightened them almost out of their wits and forced them to wear cumbersome protective devices. Given the major role that gas played in the tactically very successful German offensives of 1918, one cannot but help wondering why it has not been resorted to more frequently since then. No doubt this is one more example of an irrational attitude to technology.

Although the developments outlined above are often represented in terms of a technologically-induced victory of the defense over the offense, this is not entirely correct. As the Arab use of antiaircraft missiles during the 1973 war against Israel has demonstrated once again, the distinction between "offensive" and "defensive" weapons is largely spurious. Even if certain weapons are found to favor one side, this is hardly true of all weapons employed at a given time and place on all different levels of a war.

During the second half of the nineteenth century, while a variety of causes made tactical and operational mobility increasingly more difficult, railway-assisted strategic mobility improved by leaps and bounds. The simultaneous development of the telegraph enabled armies to make use of that mobility, with the result that although every major war between 1861 and 1905 was dotted with battles in which firepower brought tactical mobility to a halt, all of them were ultimately decided by offensives moving on external lines. Stagnation, interpreted as the triumph of defense, only reigned from the end of 1914 to the end of 1917, i.e., towards the very end of the period in question. Once this happened, it did not take long for the antidote to emerge.

Although it would be too much to say that, by the end of World War I, trench warfare in its classic form had been defeated, certainly the foundations for overcoming it had been laid. On the German side, the introduction of the flamethrower, the submachine gun, and artillery pieces light enough to be hauled forward and used in direct support of assault parties formed part of the highly innovative infiltration tactics which were developed in successive stages from the spring of 1916 on. On the Allied side, a technological solution was found in the form of a tank. This was simply an armored box on tracks that could advance up to and across enemy defenses while raking them with fire from cannon or machine guns and, incidentally, acting as cover for the infantrymen following behind. At Caporetto, at Cambrai, during the great German offensives of the period from March to July 1918, and later during the equally great Allied counteroffensives, these tactical and technological innovations permitted the defensive arrays on both sides of the front to be breached time after time. While the logistic problems of modern warfare could not be overcome by foot infantry on its own, tanks with their insatiable demand for fuel, spare parts, and maintenance, created as many new logistic problems as they solved tactical ones. In time, solutions to these difficulties would undoubtedly have been found, but by the time they were found World War I was over. This was above all a result of exhaustion in the Central Powers, rather than of a clear-cut tactical defeat suffered by its armies in the field.

Given that the armistice in 1918 put an end to experiments in tactical and technological innovation, it is perhaps understandable that the next twenty years witnessed a spirited debate concerning the direction in which warfare was moving. Though opinions were numerous and interwoven, two camps could be distinguished. On one side were those who regarded motor vehicles and tanks (and aircraft) as useful adjuncts to existing tactics, to be acquired in reasonable numbers and employed when opportune in conjunction with the existing arms, primarily the infantry and the artillery. Arranged against them were the apostles of mechanization, who considered that mechanized forces, even quite small ones, could—provided they were properly organized and trained—win the next conflict all on their own. According to them, it was the infantry and the artillery which, if they were not to be relegated to the scrapheap, would have to group themselves around the tank. These views were received with scant enthusiasm by the representatives of the traditional arms, men who, as it happened, occupied the senior commands in most countries but particularly those that had recently won the war. Neither school was proved entirely right by World War II. Mechanized forces certainly did win some spectacular victories during the early years, and afterwards they continued to play a key role. However, on their own they were incapable of deciding the conflict, let alone rendering total war obsolete as their supporters had hoped.

Though budgets during the twenties were cut back everywhere, and though tanks did not necessarily figure high on the priority list, the armies of France, England, the USSR, the United States, and Germany—the latter, proceeding in secret and on foreign soil—all experimented with a variety of tracked armored vehicles that often assumed bizarre shapes. Firepower, armor, speed, range, and reliability were all gradually improved, though for a long time the question as to what represented the best possible combination of all these characteristics remained unresolved. By the end of the thirties most tanks carried one main gun in a revolving turret on top of the hull. This configuration made them suitable primarily for fighting other vehicles and other tanks in the open, less so for dealing with infantry, especially entrenched infantry in broken terrain. Though some enthusiasts had visions of armies consisting entirely of tanks, the latter's limited firepower, as well as the difficulties in operating them in many types of terrain and at night, meant that this view never stood a chance of being accepted. From the moment the first large-scale experiments in armored warfare were made on England's Salisbury Plain in 1927, it was clear that tanks would have to be accompanied by infantry and field artillery. If the tanks were not to be slowed down by these components, the infantry and artillery would have to be motorized, or preferably mechanized, with infantry riding armored personnel carriers and the artillery being self-propelled. Add antitank artillery to enable one's own infantry to resist enemy tanks, add engineering, maintenance, logistic services, and a signals detachment to permit control of the lot, and the armored division was born. For several decades, it remained one of the most potent symbols of military power.

For a variety of reasons, at the beginning of World War II it was only the Germans who had any number of properly organized armored divisions. During the 1939 campaign in Poland, they gained valuable experience in handling them. Later, using between ten and twenty of these units, as well as a similar number of motorized formations, they were able to win a series of spectacular triumphs that have since become almost legendary. A typical *Blitzkrieg* campaign opened with a devastating blow against the enemy's airfields, aimed at gaining superiority in the air. Simultaneously, troops would be brought in by transport aircraft, or glider, or dropped by parachute in order to seize objectives in the enemy's rear and hold them until the ground forces arrived. On land, heavy attacks by massed artillery and infantry would tear open the enemy front at selected points, or else the attacks would be launched by the armor itself. Once a gap had opened up, the armored divisions would pour through. Still preceded by the air force acting as flying artillery and also in the interdiction role, and followed by motorized and infantry units to consolidate the territorial gains made, the armored divisions would take the line of least resistance much as water flows down a slope. Fanning out into the enemy's rear, their aim would be less to overcome enemy resistance than to isolate and cut off segments of his forces. Victory in a campaign was usually due less to heavy casualties on the defeated side than to confusion, disorganization, and sheer panic. To paraphrase a famous dictum of Napoleon's, lightning war was made with the tanks' tracks, not their guns.

Though there was much variety between theaters and campaigns, by and large the victories that grew out of these tactics were not due primarily to techological superiority on one side. In 1940–41, not only did all important countries have tanks but in many cases their tanks were more numerous, and of better quality, than those in the hands of the German Wehrmacht. Only in one respect, admittedly a very important one, were the Germans clearly superior. At a time when most Western tanks only carried receiving sets, and when Russian tanks frequently had no wireless sets at all, the Germans under Generals Guderian and Fellgiebel— the latter an officer in charge of the signals troops, whose contribution to the *Blitzkrieg* has been largely overlooked by historians— insisted that every Panzer should come equipped with two-way radio. Their armored divisions thus acquired very great tactical and operational flexibility such as has rarely been equaled before or since. This flexibility, possibly even more than the tanks themselves, constituted the true core of the new style in warfare.

As the Germans in 1939–42 demonstrated the devastating power of the new weapon, every belligerent in turn hastened to follow their example and set up armored divisions, corps, and even armies, uniting up to a thousand tanks under a single field headquarters. In the hands of a Koniev, a Rokossovsky, a Patton, these forces certainly played a critical role in defeating the Wehrmacht. However, they were never quite able to duplicate the spectacular German triumphs such as the six-month drive that carried them from the River Bug in Poland all the way to Moscow. The unsuitable nature of some of the theaters in which the war was later waged—notably the Italian—and a gradual decline in the effect of surprise, were probably responsible for this.

From a tactical point of view, the role of the tank had changed considerably over the years. Originally invented as a siege engine for overcoming the resistance of entrenched infantry, tanks later assumed some of the roles traditionally reserved for the cavalry. Gradually, they became specialized for fighting other tanks. In this role, what had been an offensive device *par excellence* proved itself no less effective in the defense. Indeed, a case might be made that it was more effective, as was demonstrated by the Germans on both the eastern and western fronts in 1943–45 and again—this time, conclusively—by the Israelis on the Golan Heights in 1973. Confronted with firepower which was brought to bear, not only by antitank guns and rockets (and later by guided missiles) but also by other tanks, the reaction of armored troops was similar to that of the infantry three-quarters of a century earlier. First they tried to break through regardless. When this failed, they took to fighting from behind stationary cover, digging antitank trenches, and laying minefields. More and more often they demanded that their charges be preceded by tremendous air bombardments and artillery barrages. Meanwhile, armored combat properly speaking came to consist of getting the cumbersome steel monsters to leapfrog from one firing position to the next.

During the early years of World War II, the introduction of the tank, the personnel carriers by which it was accompanied, and the motor vehicles on which it depended for its supplies, led to a great increase of operational mobility on land. Later, however, the tide turned. Armored warfare for the most part became as cumbersome as any infantry battle, and attrition rates as heavy. The logistic requirements of armored forces increased by leaps and bounds. In 1914, a typical infantry division went to war expecting to draw less than 100 tons of supplies a day, much of it consisting of fodder which could normally be had on the spot. In 1940–41, a German Panzer division engaged in active operations already required 300 tons a day. By 1944–45 an American armored division was consuming twice that amount, and the most recent estimates are of the order of 1000–1500 tons and more. Given the peculiar character of armored warfare, virtually all of these supplies have to be transported by road, a completely tracked force being beyond the means of even the richest armies. The result has been not only vast convoys of motor vehicles but even vaster supply and maintenance depots to keep them running. Already at Alam el Halfa in 1942, Rommel's convoys and depots not only impeded mobility but also provided ideal targets for British fighter-bombers roaming overhead, leading to his defeat. The situation was increasingly repeated in later years. Though attempts to protect land forces against air attack have been partly successful, at best the result has been to render such forces even more cumbersome. Their movements are restricted to areas that are within reach of the antiaircraft defenses, and so the vicious cycle continues.

To sum up the impact of technology on the evolution of land warfare in the period 1830–1945, it is perhaps best to begin with the very numerous tactical developments. Though by no means the result of technological advances only, and though various higher commands in particular committed gross errors in assessing the impact of new weapons and their use, tactics generally adapted themselves to the new technology. Together with progress in the field of nonmilitary technology, such as communications and transport, tactical changes led to shifts in strategy, such as the switch from interior to exterior lines after 1860, the declining mobility of warfare after 1871, and the gradual recovery in the power of the tactical offensive after 1917. From a wider point of view, however, it might be argued that there was very little change at all. Though the armored divisions of World War II certainly operated on a much larger scale than did the corps that formed Napoleon's army, and though even the least competent of those divisions on its own would easily have torn to pieces the entire *Grande Armée* complete with its genial commander-in-chief, in principle their operations displayed little that was really new. Strategy on land remained what it had been since the closing years of the eighteenth century, namely, a question of coordinating the movements of physically-separated forces over terrain, along lines of communication, among obstacles (both natural and artificial) and in relation to the enemy. After 1945, this situation was to undergo profound changes, and the most important factor responsible for this was air power.

CHAPTER 13

Command of the Air

SINCE THE DREAM of man soaring like a bird dates back at least to Biblical times, the beginning of the beginning of aviation is shrouded in more obscurity than that of most technological devices. Nor is it merely a question of deciding who built the first flying device, when, where, and how. The real problem is to decide exactly what is meant by such a device. Depending on the definition selected, one might include under the rubric of flying devices— imaginary or real—the wings that Daedalus allegedly made for himself and for his son Icarus; the contraption which Eylmer the Lame, a late eleventh-century monk from Canterbury, apparently built in order to leap from a cathedral tower; and of course the famous ornithopter, or flying machine with flapping wings, which Leonardo sketched in his secret notebooks. A complete catalogue of these devices would probably show that, throughout recorded history, hardly a century has passed which did not see somebody at work, somewhere, trying to translate the dream into reality. Most of these attempts were destined to remain on paper, mere dreams based on science, religion, or magic. Those that got beyond this stage often ended when the inventor suffered a few broken bones, or fell to his death.

For practical purposes, the history of aviation starts in 1783. It was in that year that the brothers Montgolfier, manufacturers of paper in Lyons, France, first built a hot-air balloon large enough to carry one or two men. A few months later, another Frenchman, J. A. C. Charles, constructed and flew the first hydrogen-filled balloon, the principles of which have barely been altered to the present day. News about these inventions caused an immediate sensation. The year had not come to an end before a tract published in Amsterdam engaged in speculations concerning the use of "flying globes" for military purposes, specifically the capture of Gibraltar from the English. During the Napoleonic wars, a great many pamphlets were brought out containing detailed descriptions of the employment of balloons for military purposes. Often these pamphlets were accompanied by printed illustrations showing huge hot air or hydrogen-filled flying devices crossing the English channel and landing entire units of the *Grande Armée,* complete with their horses and guns.

These sanguine hopes notwithstanding, during most of the nineteenth century the use of aerostatic, or lighter-than-air, devices for military purposes remained marginal at best. Against the Austrian-Prussian forces at Valmy in 1792, and possibly on one or two other occasions, the French put aloft a couple of balloons to observe the enemy armies. Apparently the balloons were not considered very successful, for Napoleon a few years later decided against keeping a balloon unit on his establishment. During the American Civil War, too, both sides sometimes employed tethered balloons for observation. During the siege of Paris in 1871 a few dozen balloons were manufactured and used to take mail and people out of the city—among them future premier Leon Gambetta. These experiments demonstrated the possibilities of balloons as well as their limitations, particularly the difficulties created by the weather and unpredictable winds. The use of balloons, therefore, was confined to siege warfare, or else to situations in which the fronts had become stationary, as for example in front of Richmond in 1865. Even so, by the last years of the nineteenth century, balloons were no longer a novelty and had become integrated into military tables of organization down to corps headquarters level. Some thought went into the possibility of using them not only for reconnaissance but also to drop explosives and, *horribile dictu,* incendiaries. This was incompatible with the existing law of war, and several international conferences were convened expressly to consider this problem.

Even as armed forces experimented with the use of balloons in war, inventors were busily at work trying to make them dirigible. As has often been the case in military history, what was lacking was not scientific understanding of the principles, but simply techniques for manufacturing light but rigid airframes, and an engine of suitable power-to-weight ratio. When these became available during the 1890s it was not long before the first airships were built and flown in Germany, Britain, and the United States. The military possibilities of the airship, like those of the balloon, were apparent right from the beginning. During World War I both sides, but the Germans in particular, were to use these devices for long-range reconnaissance, at sea as well as on land, and for what was later known as "strategic" bombardment.

The history of heavier-than-air flying devices is briefer than that of balloons and dirigibles, but resembles it in many points. Throughout the nineteenth century active experiments aimed at building such a machine, powered or unpowered, went on in several countries. Most of these experiments were not successful and a few ended in failures that were as ludicrous as they were spectacular. They did, however, contribute much by the way of a better understanding of the scientific principles involved. As in the case of dirigibles, the real problem consisted of constructing a light but strong airframe as well as finding a suitable source of primary energy. When those became available, it was only a question of time before one of the many inventors working on the problem would hit upon a proper solution. The name most commonly associated with the early days of powered heavier-than-air flight were the American Wright brothers. It was a close call, however, as is shown by the fact that H. G. Wells, who was exceedingly well-informed on scientific matters, in his 1905 book *A Modern Utopia* mentioned the Brazilian Alberto Santos-Dumont as the outstanding figure in the field.

As with balloons and dirigibles, the military possibilities of aircraft were apparent from the moment they were invented. In the United States much of the money that went into experiments with aircraft came from the Department of the Army. As it happened, the Americans put their money on the wrong inventor. After a machine built by Samuel Langley crashed into the Potomac in December 1903, just nine days before the Wright brothers made their historic flight, Congress blocked all further government expenditure so that leadership in the field passed into European hands. During the Italian invasion of Libya in 1911–12 a handful of aircraft were used for bombardment, artillery liaison, and reconnaissance, including even crude attempts at aerial photography. During that campaign, it was conclusively demonstrated that success depended as much on training, doctrine, and organization as on the flying machines themselves. Even in the age of aircraft made of wires and fabric, however, Italy was too poor a country with too small a technical and industrial base to keep the lead for long. Primacy in aviation accordingly passed to the Germans who, at the outbreak of World War I, possessed not only the world's best equipped fleet of dirigibles but also the largest number of military aircraft. Like the balloons, these were fully integrated into the military organization down to corps level. Like the balloons, too, it was thought that their primary use would be in liaison and reconnaissance.

Reconnaissance and the functions related to it—liaison and artillery observation—did prove very important during the four years of World War I, but it was soon overshadowed by missions of a different kind. Pilots going to war in the early months often carried their pistols and used them to take pot shots at each other. From these modest beginnings a series of small, but continuous, technical advances led steadily toward the great air battles of 1917–18 in which hundreds of aircraft sometimes participated. Pistols were soon replaced by rifles, rifles by swivel-mounted single- and double-barrelled machine guns. For fear of hitting the propeller, these could at first fire only sidewards and rearwards, thus requiring a second crew member. However, in 1916 first the Germans, and then the Allies, came up with aircraft where the machine guns were synchronized with the engine and which were accordingly capable of firing straight forward.

With the technical advances came increasingly sophisticated tactics, and here again the Germans pioneered. Individual pilots such as the famous Oswald Boelcke put much thought into the question of to how to catch the enemy at a disadvantage. The result was a variety of oddly-named maneuvers for getting at the other aircraft's unprotected tail or at his exposed underbelly, and these remained essentially unchanged until after World War II. Numerous experiments were also made in developing techniques for mutual support and formation-flying, but here progress was difficult to achieve because the wireless of the day was too heavy, and too cumbersome in operation, to be carried by most aircraft. By 1916 both sides flew into action in organized formations intended to prevent individual pilots from getting lost, and also to provide mutual cover. However, once the engagement had begun the formations would instantaneously dissolve into a swarm of individual machines turning, twisting, diving, climbing, and somersaulting crazily in all directions. Known as dogfights, these battles of one against one, two against one, three against two, were nerve-wracking affairs. Pilots who stood the ordeal and shot down numerous adversaries became celebrities and were widely feted. Many of those who did not swelled the ranks of the airmen who became casualties in World War I—55,000 in all.

From 1914 to 1918, thanks to an unending series of improvements in the construction of airframes and engines, the speed, endurance, range, climbing rate, maneuverability, ceiling, and reliability of aircraft increased steadily. By the time of the armistice, the best biplanes and triplanes had a ceiling of 3 to 4 kilometers which they could reach in 12 to 15 minutes. Maximum speeds were not far from 200 km per hour, although the vast majority of engagements were fought at much less than this and had their outcome determined by maneuverability rather than by linear speed alone. At any given moment in the war technological superiority was likely to be in the hands of the Germans; however, they were ahead of the Allies often only by weeks, and never by more than a few months. Under such conditions, it often happened that an aircraft which had been the acme of technological progress in the year of its first appearance became obsolescent in the next. Still, technical excellence did not count for everything. So long as the machines that they flew were not hopelessly inferior, the skill and daring of individual pilots as well as their willingness to cooperate in teams could make up for much. Everything else being equal, the side with the larger number of machines would drive the other from the sky. In the end, that was precisely what happened.

Though the available technical means were often exceedingly primitive, aircraft during the War of 1914–18 not only fought each other but carried out a variety of other tasks to which little, if anything, has been added since. Aircraft went on reconnaissance missions and brought back information from behind the enemy front. They flew liaison missions, either transporting passengers or dropping messages. Equipped with a variety of signaling devices, or using their own wings to make prearranged signs, aircraft supplemented and sometimes replaced forward artillery observers. With their machine guns, they strafed the enemy lines. Carrying first hand grenades and then more deadly devices, they tried to interdict units and supplies moving behind those lines. Though one side employed Zeppelins and the other heavy, four-engined bombers, both conducted experiments in strategic bombing of the enemy's industry and population. Aircraft were also used, albeit on a modest scale, to bring supplies to the front, and to fly back the wounded. By the time of the armistice the parachute had just been introduced into service, and plans were under way to mount what was later to become known as "vertical envelopment."

The intensive utilization of aircraft helped develop a thorough understanding of their strengths and weaknesses which, for the most part, have persisted to this day in spite of all technological improvements. The principal strengths were speed, flexibility, the ability to reach out and hit any point regardless of natural and artificial obstacles, and a great potential for achieving surprise, a potential that was frequently exploited, from 1939 on, to get in a devastating opening blow from the air. The most important weaknesses were probably a growing dependence on sophisticated ground facilities, vulnerability to attack when on the ground, limited endurance, relatively small burden-carrying capacity, and a great drop in effectiveness during bad weather or at night. As usual, neither strengths nor weaknesses worked in favor of one side. Rather, it was a question of understanding them thoroughly and using them effectively.

When war broke out in 1914, aerial operations were initially conducted on a very modest scale—all belligerents put together only had around 500 aircraft among them. This situation, however, soon changed. With the exception of the signal services, there was no arm in World War I which expanded as fast as the various air corps. In November 1918 the British service alone was made up of 300,000 officers and men, a 150-fold increase on its strength when it had entered the conflict four years previously. During the war as a whole, what was finally to become the Royal Air Force purchased no fewer than 50,000 flying machines of all types. A technical arm *par excellence,* the air corps of all the belligerents were mostly staffed by well-schooled young men of bourgeois origins. Among the aces, a sprinkling of aristocrats and other eccentrics—the most famous of whom was Gabriele d'Annunzio, the Italian poet and dramatist—lent a touch of color, but generally the prevailing values were solidly technological and middle class. The combination of these values with the spirit of adventure, freedom, and individual heroism offered by aviation proved too strong for the heads of many. During the interwar years, ex-pilots from Goering downward often sought to translate their fantasies into political action and were prominent in every fascist movement.

The frequently spectacular nature of air warfare notwithstanding, the technological limitations of aircraft were such that its role in the strategy of all belligerents remained ancillary rather than decisive. Where aircraft were available in sufficient numbers and were well employed, as during Allenby's 1917 offensive in Palestine, the contribution that they made to victory was very considerable. Very often, however, when a small number of machines attacked some target with the primitive technical means at their disposal, the effect was that of mere pinpricks. Still, as in the case of tanks on land, the men who in 1918 were trying to predict the future of armed conflict had no doubts concerning the growing role that aircraft would play. As in the case of the tank, too, there were visionaries who exaggerated the power of the new instrument and expected it to replace the traditional arms. These hopes, or fears, were never realized. However, the quality of the thought that went into some of these analyses was very high, and did much to lay the doctrinal foundations of airpower which, in one way or another, continue to shape military theory down to the present day.

During the interwar years, thanks in part to the enormous publicity that attended each improvement, aviation technology in general, and military aviation technology in particular, advanced by leaps and bounds. By 1939, lighter-than-air devices had for the most part been discarded as too slow, too unwieldy, and too vulnerable for war. Some use was still made of biplanes manufactured out of wood, wire, and fabric, but the majority of machines in every air force now consisted of monoplanes made out of aluminum, a metal that had been almost exotic in 1900 but which now constituted one of the critical raw materials with which (and for which) war was made. Though the internal combustion engine still served as the source of primary energy in virtually all aircraft, its output had been increased from under 200 to over 1,000 h.p., with corresponding improvements in reliability.

Some series-built military aircraft were capable of flying at speeds of up to 550 km per hour, though the majority, particularly the bombers, were slower. Normal service ceilings had gone up to perhaps 8 km, though a few specialized machines equipped with pressurized cabins and turbochargers were capable of doing better than that. Most aircraft were now equipped with two-way radio sets that enabled them to communicate with their base and also with each other. The Germans, followed by others, also pioneered in using direct radio communications between aircraft and land units down to division level, a vital step if effective air-ground cooperation was to be achieved. As in the case of armor, there is a tendency in the literature to overlook the role played by communications in favor of more spectacular characteristics of performance. However, communications did as much as any other factor to explain the changes that took place in the conduct of air warfare from the First World War to the Second.

The warplanes of World War II, like those during the last years of World War I, came in an endless variety of sizes, shapes, and types. Though categories varied from one country to another, most air forces had light planes for reconnaissance and liaison, single-engined fighters for interception and air combat, twin-engined light and medium bombers, and a variety of transports and gliders which could be used not only for supply but also to put fully armed units on top of their targets. In addition, some forces developed original types for their own use. The German Luftwaffe specialized in dive bombers which were very successful and remained in service until the end of the war, though scarcely in the role for which they had been intended. However, they also put much effort into heavy twin-engined fighters which did not prove a match for the smaller British and American machines and, in the end, were employed mostly as night fighters.

On their side, the British and Americans concentrated on the construction of heavy four-engined bombers. Though these machines were armed with several machine guns for defense against fighters, in daylight they did not stand up to the cannon with which most fighters were armed. This meant that they had to operate at night, which greatly reduced their ability to find their targets and drop their bombs accurately. The alternative, of course, was to provide them with escorts in the form of long-range fighters. Such aircraft first became available in 1943, and it can be argued that their development represented the single most decisive contribution made by technology to air warfare in World War II.

A cursory look at the list of the various types of aircraft in use indicates the diversity of views among the various future bellig-erents as to which were the most important uses of airpower and how it should be organized. Though by 1939 in most coun-tries—the United States being a notable exception—pilots had succeeded in emancipating themselves from the control of generals and admirals, there was much argument as to whether planes could best be used as flying artillery, for interdiction behind the front, or for bombing demographic and economic and industrial targets deep in the enemy's homeland. There was discussion, too, as to whether or not airborne operations represented a practical possibility in war. Depending on the answers that were given to these questions, each air force developed its own order of battle. Though they all possessed aircraft specialized for shooting down other aircraft, the consensus generally was that the net outcome of military aviation had been a very great increase in the power of the offense. It was assumed, as British Prime Minister Stanley Baldwin put it, that the bomber would always get through. Wher-ever it did get through, the result would be not only havoc on a previously unimaginable scale but also confusion and panic.

As the technical development of aircraft continued, means to combat them also appeared. The most important machine with which to fight an aircraft was, of course, another aircraft. Though their effectiveness had not been very great, other means also ex-isted. Even during the American Civil War, the troops of both sides had taken pot shots at the other's observation balloons. In 1871, the Germans around Paris did the same. During World War I there were many instances in which not only small arms and machine guns but cannon of various calibers were made to shoot upwards. Many of these attempts were improvised—the first French solution to the problem consisted simply of a wooden frame that held a 75-millimeter field gun, complete with its shield, pointing into the sky—but a few were carefully designed. Given the relative fragility of aircraft, as well as the volume of the fire-power that could be brought to bear against them by other aircraft and from the ground, it was clear that a solution to the problem of air defense was conceivable. But given the speed and maneuver-ability of hostile aircraft, it was also clear that everything depended on finding some means of detecting them early and then vectoring one's own forces against them. In World War I, when the speed of aircraft and the altitudes at which they could fly were still quite limited, this was often done by observers who used field glasses to detect the aircraft and telephones to communicate with each other and with base. During the years between the wars, there was much experimentation with acoustical, infrared, and radio-wave detectors.

Ultimately, the system that emerged was radar. This worked by transmitting short pulses of high frequency radio waves that then bounced back from the metal bodies of approaching enemy aircraft (and ships). Though early sets were only capable of giving range and direction, subsequent sets, relying on the so-called Doppler effect, were also able to indicate exact position, course, and speed. The first operational radar system was completed just at the time war broke out in 1939 and covered the British Isles. This, again, was one of the devices that did much to shape the face of war during the years that followed.

Though radar represented an invention of the first importance, on its own it was capable only of warning against attack. If its potential was to be exploited to the full, it had to be coordinated and integrated with other devices. It was a question not merely of setting up individual radar stations but of situating them in such a way as to cover every possible approach while simultaneously avoiding overlap and mutual interference. The signals received by these stations had to be translated into coherent information and sent to a central war room. There, a team of experts was hard at work deciding which threats were to be met, in what order, by what means, and in which way. These decisions made, it was a question of sending out the relevant orders, monitoring their execution with the aid of specialized ground control radar, and modifying them as new information about the developing battle came in.

Since many of the technical instruments employed would only work in combination with all the rest, and since it was absolutely vital that mutual interference be avoided, everything depended on close integration and on taking a systems approach in which the whole predominates over the parts. On both sides of the English Channel, these requirements gradually led to the establishment of integrated air-defense systems giving employment to hundreds of thousands, including many women who turned out to be well-suited for military jobs requiring much skill but little physical strength. The radar sets that served as the eyes of these systems were coupled, often quite literally, with radio and teleprinter links, searchlights, barrage balloons, antiaircraft batteries, fighters, and night fighters. Since speed and accuracy counted for everything, there was a constant pressure to replace human operators by machines and, as the next logical step, have those machines communicate directly with each other. This trend was reinforced by the fact that many of the considerations involved could be quantified and entrusted to automatic devices, from which the first computers were later to evolve.

Advancing in lockstep with the air-defense systems, the technology of bombers and of bombing also made vast progress during these years. In 1939, most bombers on both sides were twin-engined and capable of carrying fewer than 5 tons of bombs and armament. By 1945, the heaviest bombers had four engines, each developing over 2,000 h.p., and were capable of delivering 10 tons over much longer distances. Carrying special instruments that enabled them to follow narrow radio beams broadcast for this purpose, these aircraft gradually improved their ability to find their targets in bad weather and at night, though nothing like pinpoint accuracy was ever achieved. Bombsights also improved, and towards the end of the war, airborne radar permitted targets to be attacked even when they were covered by clouds, rain, or fog. To counter radar, bombers dropped "window"— chaff consisting of thin strips of metal foil which reflected radio waves and confused the defenders. It was also possible to mislead and jam and overload radar in other ways, with the result that the battle of bombers against air defenses was increasingly turned into a game of skill requiring not only enormous technical expertise but the kind of mind that, in ordinary life, is perhaps most commonly associated with the practical joker.

Despite these impressive technological developments, the performance of aircraft in the strategic bombing role never quite met the expectations of pioneers such as Billy Mitchell, Alexander Seversky and, of course, Giùlio Douhet; though it is possible that, had Douhet's ideas been followed, and persistent gas employed in combination with high explosive, the outcome might have been different. The German Luftwaffe, originally designed for interdiction and close support, did not have the power to bring Britain to its knees, though living through the *Blitz* was harrowing. The subsequent Allied air offensives against Germany and Japan were better planned, mounted on a vastly larger scale, and caused tremendous damage. However, they too did not break the resistance of either country or drive the population into the kind of panic that psychiatrists had forecast and prepared for. On the other hand, attempts to end the war by concentrating on "critical" targets such as ball-bearing factories proved equally disappointing. Sometimes this was because alternative resources were available. In other cases, failure stemmed from deficient intelligence, enemy resistance, inaccurate bombing, or simply the planners' blindness to the need to repeat a successful attack and thus prevent repairs from being made.

The most important factor behind the inability of strategic airpower to play a truly decisive role, however, may have lain in the gradual loss of the heavy bomber's flexibility. In turn, that loss was the result of three factors: its own technical development, the need to counter the increasingly heavy opposition, and the sheer numbers involved. If bombers were to survive in hostile skies they had to fly at altitudes that often prevented them from seeing their assigned targets, let alone engage targets of opportunity. For days in advance, their operations had to be coordinated, indeed integrated, with those of countless ground facilities, weather stations, installations for broadcasting navigational beams, antiradar measures, and, of course, mighty fleets of fighters whose flight characteristics differed markedly from their own. Thus strategic bombing not only found itself opposed by a technological system but itself assumed all the characteristics of such a system. The price to be paid for "mechanical" efficiency was, as usual, a loss of flexibility. The outcome was a slugging match as prolonged, and as deadly, as anything on land. Like the land battle, it too was finally decided by attrition acting in favor of the side that possessed the greater resources.

As increasingly integrated air defenses battled increasingly cumbersome bombers, other forms of air warfare took a very different form. Though light bombers, fighter-bombers, and fighters on both sides made use of radar and were often directed into battle from the ground, and though they often flew in large formations, they were so fast and so maneuverable as to be vulnerable principally to their own kind. Consequently, for them combat remained largely a question of individual, or at any rate small-scale, dogfights not very different from those of World War I. They did not have to be integrated into systems to quite the same extent as their bigger brothers, with the result that they kept their operational flexibility much longer. Throughout World War II, but particularly when it was used on a massive scale and in close coordination with the ground forces, the fighter-bomber proved a devastating weapon. It was capable, under favorable conditions, of isolating and breaking up entire sections of the battlefield.

The potential of aircraft in carrying out tactical and operational missions was first demonstrated by the Luftwaffe which, thanks in part to the fact that many of its commanders were ex-army officers, developed air-to-ground cooperation into a fine art. At Alam el Halfa in 1942, and later at Falaise in 1944, the Allies proved that they too had mastered it, and that even the best-equipped, best-organized armored forces in the world were hopelessly vulnerable to attack from the air. It is also pertinent to point out that what finally brought the German economy to its knees was less the concentrated might of thousands of heavy bombers than the attacks of long-range fighters upon pinpointed targets in the rail transportation network. To beat one technological system, it is necessary to direct against it another either much more powerful or much more flexible.

The period between the wars also witnessed a great many experiments in the use of aircraft for landing troops behind the enemy front or else on top of isolated targets such as fortresses, islands, etc. A mission of this type might involve either transports or gliders or parachutes. Each of these instruments was found to possess its own specific strengths and weaknesses, with the result that, when the war ended, none had succeeded in establishing absolute dominance over the others. Though transport aircraft could land troops reliably and in considerable numbers, they could do this only if and where suitable ground facilities were available. Unlike transports, gliders were cheap enough to be employed on one-way missions. However, they too required suitable terrain for making a successful landing and, in addition, were restricted in their operations by the weather. Paratroopers not only required reasonably flat terrain in which to land but were always in danger of being blown away from the target area and dispersed by the wind. To reassemble them into cohesive units might require hours. Sometimes the results were even worse, as during the 1943 Allied invasion of Sicily, when numbers of them fell into the sea and were drowned.

As against these differences, the three methods for bringing in forces from the air had some factors in common. All had a great potential for surprise, but all were also extremely vulnerable to enemy counteraction both while on the way to their target and at the moment of landing. Though each of them could be used to deliver equipment as well as soldiers, naturally their load-carrying capacity did not even begin to compare with that of land transport. Consequently, airborne troops, whatever the precise manner by which they were transported, had to be content with light arms and equipment. Unless they received support within a reasonable period of time, they stood every chance of being overwhelmed by enemy ground forces backed by vehicles, artillery, and tanks. The combination of all these characteristics meant that airborne troops were most successful against isolated targets—the occupation by the Germans in 1941 of Crete comes to mind, though it was so costly that Hitler later hesitated, and finally refused, to repeat the experiment against Malta—or else in conjunction with one of the rapidly moving *Blitzkrieg* offensives. However, where these conditions did not apply—and here the Battle of Arnhem comes to mind—the prolongation of the battle usually meant that the defender was able to wipe out the invaders from the sky.

To sum up, the greatest contribution of airpower to the development of warfare between 1911 and 1945 was perhaps the ability to overfly most kinds of obstacles. If the gearing of entire societies and economies to the war effort constituted the principal characteristic of modern total war, it was aircraft which ended the immunity of those economies and those societies and made it possible to subject them to direct attack. The obliteration of the distinction between front and rear, combatants and noncombatants, followed. The outcome was a crisis in the law of war, and a process of barbarization such as had not been seen in Europe since the second half of the seventeenth century.

During World War I, the primitive nature of the available technology meant that strategic bombing had to be carried out on a modest scale and that its effects amounted to mere pinpricks. However, as time went on and the instruments were perfected, aircraft were turned into murderous weapons indeed. Their very effectiveness meant that defenses against them were soon developed, with the result that the contest of heavy bombers against integrated continent-wide defenses increasingly developed into a struggle of attrition by one system against another. Nobody who saw the smoking ruins into which most German and many Japanese cities had been reduced in 1945 would doubt the importance of the contribution of strategic air power to the Allied victory.

Nevertheless, it may not have represented the most cost-effective form in which military power was applied during the conflict.

Since strategic bombing when properly used was capable of destroying entire industrial zones, its effects were also felt in the theater of operations. There, the side that had the machines to command the skies (as well as the fuel needed to fly those machines and to train their pilots) was able to employ tactical air power against the enemy, either in close support or in the interdiction role behind the front. Owing to a variety of technological circumstances, defenses against the fighter-bomber in particular were never nearly as effective as those developed against the heavier craft. Partly as a result, tactical airpower to the end of the war retained much greater flexibility than did its strategic counterpart. This fact does much to explain its effectiveness, which was never greater than in 1940–41 and 1944–45. Even under ideal conditions, however, the underlying technological facts of life were such that tactical airpower on its own was usually incapable of deciding a campaign. The same applied with even greater force to vertical envelopment—the deployment of troops by air behind the enemy lines. Though a number of spectacular successes were achieved through such means, the normal price was horrendous casualties, and the results never quite fulfilled the most sanguine expectations of the interwar period. By 1945, though both forms of warfare were still destined to achieve great things on selected occasions, the peak of their success was probably past. As warfare became more integrated, tactical airpower in particular was destined to follow in the wake of strategic bombing and lose much of the flexibility which had characterized it early on.

CHAPTER 14

Sea Warfare

DURING THE NAPOLEONIC WARS, sailing ships and men-of-war reached the peak of their perfection and began to press against the limits of the material used for their construction. Naval warfare between 1500 and 1800 was very largely the outgrowth of the technological means in use; however, it was the result of those means alone. Whatever the period we care to consider, factors other than technology are always involved, and these not only interact with the available technology but actually help to create it.

As frequently happens in the history of technology, the revolution that transformed naval warfare after 1830 was the result not of one but of several different developments. Each of these evolved separately, but it so happened that they all reached fruition at the same moment and, meeting each other, gave rise to new forms that were almost entirely unprecedented. The most important of these were the perfection of weapons (particularly cannon), the advent of the steam engine, and the ability to build large vessels out of iron and steel.

The idea of employing steam as a source of motive power dates back to Roman times when a Greek engineer, Hero of Alexandria, built a primitive reaction turbine. Though sound in principle, such a device would only work properly if a very high number of revolutions per minute could be achieved. This required machine tools and precision engineering, neither of which would be available until early in the nineteenth century. Meanwhile,

199

development proceeded along a different avenue. During the century after 1560 much was learned about the qualities of a vacuum, which was usually created by first heating water into steam and then letting it condense inside a container. By alternately creating and filling a vacuum, it was possible to do work. By the middle of the eighteenth century, atmospheric engines of the type associated with Thomas Newcomen were used to provide power for a variety of purposes, including the draining of mines and the supply of water to cities.

For steam engines to be used in a ship, it was necessary to make them much smaller, and also much more economical in terms of fuel consumption. These requirements were met by the work of many men, especially prominent among whom were James Watt, who pioneered the separate boiler, and Richard Trevitchik, who built the first engine utilizing steam under pressure. It remained to link the engine to a paddle wheel, an achievement that is usually credited to Robert Fulton though many others were active in the field. Vessels equipped with paddle wheels, however, were too vulnerable to serve in war. Though Frederick Turner around 1830 was already painting tugs that looked like beetles and belched black smoke as they pulled or pushed magnificent sailing men-of-war into or out of their moorings, the construction of seagoing naval craft with steam engines had to wait for the perfection of the screw-propeller. This development took place only during the 1840s.

Throughout recorded history until 1830, ships had been made of organic materials, chiefly wood. Contrary to legend, the British Admiralty did not think vessels made of iron would sink. What prevented their construction had always been, not the absence of scientific understanding, but inadequate technological means. Before the Industrial Revolution, iron as a material was comparatively precious. Its employment was accordingly limited either to the most important implements—including weapons, naturally— or else to uses where it had no ready substitute. At sea as well as on land, large-scale iron structures were unknown. They only became possible during the second half of the eighteenth century when coke replaced charwood as fuel for smelting metal, and when improved machine tools were devised.

As is usually the case when new technologies go to war, the initial steps were slow and hesitant. It seems that the Americans were the first to build an ironclad, steam-powered, floating battery designed to contest British naval dominance in closed waters. However, the completion of this vessel in 1815 came too late for it to take part in a conflict which, in many ways, represented the last demonstration of what a properly organized, properly handled fleet of sailing ships could do. The next opportunity for building and employing floating batteries presented itself 40 years later during the Crimean War. When the French discovered that their ships-of-the-line were too unwieldy and drew too much water to come within effective range of Sebastopol, they hurriedly improvised three steam-propelled, ironclad vessels and used them with success to batter Fort Kinburn. This experience, news of which was soon spread by telegraph, demonstrated that floating batteries, while hardly suitable for navigation in the open sea, could operate effectively in confined waters where seaworthiness counted for little, and where targets were either fixed to one spot or else unable to maneuver freely.

The first engagement of steamship against steamship took place during the American Civil War when the Confederates constructed a steam-propelled, ironclad vessel and sent her to prey upon shipping in Chesapeake Bay. Taking the Federals by surprise, the *Virginia* used her cannon and also a ram, and her operations initially were most successful. However, on 9 March 1862 she met her match in the *Monitor,* a Federal ironclad that had just been completed and happened to be on her maiden voyage down from New York. In an act of high drama that was watched by thousands of curious spectators, the two ships circled each other for some hours, with the *Virginia* vainly attempting to ram her opponent. Both sides also fired their cannon and registered many hits (20 on the *Virginia,* 22 on the *Monitor*), but neither proved capable of inflicting more than superficial damage on the other, and not a single life was lost. As night fell, the two ships simply drifted apart, though the *Monitor* could claim to have achieved a victory of sorts by preventing her opponent from sinking more Federal craft.

Though more than a match for any wooden sailing ship in closed waters, neither the *Virginia* nor the *Monitor* was truly a seagoing vessel. The former was an improvised affair, consisting simply of a scuttled Federal man-of-war (the *Merrimac*) that had been salvaged, equipped with a steam engine, and provided with an iron coating made from old rails. The *Monitor,* though she differed from her rival in that she was made entirely of iron, was nothing more than a floating fort carrying two cannon in a revolving turret. Not only was she driven by an engine that threatened to choke the crew at any moment, but her freeboard was so low that she was always half awash. Appropriately enough both ships were destined to be lost to the sea, the *Virginia* when she could not be moved from her home port at Norfolk during the occupation by the Federals, and the *Monitor* during a voyage around the coast. This disappointing outcome notwithstanding, it was clear to informed observers that it was only a question of time before steam and iron took over. Once this happened, naval warfare would never be the same again.

Meanwhile in Europe, the construction of ironclad steamers proceeded apace. First to be taken into service was the French *Gloire*, a warship of rather conventional design, with full rigging and broadside armament. Her launching in 1859 caused something of a panic in Britain, which saw her traditional naval superiority threatened, but it was not long before the British harnessed their unique industrial resources to outbuild not only France alone but most of her maritime rivals in combination. As invention followed invention during the next four decades, the design of battleships steadily improved. Though the name "ironclad" stuck, from the 1860s on vessels were being built entirely out of iron (later, steel). Gradually their size, and the thickness of their armor, were increased. At sea, as on land, smoothbore muzzle-loading cannon were gradually replaced by rifled breech loaders which fired armor-piercing explosive shells. Their effectiveness was demonstrated for the first time by the Russians against the Turkish fleet at Sinope in 1853.

Since the considerations of weight that limited the size of ordnance on land did not apply in the same form at sea, and also because it was necessary to penetrate the iron armor protecting their rivals' vitals, the guns carried by warships grew by leaps and bounds until they attained weights of 60 tons and more. This in turn led to a rapid decline in the number of guns that could be carried aboard, while naval architects looked for more effective ways of mounting those that could be carried. Instead of being mounted on the broadsides as previously, cannon were now put into steam-powered revolving barbettes that later developed into turrets. If cannon were to fire in all directions the rigging had to go. As successive improvements in engines reduced the consumption of fuel and increased endurance as well as reliability, rigging was progressively reduced, until the British *Devastation* of 1871 became the first major sailless seagoing warship in several centuries. Once this had been achieved, it remained to discover the most effective ways in which the various elements could be combined. Since the technological innovations incorporated were very numerous and very radical, it is perhaps natural that these combinations often took strange forms and sometimes proved not only unsuitable for combat but acutely dangerous at sea. The British HMS *Inflexible* class of warships of 1875, which depended on cork-filled chambers for buoyancy and had their guns arranged both asymmetrically and off-centerline, is a case in point.

In a period of rapid technological change, the validity of the tactical lessons that could be drawn from naval engagements was open to doubt. The number of such engagements was strictly limited, in any case, by the prevalence of the *Pax Britannica*. As often happens when practical knowhow is absent, sailors looked into history in the hope of finding useful analogies. In an age that put much store on classical learning, it is not surprising that they found the answer in ancient Greece. It was thought that, since steam-powered warships were much more maneuverable than sailing men-of-war and because they were independent of wind, current, and tide, their fighting capabilities would resemble those of galleys. This caused the ram to come back into vogue, and attempts at ramming were made not only during the American Civil War but also during the naval battle of Lissa in 1866 when the Austrians rammed and sank the Italian flagship *Re d'Italia*. Ignoring the fact that the Italian ship was rammed only after she had already been disabled by fire from heavy cannon, every major naval power hastened to equip its vessels with a mighty protruding tooth in front. The hopes put on the ram as a weapon of combat at sea did not prove justified. Its only recorded "success" came in 1893, when one ram-equipped British ship accidentally sank another during maneuvers.

Seen from a tactical point of view, each successive generation of battleships built after 1870 added speed, carried bigger guns, and had better armor protection, with the result that each was capable of blowing all its predecessors out of the water. Strategically, however, a navy made out of ironclads was rather less flexible, or at any rate more complicated to handle, than one composed of sailing men-of-war. Though successive improvements in engines permitted masts and rigging to be discarded, the endurance of coal-fueled vessels was always limited to a few weeks at most. For them to make really long voyages it was necessary to have bases, either neutral, friendly, or if possible wholly-owned. These bases had to contain not only coal but the specialized personnel, spare parts, and engineering facilities required for the resupply, maintenance, and repair of some of the largest and most complicated machines built by man. Tactical power was thus bought partly through the sacrifice of strategic freedom. Even more than before, being a first-class naval power was a question of building up a complicated logistic apparatus as well as the acquisition of as many overseas bases as possible. This factor, of course, was not without importance in the great drive towards colonization that got under way after 1871.

The new battleships' freedom of action was also constricted by another factor. Though during the age of sail men-of-war had come in many different sizes, basically they all employed the same motive power and, what is more important, the same type of armament. As a result, the big ships were normally capable of handling anything smaller than themselves. Towards the end of the nineteenth century, however, this no longer applied. The same steam engines that propelled heavy battleships at 10 to 15 knots were capable, when properly designed, of driving much smaller craft at speeds of 25 knots and more. When these craft were equipped with self-propelled torpedoes, a prototype stand-off weapon that was first introduced during the 1860s and steadily developed thereafter, the threat presented by small craft could no longer be ignored. There arose, particularly in France, an entire school of thought that claimed that the days of the battleship were over. Just as the mighty dinosaurs had been ousted by smaller, more agile mammals, so the cumbersome steel monsters would have to give way to swarms of much smaller craft. These would run circles around the battleships and, after sinking some and causing the rest to stay in port, engage on commerce-raiding on an unprecedented scale.

As it happened, the expectations of the *jeune école* were not realized, or rather, when they were realized, it was at the hands of the wrong people using the wrong instruments in the wrong war. Meanwhile, however, it was the British who had most to lose if the battleship were indeed obsolete. Careful study led them to the conclusion that this was just not so. Provided they were given small-caliber, quick-firing secondary armament, battleships were perfectly capable of defending themselves against torpedo boats. Much in the manner of present-day American aircraft carriers—which, however, have gone to even greater lengths in discarding all armaments except for their planes—the battleships of the turn of the century surrounded themselves with screens of destroyers—"torpedo boat destroyers"—specifically designed to "destroy" torpedo-armed boats. As one might expect, once destroyers had been launched by every navy, the question soon arose as to what would happen when those of one country met those of another. Under such circumstances the side carrying the heavier ordnance might expect to come out on top, a consideration which caused the size of these vessels to double in the two decades between their first appearance and the outbreak of World War I.

While all these technological changes were taking place, the Victorian peace still reigned hard. The war which the United States fought against Spain in 1898 did witness some naval action. However, since the Spanish vessels had been hopelessly outclassed and caught in port to boot, it provided little guidance beyond pointing to the extreme inaccuracy of naval shooting caught between modern ordnance on the one hand and antiquated gunlaying equipment on the other. The engagements fought by the Japanese against the Russians in 1905, culminating in the great naval battle of Tsushima, were a different matter. One lesson, emphasized by the British in particular, was that, everything else being equal, greater speed constituted a decisive advantage in a battle between ironclads. This was because it enabled the side which possessed it to catch the enemy from angles (the famous maneuver of "crossing the T") at which the number of cannon the enemy could bring to bear was relatively small. Another lesson was that modern ordnance had increased the range at which naval encounters were fought to as much as 5 to 8 km, putting an end to any speculation concerning the effectiveness of the ram. If artillery was to be effective at long range everything depended on careful, deliberate shooting based on first-class training and exercise. Torpedoes, launched from the tubes of Japanese destroyers, had played an important part in the battle, but only when their use was coordinated with the battleships' heavy cannon, or else after the enemy vessels had been badly damaged.

A question which was not settled by the engagement of Tsushima, and which was to give rise to much argument thereafter, concerned the relative importance of the main, intermediary, and secondary armament carried aboard ship since the 1890s. So long as the accuracy of the heavy cannon was compromised by the absence of suitable range-finding, directing, and laying instruments, there was much to be said in favor of closing with the enemy in order to rake him with fire from one's medium caliber guns which could be fired more rapidly.

Even as Tsushima was being fought, however, a number of inventors in Britain and the United States were laying the technological foundations for modern gunnery. By 1914 battleships no longer employed the traditional method of opening fire at the moment the movement of the ship brought the enemy into the sights. Instead, they carried gunlaying equipment that allowed the barrels to be continually trained on target. Enormous optical rangefinders, often more than six meters wide, enabled the gunnery officers on board to determine the correct elevation. Though not all vessels had as yet reached this stage, there was an increasing tendency to centralize fire control and even the actual act of firing in the hands of the gunnery officer who consequently became the second most important member of the crew after the captain. Positioned high aloft on the main mast, the gunnery officer received information from the range and direction finders. He then used a mechanical computer to make the necessary calculations concerning direction and bearing, sent instructions to the turrets, and finally pressed the electric button.

Once accurate long-range shooting had been made practical, the time came to discard a battleship's intermediate armament entirely. Apart from the minor guns used for close-in defense, the ship would then rely exclusively on the big guns comprising the main armament. The first country to take the plunge was Britain whose formidable First Sea Lord, Admiral John Fisher, provided the inspiration and the guidance. Once the first all-big-gun ship had been completed, it was immediately clear that no other ship could live with her and that all other navies would have to follow.

Since the *Dreadnought*, powered by a Parsons turbine rather than by conventional reciprocating engines, was also the fastest big vessel afloat, she at once rendered obsolete Britain's entire mighty fleet of cruisers, a grievous loss. In battleships alone, however, Britain was able to more or less hold her own against the efforts of other nations. When the Great War started in 1914 the largest and most recent classes of battleships were of 27,000 tons burden. They were armed with eight 38-centimeter cannon, each weighing almost 100 tons and capable of firing an 885 kilogram shell to a range of approximately 20 kilometers. In the British Navy, too, there was a shift from coal to oil for propulsion. This move, once again, can be interpreted as an attempt to increase operational flexibility and range at the expense of greater dependence on the grand strategic level.

The battleship as it developed from the 1870s on represented a tremendous investment in money, science, industrial capacity, personnel, and sheer skill. Every country—even Chile and Peru—with a claim to be taken seriously at sea had to possess at least a few of the latest of these behemoths. Consequently their construction not only gave rise to the first technological arms race but turned into a matter of national pride, as if a people's entire greatness could be expressed in a score or so thousand tons of steel floating on salt water. The naval intelligence departments of every power kept careful track of its own battleships as well as those of potential allies and rivals. The battleships of each country were passed in review, showed the flag, and figured large not only in a proliferating professional literature but in children's books and advertisements. Battleships, or capital ships as they were sometimes called, were commonly named after great heroes and famous victories. For this reason alone, the loss of one came to be thought of as a minor national disaster that could seriously affect the morale of the armed forces as well as that of the general public. The growing power of individual ships was matched by a steady decline in their commanders' willingness to put them at risk, a reluctance that was much in evidence at such places as Gallipoli and Jutland. To be of use in war, however, a weapon *must* be expendable. It was their inability to meet this criterion, as much as any purely technological development, which in the end caused this type of vessel to disappear.

In contrast, the submarine was destined to play a very great role during the period after 1914. Like flying, the dream of sailing under the sea is a very ancient one. Attempts to realize it date back at least as far as Leonardo da Vinci, who claimed to have produced a design but concealed it for fear that wicked men would turn it into a weapon. Numerous attempts to build underwater craft and put them to military use were made from the War of the American Revolution on. Once again, the factor that did most to delay progress was less a lack of scientific understanding than the absence of technological knowhow, specifically a suitable engine, a method for finding one's way underwater, and a self-propelled weapon capable of operating beneath the sea. The vessels actually built and tested were usually both very slow and limited in range. This accounts for Napoleon's rejection of Fulton's submarine and, later, for the failure of several other French attempts to develop submarines as a means of combating the superior British fleet. During the American Civil War, the Confederates came up with a class of miniature submarines known as Davids; these, however, proved considerably more dangerous to their crews than to the enemy. In all these attempts, there was only the outcome to differentiate between heroes and fools.

As it happened, a solution to the power problem had to wait until the 1890s, when it occurred to the American John Holland that a submarine did not necessarily have to rely on the same engine for diving and for traveling on the surface. Once this step was taken, two engines were provided, an electrical one for underwater work, and a petrol engine—later, the more economical diesel—for cruising on the surface and charging the batteries. Development of the torpedo, a weapon that was powered by compressed air driving a small turbine, had by this time reached the point where it was capable of traveling to a range of over a kilometer at a speed greater than that of most ships. Launched from small surface craft, it never quite fulfilled the hopes of its originators and was employed, as at Tsushima, mostly at close range for delivering the *coup de grâce* to an opponent who was either confined in narrow waters or else had already been disabled by gunfire. However, for underwater use it was ideal, and did much to make the submarine into the deadly craft that it eventually became.

By the outbreak of World War I, the submarine had already assumed a form which was to change little over the next thirty years. The largest craft about to enter service carried a submerged burden of just over 500 tons, had a range of perhaps 10,000 kilometers, and were armed with four to six torpedo tubes. When cruising on the surface their speed was comparable to that of most major merchant vessels, though not to that of warships. Below the surface, however, they were capable of a mere 3 to 4 knots, and even this could not be sustained for more than 24 hours. A submarine's crew numbered perhaps 30, against as many as 1,200 on a first-class battleship, and its cost was in proportion.

Submarines at first were considered most suitable for protecting the coast against attack, or else for accompanying the fleet into battle, where luck, or craft, might help them get an enemy vessel into their sights.

Where actions were fought in remote waters, as happened during the Battle of the Falklands in 1914, destroyers and submarines were usually absent and the surface ship carrying the most powerful guns usually emerged the victor. However, in narrow waters—and during the period in question this included the entire North Sea—the situation was completely different. In these areas, capital ships were surrounded by swarms of cruisers, destroyers, and torpedo boats—and the cruisers themselves were really nothing but smaller, weaker battleships and differed from the latter mainly by having thinner armor, smaller guns, or both. In addition, submarines would be lurking in front of the enemy anchorages in the hope of catching the fleet as it left or entered them. Battleships could deal with each other, and also with those cruisers that were not too fast for them. Light craft and submarines were another matter, however, particularly at night or when visibility was limited by rain or fog.

To prevent their precious dreadnoughts from falling victim to these sneaky craft, fleet commanders in World War I screened their own forces with submarines and destroyers. In addition, each side tried using its cruisers as bait for luring the enemy battleships, or preferably a squadron of them, into the maws of its own main fleet. To control the lot, increasing reliance was placed on radio. Quite apart from other strategic considerations on both sides, the combination of this technological means with an almost pathological fear of losing precious battleships made naval warfare into a highly centralized, cautious, and almost timid affair. The need to combine so many different craft, and the availability of a technical instrument for doing so, once again led to war being waged by a systems approach. As always when one system meets another that is equally well developed, the side with the bigger battalions possesses an advantage. Realizing this fact, the Germans wisely chose to remain in harbor and so the tactical issue remained undecided.

As the speed, range, and power of modern steam-propelled men-of-war caused more and more waters to be regarded as "closed," naval blockade of the type practiced in the eighteenth century was no longer practical. Though the logistic outlay required was on an enormous scale, it was therefore decided to move Britain's blockade to cover the Atlantic from Scotland to Bergen. As a device of economic warfare, this system proved remarkably effective and gradually choked off German trade, condemning millions to suffer hunger and cold. The Germans on their side sent out surface raiders to prey on Allied shipping, and some of these raiders were quite successful. However, since they had to take on fuel at regular intervals, and since the Allies were able to use radio direction-finding equipment in order to locate and intercept them, on the whole they were much more vulnerable to destruction than their sail age predecessors. In both World Wars, the operations of surface raiders yielded some good romantic adventure yarns written by their captains after the war. They yielded little else.

As opposed to the surface raiders, the cramped, oily, smelly submarines developed into a weapon which, for the purpose of carrying out a *guerre de course,* put all its predecessors in the shade. During most of World War I, there was no real defense against submerged submarines. Lying quietly in wait, they were able to send to the bottom any vessel insufficiently agile to outmaneuver their torpedoes, which included all merchantmen and most heavy warships. Reared as they were on Mahan's theories concerning the need to seek out and destroy the enemy battlefleet, the Germans in particular took time to realize that the submarines' best targets were not warships. However, once this happened and Unrestricted Submarine War was declared, the possibility of defeating Britain by starvation became very real indeed. Fortunately for the Allies, during World War I the submarine still suffered from a number of important technical limitations. Submerged craft were not only completely out of touch (all but the longest radio waves being unable to penetrate water) but too slow to do much but wait patiently in the hope that a target would present itself. Submarines that were caught cruising on the surface in order to make good speed from one position to another, or else to charge their batteries, could be attacked by gunfire or even rammed. Towards the end of 1917, the convoy—an old system that was revived by the British government much against the wishes of the Admiralty—proved very effective against submarines. Though the fact was not understood until much later, in the main this was due to the reduced number of targets presented over the ocean as a whole, and to the inability of individual submarines to take on an entire convoy at once. Active defenses, on the other hand, only improved very slowly and did not really come into their own before the war ended.

If submarines threatened shipping from below the surface, air-power soon did the same from above sea level. Even in the years before 1914 it had been clear that dirigibles and aircraft could perform usefully at sea, particularly on reconnaissance-type missions. Where distances were short they could be flown from land. From 1909 on, however, experiments were also made in putting them aboard ship. The earliest naval aircraft differed from the rest simply in that they were equipped with floats rather than sledges or wheels. These planes were lowered into the water by means of a crane, then took off using their own power. Coming down involved the same procedure in reverse. Given that operations were only possible in calm, clear weather, and also the various technical limitations that made the aircraft of 1914–18 into the fragile instruments that they were, it is perhaps not surprising that comparatively little was achieved. Still, what was achieved pointed the way towards the future.

Though it seems that few ships were actually sunk by an aircraft during World War I, the rising brand of brash naval pilots claimed that theirs was the wave of the future, and that any additional sums spent on battleships would simply be so much money sunk. Britain and the United States between the wars witnessed numerous experiments—some of them highly publicized—in which aircraft were made to drop bombs on ships. If only because the actual conditions of combat could not be duplicated, however, the results were usually inconclusive and left both sides either claiming victory or blaming defeat on the umpires' prejudices. If pilots proved that they could sink a stationary ship and inflict at least some hits on one that moved, admirals were quick to point out that in a real war the navy would be engaged in violent evasive maneuvering and would also be shooting back. To make large ships more defensible against air attack, their armored decks were reinforced and they were festooned with rapid-firing antiaircraft cannon. Even as late as 1936, the report presented by a British blue-ribbon committee appointed to look into the matter admitted its inability to arrive at firm conclusions. The issue was finally resolved only by the coming war itself; not an unusual state of affairs when new technologies are introduced.

In 1921 the first aircraft carrier, a converted cruiser, was completed and commissioned by the Royal Navy. The net effect of the 1922 Washington Treaties, which placed severe limitations on the tonnage and armament of the battleships that could be acquired by the major powers, was to stimulate the development of these vessels. Partly as a result, their number grew quite rapidly. By 1939 the typical flattop was a thin-skinned vessel—though the British showed some foresight in providing armored decks—of up to 30,000 tons burden. It could serve as a floating airfield for perhaps 40 to 50 aircraft of various types up to, but not including, medium bombers. The problems of operating under various conditions of weather and light had been solved, more or less, though making a deck landing in particular was still a fairly hazardous business and has remained so to the present day. Most naval aircraft were armed with the usual small caliber cannon and free-falling bombs. However, some were also capable of dropping torpedoes, a deadly weapon in the hands of a determined pilot. In addition, the most modern battleships now carried up to four light-reconnaissance aircraft, whereas even many cruisers carried one or two. These could be launched from catapults and, landing on their floats at the end of their missions, hoisted back aboard.

During the six years of World War II, a fair number of old-fashioned artillery duels did take place at sea, and indeed the effectiveness of the guns themselves was greatly enhanced by the addition of radar for target acquisition, rangefinding, and fire control. In most cases, however, the aircraft of each side discovered the other's ships long before they could get close to artillery range. Once this happened, and provided an aircraft carrier was at hand or the fleets were within the range of land-based planes, it would not be long before attack from the air got under way. Though airpower was often hampered by bad weather or darkness, Norway in 1940 and Crete in 1941 proved that it was a bold admiral who ventured his major units in waters where adequate air cover was not assured. Time and time again in the Atlantic, the Pacific, and the Indian Ocean it was proved that surface fleets operating without the support of aircraft were helpless when faced with fleets with planes. To coordinate the action of aircraft and warships at sea, it was necessary to have not only the right hardware but also specially trained pilots and, perhaps most important, the right kind of organization. This fact gave the British, who did have a separate and integrated naval air service, a decisive advantage over the Italians who did not.

As aircraft gradually grew in range and power, the entire character of naval warfare changed. After the battle of Midway in June 1942 it became the norm for major engagements to open while the fleets were still dozens of miles apart, visible only to the eyes of pilots or else as blips on radar screens. Once the location of the enemy had been determined it was the turn of the torpedo-carrying aircraft and dive-bombers. Meanwhile fighters, also carrier-based, would protect one's own vessels against attack. Since the endurance of aircraft was relatively limited and since they had to land for refueling, each side did its best to catch the other's planes as they were being serviced on deck. In this game the quality and quantity of the hardware in the hands of each side played a large role, but as usual that alone was not decisive. Rather, what counted was the ability and willingness to take a calculated risk, to get into the enemy's shoes and then deliver the type of blow that would catch him at maximum disadvantage without, as far as possible, exposing oneself.

While aircraft were intensively used in naval actions, they also played a very important role in reviving the art of amphibious warfare. There was nothing new in seaborne invasions; however, in the majority of cases the invaders owed their success precisely to the fact that they did not attack defended beaches and hence did not require specialized craft. The great sailing vessels of the period from 1500 to 1830 were singularly unsuited for this type of operation, much more so than the galleys that they replaced. Usually men rowing ashore in boats only stood a chance if the defenses were weak or nonexistent, or else when they took the enemy by surprise. So long as land transport depended on horse-drawn vehicles and the normal method of raising the alarm consisted of lighting a beacon on top of some mountain, finding a weakly-held coast and establishing a beachhead was often not too difficult. The introduction of railways, motorized transport, and modern telecommunications changed that equation, however, and promised that most seaborne invasions would be either thrown back or contained as happened at Gallipoli and Salonika during World War I.

Particularly as organized by the Japanese during the first years of World War II in East Asia, most seaborne descents were still launched at unexpected places against light opposition. Later, however, conditions changed. In the vast expanses of the Pacific Ocean there was usually no alternative to island-hopping, and the islands themselves tended to be heavily defended. In Europe, the Nazis both fortified the coast and operated an excellent transportation network that permitted the rapid reinforcement of any point. These facts gave air power a vital role. Though aircraft could of course fly missions against an invading armada, carriers now enabled that armada to operate its own aircraft whose performance was only slightly, if at all, inferior to that of land-based ones. Once the invaders possessed air superiority, their planes could join with heavy naval cannon in bombarding the coastal defenses and clearing the way for a landing. Unlike heavy cannon, too, aircraft could be used for interdiction behind the front, finding ideal targets in railways and, to a lesser extent, columns of motor vehicles. Add special flat-bottomed, highly maneuverable craft for landing troops and their heavy equipment, and the technological foundations for seaborne invasions of an unprecedented kind became available. The Americans in particular were to develop amphibious warfare into a fine art, but also one which, during the peacetime decades after 1945, was to become so specialized and ritualized as to represent, in the eyes of some, a waste of resources on a tremendous scale.

Submarine warfare, too, was transformed by the advent of air-power at sea. In 1939 submarines, though larger, faster, and possessed of a longer range, were still not too different from their World War I predecessors. The most revolutionary development that was to make them into such a devastating weapon was not technological but tactical. Instead of spending most of their time on station in the hope that a target would present itself, German submarines in particular now sailed long distances on the surface looking for prey. Once a convoy was located, the submarine would take advantage of its small silhouette (and of the bad weather so often prevailing in the North Atlantic) in order to follow it at a distance and use radio to inform headquarters ashore. Headquarters would summon other submarines for help, and a so-called "wolf pack" could be assembled and employed to attack the convoy in a coordinated manner. During most of the first half of the war, though there were many ups and downs, these methods were extremely effective. Had geography permitted, and had relations between the German Luftwaffe and Kriegsmarine not been

Modern land warfare differs from that of previous ages in that its drabness is deliberate and not merely the result of circumstances. Here a British heavy gun is being towed into position by a tank during World War I. *Imperial War Museum, London*

On the eve of World War II, each air force had its own unique types of aircraft. Here is a twin-engined German ME-110 *Zerstoerer* (destroyer) flying a mission over Poland in 1939. *Camera Press, London*

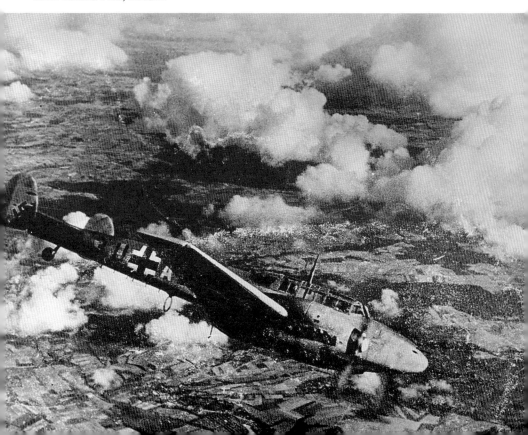

Total warfare reached its peak during World War II when nations mobilized on a continental scale and committed all their resources to the struggle. Here, massed American amphibious vehicles (DUKW's) are being prepared on the eve of the Normandy landings. *Imperial War Museum, London*

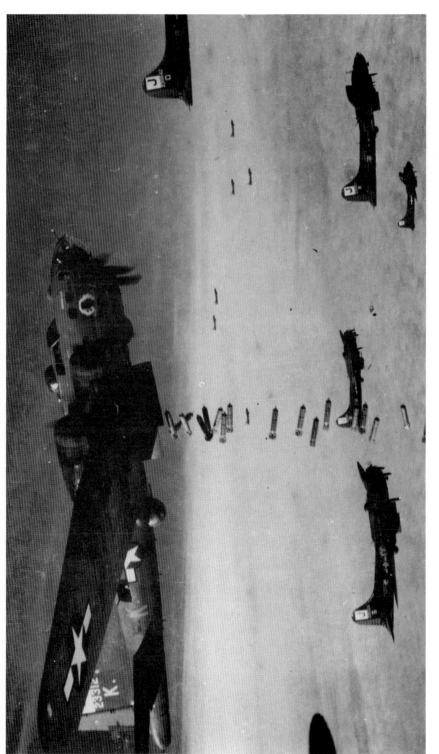

Strategic airpower has enabled modern war to reach behind the front and obliterate the distinction between combatants and noncombatants. American B-17 bombers are pictured here dropping their loads over Germany in 1944. *Imperial War Museum, London*

The introduction of nuclear weapons put an end to total war and in many ways revolutionized the nature of international relations. Here the fifth atomic bomb explodes over Bikini, July 25, 1946. *U.S. Navy Photo*

Modern warfare relies heavily on computers and is increasingly being automated. This picture shows part of the control center of the aircraft carrier USS *Nimitz*. Officers wage war at one remove from reality by watching monitors, talking newspeak into microphones, and pushing buttons. *U.S. Navy Photo*

Integrated modern warfare is shown in this sketch by an Israeli artist. Note aircraft, helicopters, remotely piloted vehicles, tanks, artillery, armored personnel carriers, light naval craft, command-posts, and early-warning stations. All are linked by electronics and by the inevitable acronyms. Note the sketch does not show any weapons destroyed, nor human casualties. *Tadiran Ldt., Tel Aviv*

Many modern weapons are TOO 6 EFIBUP: too Expensive, too Fast, too Indiscriminating, too Big, too Unmaneuverable, and too Powerful to be very useful in real-life war. The American F 4 Phantom fighter-bomber was at one time hailed as the best of its kind ever built. However, it did not help the U.S. win the War in Vietnam. It is shown here with ammunition representing alternate ways of arming. *Israel Air Force*

Though nuclear weapons put an end to large-scale conventional warfare among the most important powers, such warfare—often using second-rate equipment—retained its importance in less-developed parts of the world. Here is a dramatic shot of Israeli armor advancing into the Sinai, 1956. *Israel Government Press Office*

Numerically speaking, guerrilla warfare and terrorism have been the predominant form of armed conflict since 1945, successful partly because they are less sophisticated than TOO 6 EFIBUP weapons. Here a British patrol in Malaya wades through a muddy stream looking for insurgents. *Imperial War Museum, London*

characterized by endless squabbling, Admiral Doenitz might have used more aircraft in order to aid his U-boats in finding targets and attacking them. Under such conditions, there is little doubt but that they would have been still more effective.

Acoustic sonar came just too late to take part in World War I, but by 1939 it was available for locating submerged submarines. Location was certain to be followed by an attack of depth-charges dropped from light warships. Sonar on its own, however, had several important disadvantages. In its passive form it possessed long range but was unable to locate an enemy exactly. In its more sophisticated active form it was capable of greater precision, but gave its operator away at ranges much longer than its own, which was rather limited. Either form of the device might also mislead its operators under various conditions of pressure, temperature, and salinity, at sea, giving rise to false alarms. As a result, the use of sonar has remained tricky to the present day.

To locate submarines operating on the surface it was necessary to employ another means, and in the spring of 1943 this was found in the form of airborne decimetric radar. Aided by this apparatus, land- or ship-based aircraft could locate submarines under virtually all conditions. Once located, a submarine that did not submerge fast enough would be illuminated by a search-light and subjected to depth-charges dropped from the aircraft itself. By way of an answer, however partial, the Germans first mounted antiaircraft cannon aboard their submarines and tried to fight it out, then developed a device capable of warning the captain that his ship was being located by radar. Though both methods were partly successful, neither proved capable of restoring to the submarine anything like its previous freedom of action.

Meanwhile in the Pacific, where both sides employed carriers and also had airfields located on islands, submarine warfare took a different form. If submarines were to operate at maximum effectiveness in the vast expanses of water, the very limited capabilities for reconnaissance that they possessed had to be complemented by those of radio-locating, cryptology, and aircraft. It was a question of using technology and organization to coordinate undersea craft with surface ships and aircraft. This game was mastered by the Americans to such an extent that, by the end of the war, Japan no longer had a merchant navy and was on the edge of starvation. Assuming that, in the next naval war, space-based satellites will be added to the list of devices employed for surveillance, target acquisition, tracking and damage assessment, submarine warfare in the Pacific probably constitutes a much better model of the future than the Battle of the Atlantic.

To sum up, the development of naval warfare from 1830 to 1945 is perhaps best divided into two parts. During the first, the end of which is marked by the Battle of Jutland in 1916, battleships predominated. Sacrificing strategic freedom for sheer combat power in the shape of mighty guns, they grew steadily larger, better armored, and more precious in every sense of the word. At the same time, they were perceived to be threatened by a variety of smaller and more agile craft, both surface and underwater. Though it was not until the beginning of 1942 that battleships at sea were sunk by airpower alone, long before this the effects of the threat had made themselves felt. Capital ships came to be screened and protected by flotillas of lighter vessels, an exercise in coordination which, in view of the different speeds and seagoing characteristics involved, was often extraordinarily complex. The introduction of radio furthered the process until the whole was integrated into a system which would take no action except at the orders of the flag admiral. The result, as already said, was a style in war characterized by extreme prudence, not to say timidity.

Precisely because they were much less costly and less precious than battleships, aircraft and submarines were able to revolutionize naval warfare after World War I. Though neither was altogether independent in its operations, and though both had to be coordinated with other technologies, during combat at any rate neither formed the core of a large, integrated system. This left them much greater flexibility and, when properly employed, that flexibility was decisive. Both the aircraft and the submarine continued to make giant steps forward during the years after 1945. Performance improved by leaps and bounds, but only at the cost of enormous increases in price that threaten to make them almost as precious as battleships once were. This is all the more true of the aircraft carriers themselves which, together with their aircraft and escorting vessels, can easily cost upwards of $20 billion each. Whether, under these conditions, naval warfare is in danger of coming back full circle to Jutland is a moot question. It will be discussed in the last part of this work.

CHAPTER 15

The Invention of Invention

As THE ENDLESSLY VARIED, kaleidoscopically changing succession of equipment employed in war indicates, technological inventiveness has always played an important role in military affairs. Men from the earliest times have applied their genius to the design and production of better weapons, so that military technology has rarely stood still for very long but has been in a state of almost continuous turbulence with currents, tides, whirlpools, and eddies almost too numerous to analyze and understand. Spear-carrying infantry were superseded by arrow-firing charioteers, who were succeeded by mounted cavalry carrying either bows or edged weapons, who in their turn had to give way to the iron-armored foot soldiers who dominated the classical age. Later on, additional technological inventions played a critical role in the renewed rise of armored cavalry, but also in its decline after about 1500. Military technological innovation during the period before 1830 was normally—though not always—much slower than the rate to which we have since become accustomed, and this fact was important in dictating the nature of military organization and of war itself.

Our knowledge about invention—including military invention—during the centuries before 1830 is scanty in the extreme. The origins of such inventions as the bow, the sword, the spear, or the corselet, have long been lost in the mists of time. The first appearance of many others, such as the crossbow or gunpowder, took place during civilized times but nevertheless went unrecorded.

Though there have been some exceptions from the time of Archimedes on, the idea that inventors are worth mentioning in the company of priests and rulers and generals only dates to the age of the Renaissance, when Italian city states such as Florence and Venice first started granting patents and enacted legislation to protect them.

Seen as a mental process by which something is created *ex novo,* the concept of a technological invention is even more recent. As the process by which gunpowder was gradually differentiated from incendiaries demonstrates, people often took a long time to recognize what was new even when they were confronted by it. That, of course, is merely another way of saying that technological progress before 1800 was for the most part comparatively slow. Had it been rapid, both the process itself and its social consequences would surely have received greater attention.

The accelerated pace of technological innovation in modern times, however, was by no means the sole result of the new awareness of invention. At least as important was the fact that, at some point during the Industrial Revolution, progress became sustained. A transition took place from a situation in which inventions were for the most part not only exceptional but accidental and unexpected, to one in which technological change—and the anticipation of technological change—became the normal state of affairs. Applied to the military sphere, this meant that war itself became an exercise in managing the future, and the most successful commanders were not those most experienced in the ways of the past but, on the contrary, those who realized that the past would *not* be repeated.

In addition to becoming sustained, technological progress also became deliberate and therefore, up to a point, predictable. No longer regarding new devices as the gift of the gods or, increasingly, even as the near-miraculous brain-child of individual inventors, society began developing technology in directions which for one reason or another appealed to it. Often vast human and economic resources were expended to obtain some desired result, and the time was to come when it seemed that a goal only had to be formulated in order to be achieved. To use an analogy from the world of botany, previously technology (or rather, Technology with a capital t) had been like a fruit-bearing tree in which change takes place only very slowly by means of genetic accident. During the period here under consideration, more and more it came to resemble a potted plant. It has not been allowed to develop naturally, but is deliberately manipulated to answer the grower's needs.

When did the change in the nature of technology, which some regard as the most important historical transformation ever to be experienced by man, take place? Nobody familiar with historical processes would expect a precise answer to this question, and yet in the case of military technology the answer is fairly straightforward. When Jomini and Clausewitz wrote their great theoretical works in the 1820s, they based their reflections on the assumption that technologically things would continue much as they always had. Though neither man can be blamed for ignoring technology altogether, neither had an inkling that military technological progress might be decisive to the outcome of wars, let alone that the most tremendous technological revolution of all times was just around the corner. In the case of Clausewitz at any rate, the fact that this revolution has not caused his writings to become out of date represents a tribute to the greatness of the man. However, where Clausewitz stands, others have been unable to follow. From his day to ours he has had no successor of comparable stature, and for this fact, too, the rapidity of technological change as well as the sheer unpredictability of its effect on the conduct of war may be held co-responsible.

Though the manner in which technological progress takes place was transformed during the nineteenth century, the nature of invention as a mental act remained the same. In the absence of detailed knowledge, one can only assume that men's creative mental processes were the same before the Industrial Revolution as they are today. No invention is entirely new, and each one is necessarily made up of a combination of existing elements. As the full-rigged sailing ship demonstrates so well, the essence of invention consists of an act, which might almost be described as an act of violence, by which these elements are wrenched out of their accepted frameworks and put together in new combinations. Doing this requires a certain flexibility, not merely in the mind of the inventor, but also in the structure of the organization or social milieu to which he belongs. However, such flexibility merely constitutes a necessary condition for invention, never a sufficient one.

During military history as a whole, the organization of some armed forces has undoubtedly been more flexible than others.

Nevertheless, military organizations have tended to be even less flexible than most large bureaucratic structures, and for several interrelated reasons. The compartmentalization that is a necessary outcome of military secrecy often makes it difficult to engage in a free exchange of ideas and thus to assemble all the bits and pieces needed to create a new invention. In addition, military organizations by definition are designed to operate in a medium of very great uncertainty, namely, war. This has always caused them to put a premium on subordination, discipline, hierarchy, and rigid social structures, all of which represent the direct opposite of flexibility. Finally, the need to operate in a highly uncertain, confused, and stressful environment has caused armed forces from time immemorial to invent their own forms of communication which would be, as far as possible, cleansed of ambiguity and redundancy—from precisely those forms of language, that is, which are indispensable for free, undirected thought.

The history of individual inventions will bear this out. Though inventors from Leonardo on very often had military uses in mind (and turned to the military for financial support), all the most important nineteenth century military devices originated in the minds of civilians. This is true of the first practical breech-loading rifle, which was built by John Dreyse, a manufacturer of locks. It is equally true of the built-up, steel-made, rifled cannon (John Armstrong and Alfred Krupp), of the armored steel man-of-war (John Ericsson), of the machine gun (Hiram Maxim), of the submarine (John Holland) and of any number of other inventions. During the twentieth century, too, none of the most important devices that have transformed war—from the airplane through the tank, the jet engine, radar, the helicopter, the atom bomb, and so on all the way down to the electronic computer—owed its origins to a doctrinal requirement laid down by people in uniform, though it is fair to add that some inventors did have military experience.

If the military thus represent an exceptionally unfavorable environment for the mysterious creative act popularly known as invention, exactly the opposite is true concerning the no less important process by which an idea is taken from the drawing board and transformed into operational hardware. As the example of aircraft, radar, the computer, ballistic missiles, and a great many other modern technologies shows, very often the inventors turn to the military in order to obtain support for their ideas. Once the potential usefulness of a new concept is recognized, no organization is better placed than the armed forces to guide its development and bring it to fruition. Compared to almost all other organizations in the modern world, the military possesses tremendous technological resources. And the military is often able to deploy those resources regardless of foreign considerations, including the very important one of financial cost. As the Manhattan Project showed, necessity—particularly if it can be represented in terms of a national military emergency—knows no bounds. In the words of Adam Smith, which serve as the motto of this study, "the one thing more important than opulence is defense."

Take, for example, the case of the ballistic missile. One need only recall the American national anthem to realize that the use of rockets in war has a long history, dating back perhaps a thousand years. However, problems of accuracy and reliability for the most part have caused this use to remain strictly marginal. After World War I, motivated by reasons which had absolutely nothing to do with the military, small groups of enthusiasts set about developing liquid rocket engines. In the United States, Robert Goddard in a book called *A Method for Reaching High Altitudes* went furthest in developing the theoretical principles involved. In Germany, Wernher von Braun and his associates came up with the first practical engine. At this point, their fates diverged. In America between the wars a financially hard-pressed military establishment looked on Goddard as a freak and refused him financial support. In Germany, by contrast, the land army was not only well funded by Hitler but afraid of the growing influence of Goering's Luftwaffe. Looking for a means by which it could participate in the kind of strategic bombardment that, during the early thirties, was considered to be the wave of the future, it stumbled across von Braun and his group. Development was put under the direction of an artillery officer, Walter Doernberger, and transferred first to Berlin and then to the seclusion of Peenemünde. There a crash project was mounted to build the world's first medium-range ballistic missile, and this yielded its fruit by 1944.

The story of the V-2 serves as a good example of the way an "essentially civilian" invention for which no military requirement existed was taken over by the armed forces and developed into an operational weapon. However, it also illustrates the uncertainties involved. At the time of its discovery by Doernberger, the liquid rocket engine was a fragile contraption that exploded as often as it worked. Even when it did work, all it could do was lift a small missile some way into the air from where it would come crashing down in some totally unpredictable manner. It took tremendous vision, determination, and self-assurance—plus technical expertise and financial resources—to turn this contrivance into an operational weapon. Both for technical reasons and because nobody had a clear idea of what war would look like in five or ten years when development came to an end, success was by no means assured in advance. As it happened, a combination of excellent engineering and slave labor enabled the technological difficulties to be overcome to the extent that a missile was built capable of hitting a target the size of London from 200 or so miles away. By the time the weapon entered operational status, however, it had become clear that, per ton of explosives dropped, strategic bombing was far less effective than had originally been assumed. The payload which the V-2 could carry was much too small, and a good case can be made for arguing that the resources the Germans put into its development were largely wasted. Since the original engine was designed by enthusiasts who had their own reasons for engaging in this work, it is even possible to ask whether it was the German military who used von Braun, or von Braun who took the Wehrmacht for a ride.

To turn to a weapons system that was a military success, take the World War I tank. During the period between the invention of the internal combustion engine and 1914, several inventors—some of them, officers—in various countries raised proposals for the construction of armored, tracked, fighting machines. A few experimental models were actually built, but since a military requirement was not perceived to exist, none underwent further development. With the onset of trench warfare in 1915 it was an eccentric civilian in the British Admiralty, Winston Churchill, who ordered a concentrated developmental effort and authorized the expenditure of the necessary funds. Once the prototypes were ready they had to be forced on the military who, partly out of distrust and partly because of the desire to preserve secrecy, at first threw the new machines away by making them attack in small numbers.

Working in the tank's favor, however, was the fact that an unusually clear immediate tactical requirement, namely, breaking through the opposing line of trenches, could now be seen by all. As Samuel Johnson once said, there is nothing like a death sentence for clearing the mind. Turning the tank into a success was, from this point of view, a fairly limited enterprise, requiring many improvements in detail but no fundamentally new principles and, consequently, no very prolonged process of research and development. As one model followed another, teething troubles could be ironed out and development pushed forward rapidly by means of close collaboration between engineers and practical soldiers. The requisite logistic infrastructure was gradually set up, while that very important prerequisite for any new weapon— a coherent doctrine for employment—was worked out by J. F. C. Fuller in his capacity as chief of staff to the Armored Corps. Thus was born an instrument which, though it did not win the war on its own, certainly played a role in doing so.

On the whole, military organizations tend to be conservative in their approach to technological innovation. Their caution may sometimes be due to sheer blindness, as in the case of the World War I British General who allegedly ordered "those damn things"—his divisional machine guns—taken to the wings and hidden. A new weapon may not be accepted because it does not look nice or offer proper room for existing military ceremony, as allegedly happened to the submarine in the German Navy before 1914 and, to a lesser but not insignificant extent, in the present day American Navy. Sometimes the resistance reflects fears concerning the impact that a new technology will have on the structure of the organization, the status of the personnel involved, and indeed on their entire way of life. As the case of the replacement of sails by steam at sea illustrates, often enough these fears are only too well-founded. Even if they can be overcome, the effect that innovation will have on readiness must be confronted. Finally, realism demands that we recognize that a decision to go for a novel technology which will yield its fruit (if indeed it ever does) in, say, fifteen years, and may then be ready for the wrong kind of war, neither is nor should be lightly taken. To the reader who does not allow his vision to be obstructed by enthusiasm for technological progress in itself, it will be readily apparent that in these and similar cases it is difficult to separate the rational from the irrational, the correct from the incorrect. Often, only time will tell.

What distinguished the period after 1830 most of all, however, was that military-technological innovation became not only rapid but institutionalized and permanent. A new phenomenon, the qualitative arms race, took hold and established itself from about

1860 on. As each successive generation of sophisticated weapons and weapons systems appeared on the scene, all its predecessors were either thrown onto the garbage heap or sold to some less developed country, the difference in many cases being merely a matter of nomenclature. A process of technological competition arose, one that was sometimes relaxed but never halted, generating a treadmill effect in which all countries were compelled to run for fear of standing still. In view of the tremendous advances taking place every few years, there could be no question but that each country's effective military power depended on its armed forces continuously keeping abreast technologically. During the age of total warfare in particular, this also meant keeping pace scientifically, industrially, and economically, although—as Hitler and Stalin demonstrated—not necessarily ideologically and morally.

The military hardware that was now perceived to play such an important role in war stemmed from the efforts of engineers, scientists, and managers and could only be operated with their aid. No longer, as in the days of Frederick the Great, could these specialists be hidden away in the technical services and thrown out after the conflict was over. Henceforth they would claim, and increasingly obtain, their proper share of responsibility and power. The opening shots in the war between brass hats and white coats—engineers adopted white coats as they gained in status, to show that theirs was no longer a menial profession—were fired at sea when the engineers working below deck demanded to be given a status equal to that of the sailing officers walking above it. Between 1919 and 1939, similar struggles took place in the air forces (which constituted a technical arm from the beginning) and the land forces of many countries. During World War I, much to the chagrin of the military leadership, governments more and more were compelled to ask for scientific counsel on the conduct of operations. During World War II, the military was able to go them one better by appointing scientific advisers to the staff of every senior commander worth his salt. Finally, when Robert McNamara was appointed secretary of defense to the Kennedy Administration in 1961, the technicians and the managers had really arrived. They took over the conduct of war proper, with results that bear further scrutiny.

As military technological innovation became institutionalized, it also helped change the prevailing views concerning the nature of war itself. Armed conflict had traditionally been thought of, in Clausewitz's words, as "a mental and physical contest waged by means of the latter." The prominence of technology in the industrial age, however, pointed to the conclusion—to quote the American Field Service Regulations of World War II—that victory in modern war hinges on troops and commanders mastering a series of complex skills, which to a large extent are technical skills. Where once war was waged by men employing machines, more and more war was seen as a contest between machines that are served, maintained, and operated by men.

As this view gained ground, subtle, almost unnoticeable, changes took place in people's habits of thought as reflected by the military terminology in use. War previously had been a question of units and men being assigned objectives and seeking to achieve them by one method or another. Following the new emphasis on what technology can do, it more and more became a matter of capabilities which a word of command might actualize into missions. These two approaches represent two entirely different frameworks of thought, even two irreconcilable mindsets. The first framework makes the mind think in terms of what it wants to achieve, the second, in terms of what it already has. The first seeks to shape the present in accordance with the demands of the future, the second to base the future on what is available at present. For better or worse, the transition from the one to the other is a result, and not the least important result, of the technological revolution that has taken place.

From the idea that war is primarily a question of technology it was only a short step to the conclusion (to quote Fuller) that "weapons, if only the right ones can be found, constitute ninety nine percent of victory." This, too, was a revolutionary notion. Before 1830, though people certainly recognized good weapons when they saw them and tried to improve the quality of those actually in use, they generally did not look to advanced weapons for winning wars just as they did not look to technological innovation for solving social and economic problems. In fact, the normal view was just the opposite. When Homer sang the praise of the weapons made by the god Hephaistos for Achilles, or when the anonymous author of the *Niebelungenlied* lovingly described those wielded by Siegfried, nothing was more remote from their minds than to attribute their respective heroes' victories to technological superiority. Even to the Byzantines, who were probably as technically-minded as any society before the nineteenth century, the suggestion that victory in war was due to technological superiority would have appeared less as praise for the weapons than as an insult to their users. For the opposite view to establish itself took a major revolution—social, ideological, cultural, and moral; a revolution similar to the one that is generally associated with the transition from the preindustrial to the modern industrialized world.

The role played by technological superiority in war was nowhere as great, or as clearly decisive, as it was in the numerous colonial conflicts that took place in Africa and Asia. By 1850, the superiority of European arms over all others had been established for a long time. However, up to this point it had only enabled Europeans to dominate the seas and establish themselves in enclaves along the world's coasts. During the second half of the nineteenth century, this situation underwent a change. If European weapons continued to improve by leaps and bounds, it was a number of other essentially nonmilitary inventions above all—the steamship, the telegraph, and improved medical techniques—which now enabled their owners to penetrate deep into the interior and overrun entire continents. Time after time in this period, the advanced weapons wielded by small groups of white men enabled them to blast much larger native African and Asian levies to pieces. Time after time, too, it was shown that the only way to stop the Europeans was by adopting their weapons and, along with those, numerous other aspects of their industry and culture. Certainly, nothing would be more absurd than to attribute the explosion of emigration and imperialism that took place from 1850 to 1914 solely to the Europeans' superior arms or even to their technical superiority in general. On the other hand, whenever the chips were down it was that superiority and those arms that counted.

Inside Europe itself, as well as in other areas that adopted European technology, the effects of superior arms in the hands of one side could also be spectacular. As early as 1866, the French chassepot rifle was reported to have "wrought marvels" against the Italians during the defense of Rome. In the same year the needle gun, its firepower greatly superior to that of the Austrian muzzle loaders, accounted for the Prussian victory in every battle against the Austrians except, by an odd quirk of fortune, the most important one fought at Königgrätz. World War I began with the Germans employing giant howitzers to crack open the Belgian fortifications at Liège and Namur. It was almost at its end when the tank, essentially a bulletproof box on tracks, enabled the British to break through the hitherto solid German defenses at Amiens, and to turn 8 August 1918 into what Ludendorff called "the Black Day of the German Army." In 1939 German Panzers armed with machine guns and cannon made mincemeat of lance-carrying Polish horsemen, and torpedoes capable of hitting ships in shallow waters played an important role in the Japanese victories of 1941–42. Finally, in 1945 the dropping of two nuclear bombs on Hiroshima and Nagasaki offered a dramatic demonstration of the advantages of technological superiority by ending the war in the Pacific within as many days as the years it had previously lasted. Precisely because it was so convincing, however, that demonstration gave rise to as many problems as it solved.

With the exception of nuclear devices, the effect of which is to suspend war rather than contribute to its conduct, a survey of the successful employment of "superior" weapons to win engagements reveals that it has always involved striking a complex balance between several interrelated factors. In almost every case the weapons in question were new, and hence caught the enemy materially and—more important—psychologically unprepared to resist. They were not so new, however, as to prevent extensive prior experimentation, training, and the formulation of doctrine by the side using them. While no weapon can be successful unless it is supported by the appropriate technical-logistic infrastructure, that infrastructure should not be allowed to grow to the point where it becomes an impediment in its own right. While integration with older, existing arms is a must, that integration should not lead to a loss of independence and flexibility. Perhaps most important, the successful use of the new weapons often involves a conceptual side-stepping, so to speak, a rethinking not merely of tactics but of operations and even of the goals of the conflict. It is not a question of doing the same better, but of doing something altogether different. A good example was provided by the Prussian needle gun in 1866 which necessitated a new combination between defensive tactics and offensive strategy. Another somewhat similar example concerns the Egyptian antitank missiles during the early days of the October 1973 War.

By ensuring that every belligerent will exert itself to produce a never-ending stream of new arms, however, the very success of technological superiority in many battles and short conflicts has also helped prevent it from becoming firmly established on one side or another. Consequently, in long wars between major advanced powers a kind of seesaw effect tended to become manifest. As each side tried to leapfrog the other, the advantage obtained by each was usually too temporary, or too limited in scope, to prove decisive before countermeasures could be devised. Often, too, sheer inexperience in the use of the new arms—sometimes, inexperience compounded by the need to preserve secrecy, as in the case of the French *mitrailleuse* and the British tank—made it all but certain that, by the time their use was properly understood, they would no longer be new.

Though the seesaw effect can be observed at work in all major wars since 1861, at no time was its role greater than in World War II. Six years of conflict saw the replacement of the last biplanes by the first operational jet fighters as well as the opening up of entire new technological horizons in fields as critical as electronics and nuclear energy. Nevertheless, the war neither witnessed a clear technological superiority on one side nor was the outcome decided by it. If the British constructed the first operational air defense radar system, it was the Germans who led in the field of electronic navigational aids for bombing. If the Allies built the most powerful internal combustion aircraft engines, the Germans pioneered the revolutionary jet and rocket engines. If the Allies' lead in electronics tended to widen during the last years of the war, it was the Germans who consistently came up with the most powerful tanks as well as the best artillery and machine guns. If British and American submarine technology led the world in 1939, by 1945 it was the Germans who were drawing ahead with revolutionary new designs. Had the war been prolonged, the nuclear monopoly in the hands of the Western Allies might have changed the picture. Nothing is more typical of the character of the technological race than the fact that, in the summer of 1945, every one of the victorious powers engaged the rest in a race aimed at rounding up as many German experts as possible. Had victory gone to the other side, no doubt it would have done just the same.

The benefits of technological superiority, where it could be established and maintained, were not evenly distributed but varied according to the environment in which the war was waged. At sea and in the air, technology is required not merely in order to fight but for sheer survival. If only for this reason, and everything else being equal, the simpler the environment the greater the military benefits technological superiority can confer. By contrast, the terrestrial environment is much more complex, including as it does terrain, lines of communication, obstacles natural or artificial, and every kind of clutter. The net effect is to take away some of the benefits of superior technology, which will be of account only to the extent that it can be integrated with all these factors. Hence a complex environment, more than a simple one, tends to give the advantage to the superior tactician. That side wins that is best able to comprehend the *totality* of factors involved, and then uses them to advantage.

This conclusion, deriving from theoretical considerations, seems to be confirmed by two situations in World War II when technological superiority proved decisive. One was in the spring of 1943, when the introduction by the Allies of decimetric radar led to the decimation of the German U-boat fleet, inflicting on it a defeat from which it had still not recovered by the time the war came to an end. The other was the introduction by the Americans of the long-range Mustang fighter-bomber which, by making possible escorted daylight bombing raids, decisively aided in the destruction of much of Germany's economic and industrial infrastructure. If only because of the much larger number of individual units engaged, conventional warfare on land presents no comparable examples. Moreover, since a human population constitutes by far the most complicated environment in which war can be waged, technological superiority proved least effective in campaigns like the one the Germans fought against Tito's guerrillas. This was an experience which baffled them at first, but which other armies have since shared to their cost.

Furthermore, nontechnological factors are capable of imposing limitations on technological superiority even in cases where the disparity between the two sides is much too great for the seesaw effect to take hold. Consider the following extreme example. At Omdurman in 1896, an Anglo-Egyptian army encountered the Sudanese Dervishes, followers of the Mahdi. Since it was a case of horseflesh being pitted against gunboats, and lances against machine guns, the Sudanese never stood a chance. Within a few hours, and at the cost of a mere handful of Anglo-Egyptian casualties—some of them the victims of an ill-considered charge led by Winston Churchill against the wishes of the expedition's commander, General Kitchener—some 20,000 Dervishes were mown down whereas the rest fled in wild disorder. The rout was caused not just by technological superiority, but by the tactics selected by the Mahdi. Consisting of tumultuous frontal charges, they were the worst possible under the circumstances. Had he opted for guerrilla warfare and directed his efforts against the long and vulnerable British line of supply, the short term outcome at any rate might have been quite different. The effect of cannon and of Maxim gun would have been nullified, and the British forced to fight a prolonged campaign of attrition over unfamiliar, waterless terrain. The Dervishes might have anticipated the Libyan Senussi who, though easily defeated by the Italians and driven from Tripoli in 1911, were able to fight on for years thereafter and were never completely subdued.

Judging from this example, as well as numerous others ranging from Vietnam in 1964–72 to Afghanistan since 1979, there is no weapon but that has its limitations and no technology so perfect that it cannot, in principle at any rate, be countered with the aid of the appropriate organization, training, and doctrine. The more complex the environment in which the conflict takes place, the greater the prospect of doing this successfully. In every case, instead of tamely surrendering to the enemy's "superior" weapons, one should draw up an exact catalog of the things they can and, even more to the point, can not do. Next, it is necessary to take advantage of these limitations.

As the process of continuous technological innovation became established and sometimes yielded great victories, it also gave rise to a host of equally great problems. Perhaps the most important of these was the addition of a fresh dimension to the uncertainty which constitutes the normal environment of war. Although coping with the future has never been easy, planners before 1830 at any rate were able to take existing weapons and equipment more or less for granted. During the nineteenth and twentieth centuries this was no longer true, however, and indeed the time was to come when to base one's calculations on available hardware was to invite defeat (the growing technical failure of the German Luftwaffe after 1941 provides a good example). The long lead times of up to 15 years that often characterize the most modern technologies in particular mean that most wars have to be fought with the hardware at hand. However, those very same lead times also signify that planning has to commence years in advance and involve educated guesses concerning the nature and effect of devices which, as yet, exist only on the drawing boards or simply as semi-articulated ideas in the minds of inventors. The conflicting demands of readiness and of preparation, of present and the future, make the task extremely difficult. No wonder it has spawned an entire new industry, commonly known as technological forecasting, that has much in common with the ancient hocus-pocus.

As early as the last decades of the nineteenth century, another complaint about the effect of continuous technological innovation was being heard with increasing frequency: namely that the numerous changes in weapons and equipment would lead either to a badly trained army or to one that was well-trained but heterogeneous, and belonging to different technological ages. This problem has since become much worse. At any given moment, the inventories of virtually every modern armed force are likely to contain some arms that are really first-class (although already obsolescent in comparison with those still under development), some that are merely adequate, and some that are on the verge of obsolescence and fit for use only on secondary fronts, on second-rate missions, and in the hands of second-rate cannon fodder. Maintaining a force equipped in such a way represents a logistic nightmare, one that is not only complicated but exceedingly costly in terms of financial outlay and man-hours of training—a problem, incidentally, which has played a major part in the growth of "tails" (service) over "teeth" (combat units) during the last hundred years.

From the point of view of an army's function, which is combat, an even greater threat may be the possibility that the rapid turnover in technology will contribute to an equally great turbulence in doctrine, training, organization, and the personnel structure. Coupled with the specialization that is a necessary condition for, and an outgrowth of, the use of sophisticated technology, such turbulence may contribute to a loss of institutional memory and of cohesion, possibly even to disintegration to the point that the force will no longer be capable of fulfilling its military mission. This, it is suggested, was a cardinal factor among those that affected the performance of the American armed forces in Vietnam. Contrary to what has sometimes been suggested, there is nothing specifically American about this phenomenon. As the Israeli performance in Lebanon shows, other armies, however high their quality, are not immune to it and may eventually succumb to it.

To conclude, the most important lesson of this chapter is that the quest for technological superiority, like anything else, carries a cost; and that if this cost is not carefully studied and managed it may increase to the point where the adverse effects exceed the beneficial ones. Second, although technological superiority can be very important in war, its effect is not equally great under all circumstances, and even where it is very great, technology on its own will seldom decide a war. Third, the seesaw effect will make the establishment of technological superiority in a major war between major powers exceedingly difficult as well as costly; as the victory of the USSR over Germany in World War II suggests, there are cases where greater benefits may well be derived by stressing quantity over innovation. Fourth—and peace to those who believe that soldiers prove their stupidity by their choice of a profession—there are many perfectly good reasons why the military should beware of excessive enthusiasm for new technology. Fifth, although armed forces in many ways represent an ideal environment for undertaking technological development and forcing it through, they hardly offer a climate that is favorable for invention, and should therefore pay others to do their inventing for them.

Finally, and of the greatest practical significance, is the fact that technology does not just represent an assemblage of hardware but a philosophical system. As such, technology affects not only the way war is conducted and victory is sought, but the very framework that we use for thinking about it. By tracing the way in which technological change has affected that framework, its nature has been laid bare: far from being somehow "objective" or "given," the framework has been shown to be the product of specific historical circumstances. Since historical circumstances are always in a state of flux, a framework useful at one moment is likely to be out-of-date, even positively harmful, in the next. In the light of military technological progress, our thinking about both technology and war may need to be revised.

PART IV

The Age of Automation, 1945 to the Present

CHAPTER 16

Computerized War

ONE VERY IMPORTANT result of the invention of invention, not yet mentioned in this volume, is the extraordinary complexity of "modern" warfare as compared to all its predecessors. In part, this complexity simply reflects the growing sophistication of the hardware itself. After all, there is no comparing a modern self-propelled gun with its tens of thousands of precision-made components, to the artillery of 50, or even 15, years ago. However, the complexity of individual pieces of hardware only forms a relatively small part of the problem. Other factors are the momentous variety of equipment used in modern war; the need to back up that equipment with hundreds of thousands, even millions, of different spare parts that often require different kinds of storage facilities and have different expected life spans; the need to train, organize, and cater to the needs of the many classes of specialized personnel who alone are capable of maintaining, repairing, and operating the equipment; and the task of merging both hardware and personnel into integrated teams, capable of surviving on the battlefield and of fulfilling their missions under the tremendous pressures it brings to bear. Since there is a sense in which war has always been war, none of these problems is essentially new. Nor do I claim that they are, except to note that the degree of complexity has increased the difficulties by many orders of magnitude.

To look at the matter from a "cybernetic" point of view, the cardinal result of the invention of invention, and the accelerated pace of technological innovation, was a vast increase in the amount of information needed to "run" any military unit, make any decision, carry out any mission, conduct any operation, campaign, or war. As might be expected, this fact strongly influenced the organization of military headquarters. While Napoleon had still been able to emulate Alexander and concentrate most command functions in his own hands, the middle decades of the nineteenth century saw the emergence of a new institution, the modern general staff. The rise of the general staff is best understood as a direct outcome of the need for more and better data-processing. At the same time, it was itself the cause for further growth.

In 1870, the German General Staff consisted of some 70 officers, few of whom were so specialized that they could not, in a pinch, take over each other's jobs. Less than three decades later the number of officers entitled to wear the coveted crimson stripes had passed the 200 mark, not counting several hundred more who had been detailed to the headquarters of every army, corps, and division. Specialization and professionalization proceeded apace, the simple and flexible structure of 1870 gradually turning into a bureaucratic monster. Since similar developments were taking place in the armies of other countries, it is not surprising that the diaries and memoirs coming out of World War I are riddled with complaints concerning the way in which modern technology was helping turn war into an exercise in management. By 1918, it sometimes seemed that as many forms had to be filled out as shells and bullets were fired at the enemy.

Though some armies were notoriously more affected than others, the trend towards more increased paperwork was greatly intensified during World War II. In that conflict, so many records were produced that most of them have still not been examined, in spite of the best efforts of thousands of subsequent historians.

Because the drive towards more and more complex technology continued after 1945, and because the world's most advanced armed forces tended to be at peace during that period, free rein was given to the pressure towards overorganization that is inherent in any bureaucratic structure. As the number of fighting troops generally declined, there was a great increase in the number of services, arms, branches, departments, and military occupation specialities (MOS) into which they were divided. Sheer complexity made it impossible for officers to command as many men as they did previously, with the result that arm for arm, and level for level, the size of military formations generally declined. Everything else being equal, this in turn made for a taller command structure, and so the merry-go-round continued. The most advanced armed forces piled staff upon staff and folder upon folder. The German Bundeswehr—by no means the worst of the lot—offers a perfect example. As compared to the old Wehrmacht, it saw the percentage of *Führungstruppen* (literally "command-troops") increase fivefold between 1945 and 1975.

Thus technology gave birth to complexity, complexity to an extraordinary requirement for information, and the requirement for information to paperwork. The avalanche of paperwork that is threatening the most advanced modern armies would have overwhelmed them long ago had it not been for the introduction of mechanical data-processing equipment. This, again, was hardly an original military development. Instead, its beginnings are usually associated with the name of an American statistician, Herman Hollerith, whose ticker-tape-operated machines were developed from those used in the weaving industry (the Jackard Loom), and intended for use in processing the 1890 national census data. In 1910 one of Hollerith's associates invented the punched card as a means for storing data. Thereupon they incorporated manufacturing and selling, computing, tabulating, and recording equipment. During the period between the wars the use of mechanical calculators, data-processing equipment, and printers gradually spread in the administration of business organizations of every kind, though some organizations proved more resistant than others. By World War II, in the U.S. Army at any rate, their use had become a self-evident necessity. Their ubiquitous presence was captured in Joseph Heller's novel, *Catch-22*, where a character named Major Major was promoted to Major by an IBM machine with a sense of humor.

Another use to which early calculating and tabulating equipment was put was data processing for the purpose of aeronautical research, pioneered by a German engineer, Konrad Zuse, with his *Z 3* machine built in Berlin in 1941. More exciting was the deciphering of German military radio traffic, a task that was begun by Polish Intelligence and later taken over and developed by the British, who gave it the name of Ultra. At the heart of Ultra was the Bomba, or Bomb, which was an electromechanical calculator capable of operating at speeds much higher than those of any other data-processing device available at the time. It thus permitted the millions of different combinations formed by different settings of the wheels on the German Enigma encoding machine to be run through within a reasonable period of time, usually six to seventy-two hours from the moment the broadcasts were intercepted. Similar machines were employed by U.S. Intelligence. Known under the code name of Magic, they helped crack various Japanese diplomatic and naval codes and thereby contributed greatly to victory in the Pacific war.

Yet another military use of data-processing equipment was in antiaircraft defense work. In this field everything depended on the coordination of radar sets, searchlights, guns, and fighter aircraft, a job that had to be performed rapidly and with great accuracy. Mechanical and electromechanical calculators capable of meeting those requirements were already available, so that it was only natural to harness them for this work. For both sides, but particularly for the Germans, the goal was to construct defenses capable of covering entire countries and even continents. These defenses, comprising many different devices, had to be capable of identifying attacking aircraft, tracking their movements, ascertaining their exact altitude, speed, and bearing, and finally laying the guns in such a way that a shell leaving the muzzle at something close to 1 kilometer a second would accurately hit an enemy aircraft flying at 400 kilometers per hour at several kilometers altitude.

Since the Luftwaffe did not possess much strategic bombing capability after 1941, Allied land-based antiaircraft defenses never grew as sophisticated as their German counterparts. However, much effort went into attempts to defeat the Japanese dive-bombers and torpedo aircraft, a related and, in some ways even more difficult problem since it involved shooting at planes that not only engaged in violent maneuvering but often came in too low for radar to give advance warning. In any event, the conflict came to an end before either side was able to achieve complete integration of all systems or to develop automation very far. However, the steps already taken clearly pointed the way to the future.

The calculating machines built and employed during World War II had two principal disadvantages. First, they included numerous moving mechanical components. This meant complexity, a large size-to-power ratio, and relatively low computing speeds. Second, in so far as they were not able to choose between alternative operations—a capability known as "branching," and already envisaged by Charles Babbage for his Analytical Engine of the 1830s—they represented high-power calculators rather than true computers. The first of these problems was solved in 1946 when J. Presper Eckert built ENIAC (Electronic Numerical Integrator and Calculator), thereby doing away with cogwheels and replacing them by electronic circuits, albeit large and clumsy ones. The second problem was solved in 1947 when John von Neumann invented stored programming.

Though the development of the digital computer was now essentially complete, there followed a tremendous number of improvements in detail. In the 1950s, transistor-based machines began replacing their vacuum-tube predecessors. During the sixties, these were in turn replaced by models based on integrated circuits, which kept getting smaller and smaller in size. Progress in software and peripheral equipment has been equally tumultuous, so that the cost of per-byte data processing has been falling by a factor of 10 per decade during each of the last four decades.

Since computers were originally considered rather esoteric, one would expect the field to owe everything to civilians and nothing to the military. Nevertheless, the military, particularly in America, had been involved with computers almost from the beginning, not only as users but also as active consumers who, beginning in World War II, frequently laid down specifications and provided funds for development. Undoubtedly, one important reason behind the love story between brasshats and their computers is the sheer size of armed forces as compared to virtually all other social organizations. If the military was to be administered with anything like the efficiency of other organizations, automation represented the only way. Second and perhaps more important, computers with their binary on-off logic seem to appeal to the military mind. This is because the military, in order to counter the inherent confusion and danger of war, is forever seeking ways to make communications as terse and unambiguous as humanly possible. Computers by their very nature do just that. Had they only been able to stand at attention and salute, in many ways they would have made ideal soldiers.

The affinity between computers and the kind of mind that is cultivated by the armed forces has also been responsible for another phenomenon. Though recent issues of the *Military Review*, and the issues of 40 years ago, are both written in English, the differences between them are striking. Older articles contained a much higher proportion of verbs and adjectives. Recent ones, by contrast, seem to consist almost exclusively of nouns. These are often strung together into acronyms, most of which are used to designate machines. Thus, a jeep has now become a four-wheel all-drive cross-country-capable light-weight transportation system, or FWADCCCLWTS. The resulting language sounds as if it has been written for illiterate technicians. It is as flat, and as fascinating to read, as any computer printout.

As the military of many countries strove to automate their operations during the 1950s, the first fields to be affected were personnel administration, record keeping, and many aspects of logistics such as requisitioning, and keeping track of spare parts—in brief, the "business of war" which takes place at one remove from the enemy's hostile action. The point of the exercise was to increase cost efficiency, a term which seems to have originated in the big business firms and which now stood for all that was desirable in life. It called for the use of computers to establish constant centralized control, either directly from the Pentagon War Room, or from similar installations around the world, over the exact whereabouts, status, and condition of the last nut and bolt intended for the last tank of the last battalion.

From the administrative aspects of war, the impact of computers spread to communications, where they allowed the replacement of manual and mechanical switchboards by fully automated electronic switchboards for telephones, teleprinters, and other electronic means of data transmission. By 1964, those switchboards had become sufficiently small and reliable for the U.S. Army to pioneer the construction of a fully automatic military communications system in Vietnam, a first-ever innovation. Once integrated, all-electronic, communications networks had become available, the next logical step was to use them to link the computers employed by various parts of the organization, thus permitting human operators to be taken out of the loop to an ever-growing extent. Beginning with the Strategic Air Command, whose World Wide Military Command and Control System (WWMCCS) became operational in 1962, each individual command—navy, marines, ground forces, personnel, matériel, the lot—invested in its own worldwide, integrated, real-time communications system. Indeed, before long, having such a system at one's beck and call itself became one of the most desirable status symbols that a commander could own.

Since computers were now capable of receiving data from sources that were hundreds or even thousands of kilometers away, predicting their next success was easy. Beginning in the late sixties, computers were provided with direct links, either through wire or wireless, to a variety of electronic, optical and acoustic sensors such as cameras, television, radar, infrared, and sonar. The purpose of these sensors was to provide up-to-date intelligence by picking up the "signature" left by the opponent's operations, which in practice meant anything from the patrols of his missile-launching submarines to the state of his crops. Sensors in an endless variety of types and sizes could be located on the ground, at sea, in the air or, from 1965 on, aboard spy satellites that were put on the top of rockets and shot into outer space. By linking them with computers, it was possible for incoming data to be continuously gathered, automatically stored, and held in constant readiness for instant monitor display and printout.

Computers, however, could do more than this. Provided they were fed with the necessary software, there was no reason why they could not classify incoming signals according to predetermined criteria, thus taking over some of the functions previously allotted to intelligence analysts. Furthermore, if a computer was capable of identifying a threat—if, that is, the difference between an American and a Soviet soldier could be formalized—there was no reason why it could not sound the alarm. It could even cause the appropriate weapons to be directed and activated automatically without any need for human interference. Throughout the sixties and the seventies, the automatic battlefield has been the subject of much speculation. Things have not yet proceeded that far, in large part because many potential war environments turned out to be much too complicated to be "understood" even by the best available computer programs.

There were two important exceptions. Complete automation, or something very near it, appeared both practicable and necessary in air warfare where the environment is very simple and speeds very great. The radar-linked, computer-guided missile systems that became operational from the mid-sixties occasionally proved themselves very effective. However, they could also be too effective. The problems associated with automated warfare received an interesting demonstration in the 1973 Arab-Israeli War, when the most advanced air defense system built until that time was activated on the Golan Heights. It defeated, or at any rate helped neutralize, the redoubtable Israeli Air Force, but only at the cost of bringing down dozens of Syrian aircraft as well. The Egyptians, who were operating a similar system over the Suez Canal, fared even worse.

Since they rightly feared hitting their own planes, the latter for the most part remained on the ground.

Complete automation could also have been applied to the kind of strategic nuclear warfare associated with land-based missiles. In the late fifties, the construction of a "doomsday machine" had been regarded as technically feasible. Such a machine would identify an enemy attack, and respond by firing warheads at stationary, predetermined targets. However, the risk of a breakdown was considered too great, rightly so if one thinks of the numerous false alarms that have been caused by malfunctioning computer chips and by radar mistaking flocks of geese for enemy missiles. Acting on the assumption that humans possess better judgment than any machine yet built, the United States (and, as far as we know, the USSR as well) have accordingly decided to desist from taking the final step towards automation. The pressing of the firing button has been left to men of flesh and blood who, in order to be on the safe side, always operate in pairs so as to prevent unauthorized action by an individual. As an additional safeguard, they also carry pistols with which to shoot each other in case either one of them should go berserk.

The shining goal which computers, purchased at enormous expense, were supposed to attain was cost effectiveness in administration, communications, intelligence, and ultimately in operations. However, these results were not always achieved in practice. As many horror stories from Vietnam in particular attest, the administrative overcentralization that is always a possible outcome of good communications often led to gross waste and inefficiency, impossibly long reaction times, and a loss of initiative at the lower levels of the military hierarchy. Part of the blame for the frequent failure of automation to achieve many of the claims made on its behalf can be laid on human error, administrative inefficiency, and the incompleteness of the systems themselves (one of the cardinal consequences of the invention of invention is precisely that all systems are necessarily incomplete all of the time). However, the most important causes for failure must be sought on a deeper level.

The original reason for introducing computers into the military, and for linking them to each other, was the amount of information needed to manage modern armed forces and modern warfare. Once computers and the networks linking them were available, however, their very existence led to further huge increases in the volume of information to be processed. To reduce that information to a form usable by top-level decision-makers, it was necessary to set up additional staffs who, of course, promptly demanded that they be given their own computers. So it went, in an escalating spiral to which there was no clear logical end. Theoretically the object of the exercise was to attain that kind of perfection of which only technology is capable. In practice, it became increasingly clear that this goal would only be achieved when there was nothing left to perfect at all.

If present-day computers are to be used at all, it is first of all necessary to model and quantify the fields with which they deal. This explains why the first military domains penetrated by computers have been those which are easiest to quantify, namely personnel administration, logistics, intelligence, and finally the operation of certain weapons in certain environments. However, the process did not stop at this point. As the role of computers grew, this fact itself compelled people to quantify and model war. By so doing, automation helped modify their thinking about it.

Long before the advent of computers, people were perfectly aware of the importance of numbers as a variable of military conflict. Indeed there are many historic battles where the sources record (however inaccurately) the number of combatants and virtually nothing else. Weapons, too, were sometimes analyzed in quantitative terms: in particular, firearms could not be effectively used except on the basis of detailed calculations concerning range, rate of fire, lethality against various types of targets, and so on. The earliest of these attempts already date to the sixteenth century when they coincided with the establishment of the first gunnery schools in Spain. Later, the tendency towards quantification received additional impetus from the rise of the mathematically-based natural sciences, which carried all before them from the middle of the seventeenth century on. Accordingly, about 100 years ago, even as fanatical a believer in *l'esprit guerrier* as Foch felt compelled to present his arguments in favor of the offensive power of quickfiring weapons in mathematical terms, however elementary and however wrong.

Linked with the attempts to quantify warfare, and originating even longer ago, are the games by which, at various times and places, people have tried to simulate various aspects of war for the purpose of training, entertainment, or both. Played on the board or in the open air, and with the aid of devices ranging from papier-maché figures to real arms, these games were nothing but models that represented real-life warfare more or less accurately. Originally only a few were consciously based on mathematical calculations. Nevertheless, when examined by mathematicians, many of them proved capable of being analyzed in mathematical terms. Chess, go, and similar games, whose original purpose was to simulate war and, in a few cases, to act as a substitute for it, are prime examples.

During most of history these two efforts developed more or less separately, one aimed at the quantification of war and the other at modeling it. During the nineteenth century, however, they were increasingly brought together, with the result that people began to suspect that warfare itself might be capable of mathematical representation. In particular, the British mathematician Frederick Lanchester produced a series of equations named after him. Based on World War I trench warfare, they purported to establish a quantitative relationship between the quality of units, their size, and the rates at which they suffer attrition when confronted by each other.

While Lanchester's equations, and others that have been derived from them, can barely be made to fit the extremely complicated operations of ground combat, they are much more applicable to war at sea and in the air. As a result, the mathematically-based operations research which was applied to these forms of war registered marked progress and soon went beyond questions pertaining to individual weapons. Increasingly during World War II, and particularly on the Allied side where the military was not too proud to take advice from civilian scientists, sea and air tactics ceased to be the sole product of military men operating by experience and rules of thumb. Instead, they tended to proceed according to laws laid down by men clad in white coats and armed with slide rules, which themselves were destined in short order to be replaced by computers. Operations research at its best—which implies not only that the mathematics had to be correct but that the scientists had to maintain the closest contact with practical officers—was able to provide answers to vital questions: for example, whether the convoys crossing the Atlantic should be few and large, or the other way around, or how to operate the maximum number of aircraft from a single base without producing mutual interference.

To draw the threads of the argument together, the first 15

years after World War II saw the confluence of two mutually-reinforcing trends coming from opposite directions. On the one hand, advancing technology brought computers capable of rapidly processing huge amounts of data which, however, had to be presented in mathematical form. On the other, developments in the science of war led to the application of mathematically-based methods, originally taken from the natural sciences, to the conduct of operations. Nor should it be thought that, just because hindsight enables us to see the "objective" pressures building up, people had nothing to do with them. On the contrary, few people were more convinced of their ability, not to say right, to make history than the bright young men who programmed the computers that were already helping run military administration and play wargames. Not content to remain on the sidelines, they vociferously demanded that they also be given a hand in the management of war; indeed, they came close to claiming that war itself was nothing but an exercise in management. Precisely because breathtaking technological progress was thought to have rendered the past obsolete, actual military experience came to be regarded as superfluous, even harmful. When Robert McNamara took over at the Pentagon early in 1961 the time of the so-called systems analysts seemed to have arrived. Most of them were trained as economists, and hence had experience with computer-based modeling and data processing. Confident of their own intellectual abilities, they tended to regard warfare as a game of skill. On this subject some of them even wrote volumes that were learned, if sometimes a little difficult to understand.

In one country after another, military establishments came to be dominated by managers—some with uniforms and some without—with computers at their fingertips. This development did not proceed with equal speed at all places. If traditional American attitudes towards technology on the one hand and military institutions on the other made it comparatively easy for whiz kids to defeat brasshats in the Pentagon, in other countries things were not so simple. Generally the higher the social prestige of the military in any given place, the longer they were able to resist intrusions into their domain. Forced to give way eventually, they frequently counterattacked by themselves acquiring computer-age devices, jargon, and sometimes real expertise. Regarded from this point of view, there is nothing especially new about the computer. Throughout modern history, the introduction of new technological devices to war has been followed by claims for power on the part of those who design, produce, and operate those devices. Throughout history, too, the fights that ensued were eventually resolved when the technicians were turned into soldiers (here, artillery provides a good example), or when the soldiers mastered technological skills (such as maintaining and operating fleets of motor vehicles). Already there are signs that the present conflict will end in a similar way.

Thus, the military effect of cybernetics and computers did more than bring about changes in administration, logistics, communications, intelligence, and even operations. They also helped a new set of people to take charge, people who thought about war—and hence planned, prepared, waged, and evaluated it—with the aid of fresh criteria and from a fresh point of view. With computers acting as the stimulus, the theory of war was assimilated into that of microeconomics. Instead of striving to make the United States as strong as possible, McNamara and his team looked for ways of calculating how much was enough. Instead of evaluating military operations by their product—that is, victory—calculations were cast in terms of input-output and cost effectiveness. Since intuition was to be replaced by calculation, and since the latter was to be carried out with the aid of computers, it was necessary that all the phenomena of war be reduced to quantitative form. Consequently everything that could be quantified was, while everything that could not tended to be thrown onto the garbage heap. Among the things that were discarded in this way were precisely those factors that make war into what it is.

During the years when the Vietnam conflict was being fought, and for quite some time afterwards, the blame for the doubtful results achieved by the United States was often attributed to American military technology which was seen as unsuitable for, if not irrelevant to, guerrilla warfare. The accusation is pertinent enough, up to a point; but it does not tell the whole story. If eight-engined B-52's and 45 ton M-48 tanks hardly represented the ideal hardware with which to fight an enemy whose natural habitat was the jungle and the rice paddy, from certain other points of view the conflict was tailor-made for the new technology. Vietnam was a guerrilla war that saw neither great advances nor deep retreats. Precisely because it was *not* decided by a few statistically meaningless "great battles," it could be quantified with relative ease. In fact the "war without fronts" was a long-drawn-out struggle consisting of an endless series of repetitive operations. Over time, these operations—as well as their most important output, the notorious body count—became stereotyped to the point that they could be assigned collective nicknames such as "search and destroy" or "eagle flight" or "bushmaster." Once this had happened, the strategy—if that indeed is the right term for a process of attrition pure and simple—made up of these operations could be, and was, reduced to quantitative terms.

Under the direction of General Westmoreland, significantly himself a graduate of the Harvard Business School in which McNamara had at one time taught, the computers zestfully went to work. Fed on forms that had to be filled in by the troops, they digested data on everything from the amount of rice brought to local markets to the number of incidents that had taken place in a given region in a given period of time. They then spewed forth a mighty stream of tables and graphs which purported to measure "progress" week by week and day by day. So long as the tables looked neat, few people bothered to question the accuracy, let alone the relevance, of the data on which they were based. So long as they looked neat, too, the illusion of having a grip on the war helped prevent people from attempting to gain a real understanding of its nature.

This is not to say that the Vietnam War was lost simply because the American defense establishment's management of the conflict depended heavily on computers. Rather, it proves that there is, in war and presumably in peace as well, no field so esoteric or so intangible as to be completely beyond the reach of technology. The technology in use helps condition tactics, strategy, organization, logistics, intelligence, command, control, and communication. Now, however, we are faced with an additional reality. Not only the conduct of war, but the very framework our brains employ in order to think about it, are partly conditioned by the technical instruments at our disposal.

Since numbers are all that computers can work with, there is a tendency of computer-based quantitative analysis to disregard every factor that cannot be quantified. Armed conflict, however, is dominated above all by stress, danger, hardship, suffering, deprivation, and pain. Everything else being equal, the best army will be the one which possesses a thorough understanding of these factors and uses that understanding in order to cope with them. The failure of the American armed forces to match the Viet Cong and North Vietnamese Army in this respect was not due solely to the effect of modern technology. However, it is certainly true that factors such as morale, resolution, fighting spirit, and endurance, which could not be easily quantified, tended to be overlooked by the systems analysts. Had greater attention been paid to them, the outcome might have been different. Or perhaps, the conflict might not have been fought at all.

As these words are being written, the end of the war in Indochina is not yet a decade and a half old. An attempt to draw "lessons" from it is therefore an act of considerable temerity. On the one hand, not enough time has passed to make it possible to write *sine studio et ira*. On the other, in the field of computers in particular, technological progress during the time that has passed has been so spectacular as to almost relegate the war to a different age. Perhaps a starting point for thought may be the fact that, although other armed forces around the world have by no means remained immune to the impact of computerization and quantification and modeling, nothing like the American performance in Vietnam has been seen again. This may be because no other armed forces, not even the Soviet forces in Afghanistan, had anything like the technological resources available to the United States. Or, perhaps, it is because people have actually succeeded, to quote Bismarck, in avoiding an error by learning from those committed by their predecessors.

Even in the United States, there are some signs that a reaction has set in. If computers are still very much in evidence around the Pentagon, students at the Annapolis Naval Academy are now also supposed to study Thucydides and Clausewitz. If many decisions continue to be made by people trained in engineering and economics and management, there has also arisen a considerable body of "Reformers," one of whose main points is precisely that war represents a science (or an art) in itself which neither can nor should be reduced to any other. All these are signs that some military people at any rate are coming to terms with the new gadget. A new balance between technology and war seems on the way—one which, it is to be hoped, will combine the virtues of the new approaches and the old.

Perhaps, too, the story of the way in which computer-technology affected warfare may give rise to a more profound insight. In the sixties, the demand for new methods for thinking about war owed much to the emergence of new technological instruments.

The people in charge of those instruments were able to innovate precisely because they came from outside the military establishment, and thus felt themselves bound neither by sentiment nor by institutional affiliation. If they sometimes went too far, this was partly because they allowed themselves to be carried away by the very novelty of the concepts they were suggesting, and by the possibilities of the equipment they were using. The systems analysts, those brash young men, were the military reformers of the sixties. They did much harm, but they also did much good. That will become clear as we consider the problems posed by nuclear weapons.

CHAPTER 17

Nuclear War

IF COMPUTERS represented one new technology to emerge out of World War II, forever changing the course of history, nuclear energy was another, and militarily it was even more important. Like the majority of man's more esoteric discoveries, the origins of nuclear energy owed little either to war or to men in uniform. The work that started with the discovery of radioactivity by Becquerel in 1896 was carried on by Planck (quantum mechanics) and Einstein (relativity theory) early in the twentieth century. Centering around the University of Goettingen, research into the nature of the atom proceeded during the 1920s. It resulted in many fresh insights, such as the Schroedinger equations and Heisenberg's Uncertainty Law. The first cyclotron, or atom-smashing machine, was built during the thirties. Finally, uranium was artificially split for the first time in a Berlin laboratory in 1939. Though the meaning of this achievement was not immediately grasped even by those who brought it about, it later turned out to be a critical turning point.

Possibly because few people were capable of seeing the atom's practical uses, least of all its military uses, nuclear research before 1939 had been completely open and international. In 1940, this situation came to an abrupt end. As people already noted at the time, this was itself a sure sign that the military was waking up to its significance. The story of what happened next is, again, fairly familiar. If Germany held the lead initially, this was rapidly lost owing to a number of critical scientific errors, combined with a failure of vision on the part of the German military, industry, and government. The American government and military, too, had to be prodded by Leo Szilard and Albert Einstein before they agreed to go into atomic energy research. Once the decision to do so had been made in 1941, however, there was mounted a scientific and industrial effort that was far beyond the resources of any other country at the time. If only because it alone could afford the tremendous duplication and waste associated with any crash program, the United States was able to build the first bombs. These were dropped on Hiroshima and Nagasaki in August 1945.

Early reactions to the appearance of the bomb were, as might be expected, marked by considerable confusion aggravated by the fact that, right from the beginning, every kind of institutional interest was mixed up in the debate. On one extreme were those who insisted that nuclear weapons, though undoubtedly very powerful, were basically no different from any others; hence, that the fundamentals of war and of war-making potential would not be affected by them to any considerable extent. On the other hand, as early as 1945 there emerged a school of thought that tended to regard nuclear weapons not only as unprecedentedly powerful, but as qualitatively different from any of their predecessors. It was argued then, and still is often argued today, that there can be no effective defense against these weapons. Consequently, their only rational use—if that indeed is the right word— would be for the purpose of deterrence and preventing war.

Looking back at the debate with the benefit of hindsight, a strong case can be made that both sides were right. So long as they were relatively scarce, but assuming both sides had them, nuclear weapons would greatly increase the destructiveness of military conflict without, however, altering its fundamental nature. Indeed, the failure of the United States to derive any critical benefits from its four-year monopoly over these weapons suggests that, provided the gap in other resources was not completely unbridgeable, war would not even change its nature if the bomb were possessed by one side only. Had the United States heeded the advice of extremists and used its relatively small stockpile of atomic weapons to bomb the Soviet Union in 1945–49, no doubt the latter country would have suffered horrendously. However, assuming she would not have been brought to her knees, the war would have been decided by the balance of both countries' overall resources, and here the advantages were by no means all on one side.

On the other extreme, assume a situation in which one side (or each side) possesses enough bombs to completely and instantaneously destroy the other, regardless of any defensive measures that the latter might take. In that case victory would go to the side that was the first to strike, though in the absence of a defense there could hardly be a question of war properly speaking. Next, assume that each side is unable to prevent his own destruction by an enemy first strike, but is fully capable of destroying him even after absorbing such a strike. In that case, the use of nuclear weapons to achieve "complete" victory will have the effect not only of revolutionizing war but of turning it into an unprecedentedly effective form of suicide.

Thus, the bomb could be used in war only if its power to destroy were not absolute but either limited or capable of being resisted. If its power were absolute, then there would be no war, though a one-sided act of destruction might still take place. Almost incidentally, the old truth that any weapon can be countered is thereby stood on its head. In a situation where two opponents have enough nuclear weapons to destroy each other, these weapons will be useful *only* if they are capable of being countered in one way or another.

These ideas already reflect the strangely unreal, talmudistic character of the nuclear debate. They also draw attention to the fact that, as in the case of any other weapon, the actual capabilities of the bomb in war—even whether it can be used at all—is very much a function of the number of available devices, their yield, the delivery vehicles by which they are carried, the defensive measures taken by the enemy, and finally the type of target against which they are employed. Since war by definition represents a two-sided contest, a listing of one's own capabilities is never enough. What matters is the interaction between both sides, including the way in which they perceive each other and themselves.

To look at the question from another angle, it is clear that the weapons, their delivery vehicles, and the defenses that may be built against them—in brief, technology—only comprise a fairly small part of the nuclear equation. Compared to the remaining parts of the equation, however, the technological considerations involved are relatively simple, a fact which turns it into a suitable starting point for thought. To proceed in chronological order, the construction and dropping of the first atomic bombs was followed first by their proliferation in the hands of the United States and then in the hands of other countries as well. Many of these bombs had much greater yields than the original ones, but a real breakthrough in this field was only achieved in 1952 when the first hydrogen device was exploded. Unlike their atomic predecessors, hydrogen bombs are based on fusion rather than fission processes. This means that, provided one is prepared to pay the price in size and weight, their yield is essentially unlimited. Theoretically, and probably in practice as well, it was possible to build a weapon sufficiently powerful to annihilate a small country in a single blow, although the construction of a bomb large enough to do the same to a medium-sized nation seems unfeasible (or undesirable) at present.

In any case, it was only during the early years that designers and engineers concentrated on maximizing yield. Since at least the explosion of the first hydrogen device, greater efforts have gone into three directions. First, successful attempts were made to produce low-yield weapons which could be used selectively (in the vicinity of one's own troops, for example) and without necessarily unleashing the full fury of the enemy's reaction. Second, development focused on maximizing some of the effects of nuclear weapons, such as blast, while minimizing others such as radiation. These attempts have also been successful to the point where bombs, like ice cream, can be had in a variety of sizes and flavored to the user's tastes. Third and technologically most difficult, bombs have been progressively miniaturized. Understandably, the data on this subject are among the most classified of all. Nevertheless it is known that, if the original bomb dropped on Hiroshima weighed some 10 tons and had a yield of under 20 kilotons, devices can now be made weighing under 500 kilograms and yielding perhaps 200 kilotons.

At the time of their first appearance, the size and bulk of nuclear weapons made them capable of being carried only by heavy bombers. Their miniaturization since then has made them deliverable by many different vehicles, including fighter-bombers, missiles, cruise missiles, artillery shells and—one shudders to think—even by an ordinary car or van. Over time, the various delivery vehicles in use by armed forces around the world have tended to become not only smaller but much more accurate. This in turn made possible further reductions in yield, until the smallest weapons now deployed probably have an explosive force equivalent to perhaps one or two kilotons or even less. Even so, a weapon of this size is an awesome thing. By comparison, the so called blockbusters of World War II fame only contained 10 tons of TNT.

Traditionally, the most important way in which countries defended themselves against bombing attacks was by whittling down the other side's bomber force. However, since many an individual nuclear weapon is quite capable of reducing an entire city to ashes, it was clear that attrition rates much higher than any attained in World War II would be required if the defense was not to be altogether hopeless. During the decade and a half after 1945, early-warning and antiaircraft defense systems improved very greatly and were extended to the point that they covered entire hemispheres. Nevertheless, no side felt so confident of its ability to escape destruction as to risk an all-or-nothing confrontation. During this period, too, the difficulties of the defense were multiplied by the introduction of numerous new vehicles, each possessing different characteristics, and capable of delivering warheads to their targets. Particularly when intercontinental ballistic missiles, or ICBMs, reached operational status in the early sixties, the problem of defending a country against total destruction began to look insoluble.

Depending on one's understanding of nuclear devices either as more powerful versions of ordinary weapons or as completely different and revolutionary ones, this perceived vulnerability to nuclear destruction could lead to either of two different conclusions. The first, especially prevalent in the Soviet Union where military policy tends to be made by the military, was that war if it came would have to open with a crippling first strike against the other side's nuclear weapons and delivery vehicles. The second, more congenial to the United States (which allows civilians a greater role in formulating military policy), was that the most powerful "strategic" nuclear warheads at any rate should never be used except for the purpose of deterrence which, to be on the safe side, had to be reinforced by all possible means. Thus, a given way of thought when combined with an institutional interest led one side to concentrate on constructing a first-strike warfighting capability which would be activated if war came. Following a different logic, and reflecting a rather different institutional setup, the other side concentrated on establishing a second-strike force which, by threatening instant and overwhelming retaliation, would hopefully prevent war from taking place at all. The distinction between the two views is subtle, but important when it comes to force-structure and consequently to technological choices and the allocation of resources.

If a country's purpose is to be capable of fighting a war, the means for doing so have to be safeguarded against the worst the enemy can do. If the aim is to prevent war by deterrence, then too a force is required that is capable of surviving the worst that the enemy might do, and still inflicting "unacceptable" damage. Either way, it is necessary to set up on the ground, or launch into space, an immensely complicated array of electronic systems, whose task is to offer round-the-clock surveillance, real-time early warning (at the speed ballistic missiles travel, even real-time warning cannot offer more than half an hour's breathing space), and hardened command and control facilities capable of sending one's own delivery vehicles on their way. The vehicles themselves have to be physically protected against a possible disarming first strike by the enemy, a protection that might take any of a number of forms. At its simplest, all that is necessary is to multiply their number and keep them well dispersed. Next, the vehicles in question can be made more difficult to hit by shifting them from one place to another, putting them on permanent airborne patrol, mounting them in superhardened underground silos, hiding them under the surface of the sea, or using any number of even more esoteric techniques. Given a will and sufficient resources, and disparate military services each clamoring for possession of its own nuclear delivery vehicles, there is nothing to prevent all these methods from being applied at once. If no individual method is capable of offering an acceptable degree of security, several of them together probably can. If it is not possible to protect all one's delivery vehicles, it is certainly possible to protect enough of them to kill the enemy not once but many times over.

Thus security, interpreted in somewhat different ways on each side of the Iron Curtain, was the slogan in the name of which the decision-makers of the 1960s went to work. It was a task in which they were remarkably successful, producing as they did a system which, in its main outline, has lasted to the present day. However, seen from a different perspective the outcome has been that both superpowers enjoy less, rather than more, security than ever before. This is because peace was bought at the expense of instituting a modern sword of Damocles. Taking the form of many tens of thousands of megatons, the sword was hung above the rivals (and much of the remaining world as well) and could come crashing down at any moment. Furthermore, as nuclear weapons became more numerous and were put into the hands of different states and organizations, the risk of an accidental or unauthorized release was probably increased. The United States, and presumably the Soviet Union as well, has taken numerous and infinitely complex precautions to prevent this from happening. Some precautions, in the form of "hot" or "red" lines linking the national command centers, have also been taken to minimize the damage if it does happen. Nevertheless, at the moment of writing, a nuclear war triggered off by an accident or misunderstanding remains a possibility which, however remote, need happen just once for civilization as we know it to come to an end. Given the law of averages, which modern science tells us governs all seemingly random events, one might argue that such a possibility is bound to arise sooner or later.

The possibility that nuclear war, whatever its origin, would literally mean the end of the world led to yet another outcome. If only because neither side was completely immune to the pressure of domestic and international opinion, and because both sought to impose some limits on the other's forces, the years since 1958 have been characterized by almost continuous talks aimed at various sorts of arms limitations. These efforts have brought some results, as may be seen from the Nuclear Test Ban Treaty, the Nonproliferation Treaty, SALT (Strategic Arms Limitation Treaties) I and II (the latter unsigned, but more or less observed by both sides), and the recent agreement limiting medium-range missiles in Europe. The most important treaties have put limits on the size of the superpowers' nuclear arsenals and also on the kinds of weapons and delivery vehicles that could be deployed. In the United States, critics of the treaties have argued that they tend to freeze some of the advantages in the number and power of delivery vehicles that the Soviets are believed to have enjoyed since the early seventies. Supporters, on the other hand, emphasize that the treaties only refer to existing weapons and therefore tend to work in favor of the technologically innovative side. Both arguments are probably correct.

Complicated as it is, the SALT I Treaty reflects the technology of the sixties. At that time it was widely felt that each side's force of missiles, whether ground- or submarine-launched, was invulnerable to a first strike, hence that mutual deterrence—sometimes referred to as MAD, or Mutual Assured Destruction—was securely established. The ink on the treaty had scarcely dried, however, when further technological advances began to undermine this belief. The most important single development took the form of ballistic missiles carrying multiple independent reentry vehicles, or MIRV. Entering operational service in the early seventies, MIRV contradicted SALT I and the assumptions on which it was based in two ways. First, the new warheads were sufficiently accurate to knock out not only cities and industries but missiles in their silos. Second, the sheer number of reentry vehicles mounted on top of each missile now made it possible to knock out several enemy missiles by using just one, thus eliminating the enemy's missiles and still retain a large number of one's own ready for use. The combination of great accuracy and an exchange ratio unfavorable to the defense was perceived to endanger the survivability of second strike forces, or at least those parts of them that were land-based. This was known as the window of vulnerability.

The second technological development that threatened each side's force of ICBMs was the introduction of the cruise missile. First developed by the Germans during World War II, cruise missiles were subsequently experimented with by the armed forces of various nations, but for a long time were not perceived to offer any special advantages as compared to manned bombers and ICBMs. During the seventies, however, the simultaneous maturing of several new technologies made it possible to build small, pilotless craft powered by miniature jet engines and capable of carrying a payload over ranges of up to 2,000 km. Unlike many present-day manned bombers, modern cruise missiles are capable of flying so low over the ground as to be detectable only by immensely complex, immensely expensive airborne detection systems. Unlike ICBMs, they do not rely on inertial guidance but are guided to their targets by a system known as TERCOM (Terrain Contour Matching) which consists essentially of a radar scanning the area overflown and comparing it to a digital map stored in an onboard computer memory. Like the MIRVed ICBM, cruise missiles are exceedingly accurate. Like the MIRVed ICBM, too, this accuracy should permit them to destroy missiles in their silos.

As is almost always the case when a new technology arises, reactions to it were mixed. In the eyes of some, the capability for knocking out missiles in their silos and thus of eliminating one side's deterrent forces (even if it were only the land-based deterrent forces that were being threatened) appeared so awesome that they wished to turn the clock back and revert to the "one missile, one warhead" technology of the sixties. Others, perhaps more realistically, emphasized that cruise missiles in particular may actually strengthen deterrence. This is because these weapons, being small and provided with their own guidance system, are capable of being launched not just from stationary silos but also from ground vehicles, aircraft, ships, and even the torpedo tubes of submerged submarines. This makes them difficult to find, and hence invulnerable to a disarming first strike. Furthermore, cruise missiles sufficiently accurate to hit missile-silos should also be capable of scoring a bull's eye on individual command centers. This prospect, it is argued, presents decision makers at all levels with the strongest possible incentive to refrain from going to war because, in that case, they themselves will be the first to be vaporized.

The basic assumption on which MAD rests—namely, that in an age of nuclear abundance no means in the world can save a country's population and industry from being wiped out by a determined adversary, and that this is a good thing because stability will result—this assumption itself has its critics. Attempts to build anti-ballistic missile defenses were undertaken by both superpowers during the late sixties but, particularly in the face of the rise of MIRV, appeared sufficiently unpromising for a ceiling to be put on them by SALT I. A decade later, however, the prospect arose of one day defeating ICBMs with the aid of much more sophisticated technology that has been appropriately dubbed "Star Wars." If it is ever built, a ballistic missile defense system (BMD) will be based either on earth or in space aboard satellites. It will consist of an immensely complex array of sensors and computers, whose task will be to identify missiles after launch, distinguish them from decoys, and track them. This accomplished, the missiles will be destroyed by firing lasers, beams of charged particles, or so-called rail-guns which are devices for firing minuscule pellets of metal at velocities far in excess of anything attainable by ordinary guns. Any missiles that get through, or else the warheads which they release, will be engaged by earth-based guided missiles now under development.

The merits of building a ballistic missile defense system are very much in dispute. Advocates claim that, in a crisis, even a partial ballistic missile defense will be better than none and that the side possessing such a defense will accordingly be in a better position to raise the stakes ("achieve escalation dominance," is the technical term for this) in a game of nuclear blackmail. Opponents reply that such a defense probably cannot be made to work. Even if it can, its effectiveness against a well-coordinated first strike will be marginal. At most, so the argument goes, the defense may be effective against a "ragged" second strike; however, it is precisely here that the danger lies, for a defense that puts the Soviet Union's retaliatory capability in doubt might compel that country to adopt the first strike strategy that the United States fears most. The debate, consisting of an endless series of arguments and counterarguments none of which can really be "proved," goes on. It at least has the merit of filling the pages of professional journals and of feeding the defense consultancy business.

Since agreement is lacking on the conceptual level—it is not even clear whether the Strategic Defense Initiative (SDI) is intended to protect America's cities or her missile sites alone—BMD at present appears to share the fate of many past military technological innovations. These, precisely because they were so new, were driven less by any clear idea as to their usefulness or even desirability than by the foibles of the powers that be. To give the matter an additional twist, those powers are said to be engaged in a deliberate attempt to create institutional support for the program by sinking tremendous resources into research and development. However, neither the size of the enterprise nor the excellence of the scientific research which it involves are in themselves sufficient to guarantee its ultimate usefulness. Even if a BMD system is built and is successful, or indeed particularly if this should happen, the other superpower will not be far behind. Ways of defeating SDI are, as a matter of fact, not difficult to think of: among numerous other possibilities, many more missiles might be built to swamp the system, or the boost phase in which missiles are particularly vulnerable might be reduced by introducing new fuels, or else that phase can be eliminated altogether by placing warheads permanently in orbit. As these examples show, there is no reason to think that the Soviet reaction will necessarily be symmetrical to, or as expensive as, the American challenge.

Almost from the day of their inception, nuclear weapons were regarded in two distinct ways. On one side were those who regarded them as qualitatively different and, therefore, as too terrible to use for any purpose except deterrence pure and simple. On the other, there were those who conceived them as fundamentally similar to, if much more powerful than, all previous weapons. Over the last 40 years, and in spite of repeated warnings that some novel technology just around the corner was about to change everything, by and large the former view seems to have prevailed. The result has been that no nuclear weapons have been used since Nagasaki and that the world has greatly benefited from what appears to be a fairly stable balance of terror. Though not excluding crises, some of them nerve-wracking to participants and spectators whose fate depended on issues about which they knew little and cared even less, this balance has at any rate kept the nuclear powers from going at each other's vitals.

The threatening presence of nuclear weapons thus seems to have contributed to the rise of a form of strategic stability which, though certainly capable of being disrupted at any moment, looks real enough to most people. Precisely because it does, however, decision-makers have been wondering how far they—and, of course, the other side—can go without upsetting it; and, specifically, whether the balance of terror necessarily precluded the use of *any* nuclear weapons under *any* kind of circumstances. The question was largely academic so long as bombs were huge and strategic delivery systems scarcely capable of hitting anything smaller than cities. Since the mid-sixties, however, the growing accuracy of delivery vehicles has permitted much smaller warheads to be fielded, with the result that the problem has been put at the very center of strategic thought. In the United States, and to a lesser extent in the USSR as well, it has led to much talk of "flexible options" and "surgical strikes," neither of which are anything but euphemisms for nuclear attacks against "limited" targets. The underlying idea is that, by destroying no more than a few million people out of a superpower's population, such attacks will hopefully not provoke the injured party to retaliate with all his might. Of all the debates that have been called forth by the prevailing nuclear equilibrium, this one is in some ways the furthest removed from reality, which is not to say that it is also the least dangerous.

When people talk of surgical strikes, possibly directed against bombers on their runways or against missiles in their silos, they seem to have in mind warheads with a yield in the 100 kiloton range. We have seen that much smaller nuclear devices have also been built, however, which are now deployed by the thousand on both sides of the Iron Curtain. Tactical nukes, as they are popularly known, were developed for use in the Western European Theater where NATO has always felt itself threatened by the supposedly overwhelming conventional superiority of the Warsaw Pact. The yield of these weapons varies from a kiloton or less to the equivalent of the bomb which destroyed Hiroshima. They are capable of being delivered by fighter-bomber, short- or medium-range missile, cruise missile, or medium caliber artillery shell.

Tactical nuclear weapons are theoretically intended for battlefield use, including presumably battles taking place on one's own national territory. Hence, even more than in the case of so-called strategic weapons, much ingenuity has gone into attempts to tailor them to the user's requirements by maximizing blast and minimizing radioactive fallout, or—just in case—the reverse of this. Much thought, and at least some exercises, have also gone into attempts to devise tactics which will enable armed forces to survive and operate on a nuclear battlefield. Since they have never been tested under operational conditions, it is not even known whether troops can be made to cope with them at all, or whether the mere threat of their use will cause entire armies to break and run. Even if the second of these answers should prove to be correct—some would say, particularly if it is correct—an aggressor could make first use of these weapons in order to strike at the victim's infrastructure, including particularly his command centers, nuclear-arms depots, supply bases, and airfields. By contrast, the best defensive use could well lie in a strike against the attacker's massed second-echelon forces and communications.

The debate on tactical nukes, like that which surrounds their big brothers, sometimes assumes a strangely unreal character. On the one hand it is easy to imagine ways in which these weapons could be used, if only this could be done without fear of escalation. But fear of escalation is precisely the point. No number of speeches to the contrary can ever exorcise its specter. Hence it has been suggested that the logical way to deploy tactical nukes would be in the form of mines in the ground. There, at least, they would threaten nobody except those actually passing over them in the course of an invasion; although even then, according to most scenarios, the ratio of friendly civilians to hostile troops killed might well be such as to make their employment more than questionable.

Thus, to date, the fear that all nuclear weapons would be unleashed if even one were used has meant that none has been used. This, however, is not to say that their existence has not affected the conduct of war. On the contrary, war has been revolutionized by them. Specifically, and much to the surprise of those who interpreted modern history since the French Revolution as inexorably tending towards total war, nuclear weapons seem to have put an end to that kind of conflict. This is because the fear of escalation has extended downward until it has reached most, some would say all, conventional weapons as well. In the nuclear age, there simply is not enough elbow room for total war of the kind that characterized the period between 1919 and 1945. Henceforward nuclear powers trying to wage war on each other (something that, to date, has not happened even once) would be compelled to put strict limits on their military efforts. Far from exerting themselves to the utmost in order to attain complete victory, the aim will have to be to convince an opponent that, for him, there would still be life after defeat. If this is not achieved, then that opponent, driven into a corner, might end up by literally destroying the enemy, himself, and perhaps the rest of the world as well. Limited war with limited forces for limited objectives—that, paradoxically though perhaps not altogether surprisingly for those familiar with some of nineteenth-century science fiction, has been the outcome of the realization of the ancient dream concerning unlimited numbers of weapons of unlimited power.

Though probably as many as 90 percent of all the nuclear megatonnage at present in storage on earth is concentrated in the hands of just two countries, the phenomenon of limited war has by no means been restricted to them alone. Some of the remaining states have themselves acquired nuclear weapons. Others, since they were reluctant or unable to take that step, formed close alliances with the nuclear powers. To a greatly varying extent, they have become subject to the rules of the nuclear game. Those rules have spread like an inkstain, making their effect felt first on the superpowers' clients and allies, and then on many of the world's remaining states. In today's increasingly crowded global village, it is seldom possible for a country of any importance to go to war without touching upon at least some superpower interests. Every country must consider the possibility that its actions—particularly if they should appear to lead towards a decisive victory—will escalate into nuclear war leading not only to its own destruction but to that of everybody else. As these lines are being written, a new paradox seems to be well on the way to establishing itself: if a political organization is still capable of engaging in unhindered "total" war, this in itself constitutes sufficient proof of its relative unimportance in world politics.

Thus, over the last four decades, a nuclear balance of terror has established itself, and at present probably covers most countries to some extent. Though regarded as delicate by some, and lacking any guarantee that it will not be disrupted at any moment, so far that balance has prevented another global war from taking place. What is more, the risk of nuclear escalation seems to have put certain limits on many of the wars that did take place. Since one side at least has usually no longer been able to exert his forces to the utmost, it is questionable whether we are still dealing with the same phenomenon which, according to Clausewitz in the first pages of *On War,* inherently tends towards extremes of violent action.

This situation is no cause for complacency. The stability of the central strategic balance should not put an end to attempts aimed at abolishing war or, failing this, at coping with it should it come. Furthermore, merely because certain analysts have elected to describe most of the wars that have taken place during the last four decades as limited, it does not follow that they have also been markedly more humane, or less ferocious, than their predecessors. Finally, the mere fact that war, taking place against the ever-present background of a nuclear threat, has been compelled to pay more heed to politics than ever before does not necessarily mean that it has turned into a less effective instrument for the realization of political ends. In the right hands, and particularly if served by the right technological tools, it may still be a very effective instrument indeed.

CHAPTER 18

Integrated War

PERHAPS THE MOST important single contribution of military technology during the period from 1830 to the outbreak of World War II was the trend towards greater and greater firepower. That trend reached its climax in the great battles of attrition of 1914–18. Verdun, the Somme, and countless other mammoth engagements were characterized above all by the expenditure of millions of shells and hundreds of millions of small arms rounds by attackers and defenders alike. As the consumption of ammunition rose to previously unimaginable heights, the outcome was a revolution in logistics, one that, as clearly as any turning point in history, separates what came after from what went before.

In retrospect, one might wonder how any living being could survive in the storm of steel unleashed by rifled, quick-firing, automatic small arms and artillery. At the time, however, several solutions were found to the problem. Of these, the most important was probably extreme dispersion, which caused each soldier and each unit to spread out much more than before. Dispersion in its turn led to problems in command and control, particularly on the move and in offensive warfare, when wire-bound communication systems could only be used with difficulty, and sometimes not at all. Though few historians have discussed these problems at any length, they did as much to shape trench warfare in World War I as did barbed wire and the machine gun.

From the days of Passchendaele to those of Vietnam, the normal justification for expending vast quantities of ammunition was the need to save lives among troops on the attack. Saturation sometimes did achieve that objective, but in other cases it was tantamount to an admission of military impotence. At the heart of the problem was the fact that, given the available gunlaying equipment, the range at which the new weapons were fired was simply too great to give them a good chance of hitting their targets with the precision required to achieve a kill. As dispersion and entrenchment caused the battlefield to assume an eerie, empty look, hitting an enemy who refused to leave cover became an almost insoluble problem. This was all the more true because, as during the famous World War II battles of Monte Casino, the same shells and bombs that destroyed trenches and fortifications also created craters and rubble which provided even better shelter for the defenders. Towards the end of World War I, the gap between range and accuracy had grown so large that it even permitted armor to reassert itself on the battlefield—the tank itself being of course nothing but a lumbering, rumbling testimonial to the ineffectiveness of indirect fire.

At sea and in the air, the problems of modern warfare were in principle similar to those encountered on land. Since distances and speeds in these media were often much greater, radio if anything was even more vital for communication. As to accurately hitting the enemy, each of the two environments presented a slightly different puzzle. At sea, the introduction of optical rangefinders coupled with mechanical calculators early in the century enabled gunners to compensate for the relative movements of firing platform and target, but did not provide an answer to the question of bad visibility which might be caused by darkness, fog, smoke, or the spray thrown up by the sea and by shells that had missed their mark. On the other hand, the problem of hitting an enemy in or from the air consisted not only of varying conditions of visibility but of the high angular velocities involved; in air-to-air combat, this difficulty was aggravated by the limitations on the size and weight of the instruments that could be carried. Consequently, throughout World War I, aircraft of every type were limited to simple (read: primitive and often ineffective) optical sights both for fighting each other and for ground attack. By the time World War II broke out these sights had been improved to compensate for deflection, but were otherwise basically unchanged. The result was a vast expenditure of ammunition, even to the point that it became almost the norm for bombers to miss their target by miles, and for fighter aircraft to return from sorties with the belts of their cannon and machine guns empty and not a single hit registered.

The outcome of firepower was dispersion. At sea and in the air, and to some extent on land as well, it also led to the adoption of rapid evasive movements that were made possible by new and unprecedentedly powerful engines. Whatever the method in use, the side doing the dispersing or the moving was faced with severe problems of communication. The other side, in turn, was often left incapable of hitting the enemy at all. To deal with the situation, different countries tried different approaches at different times. However, by far the most important answer to both sets of problems was found in the realm of electronics—a new technology, the foundations of which had been laid in the nineteenth century by men such as Faraday, Maxwell, Hertz, and Marconi.

The introduction of the wireless in the field of communications was truly revolutionary. For the first time in history, armed forces were equipped with hardware that, in principle at any rate, enabled them to communicate from any place to any other regardless of distance, topographical obstacles, weather, time of day, and the movement of headquarters respective to each other; and all this could be done in what was later to become known as "real time." In the field of target acquisition, electronics realized the ancient dream of building guided weapons and thus provided a substitute for magic. As Churchill's memoirs indicate, very often the guided weapons were regarded as magical by laymen who did not understand the intricacies involved.

Regardless of the purpose which they served, initially the boxes containing power sources and circuitry were large and cumbersome. Their use was thereby restricted to the immobile headquarters of major military units. The early sets also suffered from weak power, with corresponding limitations on range, and from poor resolution in the case of World War II radar and similar devices. The process which enabled these limitations to be overcome was slow and painful. It did, however, result in a situation where towards the end of World War II not only ships but much smaller platforms such as vehicles and light aircraft were being equipped with wireless almost as a matter of course; possession of a call sign was now considered a high class status symbol. Over the years, too, successive technological advances reduced the size of target-finding devices and improved their resolution, a feat achieved principally by a shift to shorter and shorter wavelengths. By 1943 the most advanced radar in service was capable of detecting and acquiring targets as small as individual aircraft and submarines surfacing to recharge their batteries. Equipped with sets such as the famous H2S, aircraft and ships were increasingly able to find their targets in the air, on the ground, or at sea before they came into visual range, regardless of obstacles to visibility such as darkness, fog, or cloud.

If electronic circuitry could be built into manned platforms and used to guide them to their targets, then in principle they could also be put into unmanned weapons, thus doing away with the need for human operators together with all the complications that they present. The problems in miniaturization that this involved were formidable, but not insoluble. By the middle of the war, the British came up with radar-operated proximity fuses small enough to fit into antiaircraft shells. On the other side, the Germans built bombs which, with or without an engine, incorporated a radio-operated remote control system. Though both devices were used with some success (the Germans used theirs to sink Italian warships at the time of their surrender to the Allies in 1943), both had their problems. If the amount of explosives that could be carried inside shells was too small for many purposes, unmanned radio-guided aircraft such as the V-1, carrying more explosive, were vulnerable both to fighters and to ground fire; in addition, they were too slow for use against any but the largest stationary targets. By the time the war ended, both sides had therefore concentrated their attention on rockets as a means of propelling guided missiles. Whether they were fired from aircraft or from ships or the ground, these missiles would be guided to their targets by electronic devices.

Thus, at the heart of the military use of electronics there was a persistent drive towards miniaturization. It was greatly intensified during the decades after 1945, when vacuum tubes were replaced first by transistors and then by solid state circuitry which, rather than being soldered, could be manufactured much more cheaply by etching or printing onto chips made of silicon. Miniaturization enabled smaller and smaller weapons to be equipped with their own electronic brains; more and more sensing and computing power was being built into the same amount of space. As a result, from the 1950s on, successive generations of guided weapons appeared for use on land, at sea, and in the air. Bases, fortifications, ground vehicles, naval vessels, and aircraft all found themselves subjected to a growing threat from guns that relied on radar to acquire targets and from missiles that homed in on them. Corresponding closely to advances in electronic technology, a new generation of guided weapons made its appearance every 10 years on the average, their number and variety being such that even a short catalog would require a separate volume.

The original purpose of guided weapons was to economize on the size of forces by substituting accuracy for saturation, and also to provide a method for combating targets (such as supersonic aircraft) that were too fast and maneuverable to be hit by any other means. As each new generation of weapons entered service, the lethality of combat increased by leaps and bounds. However, nothing even remotely resembling the "one shot, one kill" capability frequently advertised by the designers has ever been achieved in practice, and this for two reasons. First, the results attained in laboratory tests often turned out to be much better than anything that could be done on the battlefield, where troops had to find the targets and operate their weapons under conditions of dust, smoke, noise, and extreme stress. Second, and perhaps even more important, if one side employed electronics to acquire targets and guide weapons to them, the other could use the same means for the opposite purpose—to prevent the targets in question from being discovered and hit. The result during the last 40 years has been a complex race between offensive and defensive blips; a race which is commonly known under the name of electronic warfare.

A detailed technical analysis of the complex apparatus used in electronic warfare does not fall within the scope of the present work. Nevertheless, it is essential to understand that everything depends on electromagnetic signals being passed from a transmitter to a receiver, which according to the type of device may be carried either on the same platform or on another one. Thus, one-way electronic communications gear requires a transmitter at one end and a receiver at the other. For two-way communication, it is necessary to have both a transmitter and a receiver at each end. In radar used for surveillance and target acquisition, transmitter and receiver are usually mounted side by side, though there is no technical requirement that this be so. With guided weapons, the simplest solution often adopted in air-to-air and ground-to-air missiles is to use the target itself as a source of electromagnetic (infrared) radiation, so that the missile itself only needs a receiver which can then be coupled to a guidance mechanism. However, the simplest solution is not necessarily the best. It is also possible to have the missile ride an electronic beam transmitted by a source mounted in the launching platform and reflected from the target. Finally, as in the case of the proximity fuses mentioned above, the weapon itself may contain its own power source and transmitter, in which case it will be able to illuminate its own target.

Whatever the respective positions of the transmitting and receiving devices, and whatever the precise division of the workload between them, it is not only one side that may detect electromagnetic radiation passing through air or space. If that radiation is used for communication, then it will be necessary to introduce additional complexity in the form of a code that will prevent the enemy from listening in. Even if this is successfully done and the code guarded against penetration, the enemy may still use direction-finding apparatus to locate the source of the transmissions and statistical methods to analyze their numbers, thus possibly obtaining important clues concerning the amount of activity that goes on at different places at different times. Collectively known as ELINT, for electronic intelligence, these methods were intensively used by both sides throughout World War II. During the Battle of the Atlantic, for example, ELINT provided the Germans with vital information concerning the whereabouts of Allied convoys, whereas the Allies were able to obtain equally vital information on the German U-boat fleet. Both sides also introduced a variety of esoteric techniques aimed at interfering with the other's ELINT. At a much higher degree of sophistication, the game still goes on day by day and night by night. The only way to prevent it altogether is to switch off one's electronic apparatus, to observe what has become known as radio silence.

If ELINT may be defined as exploiting the enemy's communications for one's own purposes, the simplest form of electronic warfare involves the detection of the enemy's broadcasts in order to sound the alarm. Just as the headlights of an approaching car may be seen long before they enable the driver to see anything, so the range at which the enemy may detect the beams of a radar used for target acquisition or weapon guidance is much greater than the range of the system itself. In World War II, this phenomenon had already been exploited by the German Luftwaffe, whose first warning of an impending Allied air attack often came when the bomber crews experimentally switched on their radar sets while still over the North Sea. At sea, too, German submarines were equipped with several successive versions of a special device known as Naxos. Its purpose was to warn the skipper that his vessel was being illuminated by the beams of an Allied radar, thus giving him time to crash-dive.

There is much more to electronic warfare than simply detecting enemy transmissions. As the next logical step, it is often possible to interfere with those transmissions, jam them, or spoof them. The earliest form of interference, dating to World War II, was "Window," now known as chaff and still in occasional use. This consists of thin strips of tinfoil which are dropped from aircraft to reflect the beams of radar and fool its operators. Jamming is carried out by transmitting beams of the same frequency as those of the opponent but at a different phase. During the Battle of the Marne in 1914 the French, employing a transmitter mounted on top of the Eiffel Tower, successfully jammed German wireless communications. In World War II, the Allies resorted to electronic jamming to defend Malta against the Luftwaffe. Finally, spoofing is in some ways the simplest form of electronic warfare. Applied to passive systems, it consists of substituting a fake target for the real one. For example, a fighter-bomber coming under attack by an air-to-air or ground-to-air missile may release flares, the purpose of which is to emit infrared radiation stronger than that released by the aircraft's own engine.

Though it is thus apparent that the principles of electronic warfare were already understood during World War II, this is by no means the end of the story. Beginning at the time of the War in Vietnam, missiles were developed that used the enemy's own electromagnetic transmissions as a target. Confronted with these homing weapons, as they are known, the simplest response available to the enemy was again to shut down the radar sets. Another possibility, also useful to guard transmissions against other forms of interference, was to resort to frequency hopping. This meant that, instead of continuously transmitting over the same wavelength, radar and other electronic equipment would be made to switch rapidly from one electromagnetic wavelength to the next. As might be expected, it was not long before the switching operation was taken away from human hands and entrusted to computers. In their turn, these were confronted by other computers, which detected the changes and responded to them. The deadly game continues.

The discussion so far has focused on devices that work by transmitting electromagnetic signals by wireless, but this is by no means the only possibility. Such signals may also be transmitted over wires. Since this method is immune to enemy interference, it is often preferred for short-range tactical missiles such as the ones that helicopters, vehicles, or infantrymen fire against tanks. In recent years much attention has also been directed to lasers. Since lasers are essentially nothing but highly focused monophase beams of light, they can be utilized to transmit signals in the same way that other electromagnetic waves can, and again the most important uses are in communication, target acquisition (including the very important function of rangefinding in tank guns), and guiding weapons to their targets. Like other forms of radiation, lasers may be detected, a fact that has been used in instruments serving to warn tank crews that their vehicle has been targeted by an enemy range finder. Nevertheless, the highly focused laser radiation is very difficult to interfere with, and this comprises its main advantage. Its principal shortcomings are two. First, an uninterrupted line of sight between source and target is required. Second, the beams are capable of being obstructed by certain atmospheric conditions, such as moisture and smoke.

To reiterate once again, other things being equal, the simpler the environment in which war is waged the greater the advantages offered by high technology. This explains why electronic warfare first made its impact at sea and in the air. At sea, the sinking of the Israeli destroyer *Elath* in 1967 by a relatively primitive Soviet-made homing missile, the Styx, proved to be a turning point which sent the world's navies searching for better missiles and better means to counter them. In the air, the capability of missiles against aircraft received a spectacular demonstration in 1960 when the Russians shot down an American U-2 spy plane. Vietnam, and also the so-called "War of Attrition" that Israel and Egypt fought over the Suez Canal, saw the first large-scale use of missiles and electronic countermeasures in air warfare. Technologically speaking, the most important conflicts waged since then were the Yom Kippur War of 1973, the Falklands War of 1982, and the Israeli invasion of Lebanon in 1982. Each saw the use of more and more sophisticated equipment, but none seems to have brought to light any revolutionary principles in electronic warfare.

In the case of electronic warfare, as in any other kind of warfare, no weapon and no method is sufficient on its own. Not one is suitable for use under all conditions, and each separately is capable of being countered in ways which, if far from simple, are often obvious enough. With military organizations around the world strongly committed to research and development, over the last 40 years every new technological development was promptly followed by another designed to neutralize it. As the successful Israeli strike against the Syrian missiles and air force in Lebanon particularly demonstrated, each generation of weapons was constantly in danger of being rendered obsolete by its more effective successor. Though technological superiority did play a very important role in winning some conflicts, on the whole the dream of producing a decisive conventional weapon has not come true. Above all, progress towards making conventional warfare more "cost-effective" has been infinitesimal. On the contrary, in every case where it was tried, the net result of electronic warfare coupled with guided weapons was the expenditure of vastly increased quantities of ammunition which was *also* much more expensive.

Usually, each successive advance in electronic target acquisition and weapon guidance tended to raise the signature of the weapons employed. The electronic instrumentation itself made these weapons easier to detect and destroy. The result was that, almost as soon as information about these weapons became available, the type of countermeasures needed became readily apparent, though development and deployment took longer. Meanwhile, the emphasis on electronics probably caused military technological progress in other fields to be slowed down. This was particularly noticeable on the ground, where the majority of the principal systems in use today are lineal descendants of those fielded in 1945, starting with what is still the most important single weapon, the tank. It is of course indisputable that the punch delivered by guns, the power of engines, and the quality of the armor, have all increased very greatly. As compared to those in use during World War II, modern tanks incorporate a very large number of technological refinements, beginning with gas turbine engines (if that constitutes an advance) and ending with stabilized turrets, laser range finders, automatic fire-suppressors, and many others. Nevertheless, the basic elements comprising a tank are still very much as they were 40 years ago, and so are its maximum dimensions and its overall configuration.

Much the same considerations apply with most other weapons. This applies to heavy reconnaissance vehicles, most of which are nowadays tracked rather than wheeled as they formerly were; to combat carriers, where the most important single advance has likewise consisted of a switch from half-tracked, half-closed vehicles to fully tracked, fully closed ones; to artillery, where the present trend towards mounting barrels on self-propelled, tracked platforms was already pronounced in 1945; to most types of small arms such as assault rifles, machine guns, and mortars; to portable antitank weapons, which all date back to the original wire-guided missiles that were developed by the French during the 1950s; to auxiliary gear such as infrared night vision aids which were tried out in Germany during World War II; and of course to most classes of engineering equipment.

At sea, too, since the imminent demise of the big-gunned battleship and its replacement by the carrier were already certain by 1942 at the latest, a case might be made that development since then has been conservative at best. The most visible element in that development was a tripling in the size of carriers for which, in the view of some, considerations other than simple military effectiveness were partly responsible. Though the growing size of carriers permitted those navies that could afford them to deploy progressively bigger and more powerful warplanes, the number based aboard each vessel has, if anything, declined. At present a large, nuclear-propelled carrier has the capability to launch perhaps 70 attack-aircraft sorties a day for a few days on end—hardly enough to make much of an impression even on a third rate military power.

As carriers became by far the most powerful weapon at sea, large gunned warships were regarded as superfluous and retired even though a few of them are now making a partial comeback. The smaller vessels that remained tended to specialize in such roles an antiaircraft and antisubmarine warfare, vital in order to protect the carriers which were themselves becoming more and more specialized. Aboard these vessels, guided missiles have for the most part replaced guns, though again there has been a tendency to reintroduce gunned ships into service in recent years, with their guns now much improved and provided with radar guidance. Whatever their primary armament, the various classes of frigates, destroyers, and cruisers were constantly getting bigger and bigger. Unable to afford them, some small navies decided to rely entirely on missile boats for both sea-to-sea and sea-to-ground combat. Notwithstanding these and other developments, the fundamentals of surface warfare remain the same. Which is why the carrier-centered task force, the backbone of naval warfare in the Pacific in 1941–45, continues in service today.

With submarines, too, development has been evolutionary rather than revolutionary. Thanks in part to the introduction of nuclear propulsion, the range of attack submarines, their ability to remain submerged for extended periods, and the depths to which they can dive have been greatly increased. Possibly more important still, the speed with which submarines travel underwater now equals or exceeds that of most major surface vessels, dramatically reversing the odds. Thanks in part to onboard computers, programmed to rapidly process the echoes which sonar picks up and to distinguish them from ocean noises, underwater target acquisition has also improved dramatically. So has the accuracy and, in particular, the range of weapons, some of which now make their way above the surface rather than below it and are capable of hitting their targets dozens if not hundreds of kilometers way. In the view of some, these developments will soon enable the submarine to take the place of the aircraft carrier as the capital ship of the future.

On the other hand, much the same weapons and computers that are used by submarines have also been placed aboard aircraft, helicopters, and surface vessels adapted for hunting and destroying them; in addition, the U.S. Navy in particular has engaged in a massive attempt to cover the world's most important ocean approaches with a network of listening devices resting on the bottom of the sea. Since the submarine capable of launching ballistic missiles, or SLBM, currently is the platform offering the greatest security against a nuclear first strike, developments in the field of submarine and antisubmarine warfare are everywhere kept a closely guarded secret. To date, however, a reliable way to detect and destroy *all* the enemy's submarines has not been developed, and no change is expected in the foreseeable future.

Though both the jet engine and the helicopter were already entering service in 1944, superficial technological development since then has been more rapid in the air than it has been on the ground or at sea. The rise of jet engines has revolutionized the speed of combat aircraft, their range, endurance, and other capabilities, all of which are now much greater than anything available during World War II. However, after about 1960 it was found that speeds in the order of Mach 2 were only useful under a limited range of circumstances and could actually constitute a handicap in others. Accordingly, development has changed direction. Great efforts were made to improve the maneuverability of aircraft, for which purpose it was necessary to develop new synthetic materials and entrust part of the pilot's job to a computer. Even more important were advances in the missiles and, above all, the electronics carried by aircraft. As a result, the most modern planes in service are best described as flying complexes made up of missiles and computers. With their HUDs (Head Up Display), FLIRs (Forward Looking Infra Red) and so-called "look down, shoot down" instrumentation, they are said by their manufacturers to be capable of identifying and destroying anything that moves in the air or on the ground, within visual range and outside it, singly or in groups. In practice, it is a matter of course that none of these capabilities is available under all conditions, while some are only available under quite exceptional circumstances. Sometimes, too, the adjective "advanced" simply serves to camouflage the fact that the technology in question is not working yet.

At the time of this writing, the use of helicopters for air-to-air combat is in its infancy. The earliest machines were fragile, small, and had a limited load-carrying capacity. Hence their main uses were in reconnaissance, liaison, and casualty evacuation, and as flying command posts. Larger models were built and, beginning in Vietnam where the Americans fielded an entire division of "airmobile cavalry," provided unprecedented mobility to small bodies of lightly armed troops. Since helicopters can get men and equipment out of the battlefield as well as into it, they have largely replaced the paratroopers and gliders of World War II without, however, fundamentally changing the general considerations pertaining to airborne versus ground warfare.

Since about 1975, the role of helicopters has changed. Many types of fighter-bomber in service had become much too fast, too unmaneuverable, and too large to be used against most kinds of ground targets. Nor, for the same reasons, were they of much use against helicopters. Consequently helicopters began to be equipped with short-range guided missiles similar to those fielded by the ground forces. This enables them to hover on the edge of the battlefield, pop up, fire at pinpoint targets, and get away. To judge by the analogy of aircraft in World War I, which were used for reconnaissance and liaison before they were quipped with weapons, it is now only a matter of time before we shall witness the first helicopter-to-helicopter battles. Such battles, in fact, are already a perfectly normal part of children's adventure films shown on TV.

Though military technological progress has been startling in many ways, a strong case might be made that, in all environments where late twentieth century war takes place, its impact has been less revolutionary than one might expect from the huge outlays involved. In spite of endless improvements in detail, or, perhaps because of them, the most important types of hardware remained essentially the same from 1945 to 1973, even 1982. Repeated claims concerning their imminent replacement by new generations of "smart" and "brilliant" weapons have not been substantiated, whereas the effects of those now entering service remain to be seen.

Partly as a result, too, tactics and strategy have been equally conservative. To substantiate that claim, it is enough to note that most experts on conventional warfare until very recently still considered the German *Blitzkrieg* campaigns as the highest model to follow, though the prospect of doing so on the fire-drenched modern battlefield appears increasingly remote. Moreover, virtually all present-day discussions of conventional warfare are still conducted in terms originally coined by Douhet, Ludendorff, Seeckt, Fuller, and Liddell Hart in the years before 1939. Symptomatically, there have been in the postwar world no worthy successors to these men. This fact may serve as an early indication that large-scale conventional war may have reached the end of its tether.

To this suggestion, it might of course be objected that our vision is distorted by the historical approach we have adopted. Since many of the weapons in question have never been seriously tested in large-scale combat, expectations concerning their performance tend to be based on the way similar weapons performed in the past. The next war will probably open with a series of technological surprises, involving not only the introduction of completely new weapons, but also the unexpected effects and interactions of existing ones; the objection is not without force.

Military history can tell us how, in the past, people coped with problems which in some ways resembled our own. By serving as a basis on which theory is built—in fact, as the only possible basis— it can help us learn how to think about technology and war. It cannot, and does not, make any further claim.

Putting speculations about the future aside, let us return to the actual, observable, facts. Perhaps the first development deserving notice is that, against the background of breathtaking advances in electronics, military technological innovation in other fields has not only been slowed down, but has also assumed a new character. In the period between 1830 and 1945, innovation took the form of successive weapons systems replacing each other every few years. Since about 1960, however, the more expensive type of weapons systems, in particular, came to be regarded simply as hulls, or platforms, on which to mount black boxes filled with circuitry. This meant that tanks, ships, and aircraft, instead of being consigned to the scrap heap by the appearance of their respective successors, could often be renovated by taking out one type of black box and putting in another. Since renovating equipment in this way was easier than building it from scratch, it attracted Third World countries which were thus able to get their defense industries going before proceeding to bigger things. Moreover, the continuation of technological progress in the future was now taken for granted. Hence, a premium was put on designing weapon systems in such a way that they would be easily capable of renovation when the time came.

During the last few decades, accelerating technological progress has ceased to speed up the replacement of old systems by new ones. More and more it has led to the opposite result, namely, longer and longer intervals between one generation of systems and the next. The term "life cycle" as applied to weapons and weapons systems therefore acquired a new meaning. The planning approach that it demanded differed from what had gone before, and often also from the best civilian practice as manifested, for example, in electrical appliances or motor cars which nobody bothers to upgrade, but instead replaces.

A very important consideration that governed the development of new weapons was, as always, cost. Mounting cost played a critical role in the process which is transforming many weapons into containers for black boxes that keep changing all the time. Even so, its inevitable outcome was that fewer and fewer weapons of each type were being fielded. In most cases there was no doubt that, on a one-to-one basis, the tanks, ships, and aircraft of each successive generation were more than a match for their immediate predecessors. If numbers were also taken into account, however, it was by no means obvious that a small number of very advanced weapons was necessarily "superior" to a larger quantity of weapons that were less sophisticated, but still adequate. The question as to just which "hi-lo" mixture offered the greatest combat power at the least cost was a difficult one to answer, particularly since it did not depend on technology alone but also involved doctrine, training, organization, and any number of other factors. Hence each country tended to strike a different balance, which was perceived as most suitable to its defense requirements and potential.

Since no country could afford to retire all older weapons upon the appearance of their successors, generally the effect of accelerating technological progress was that each decade saw more and more different types of weapons in service. With more different weapons around, and as each one separately was countered and then countered again, integration-into-systems became the order of the day. Instead of operating on an individual basis, there was a tendency for weapons to be linked to each other by intricate networks of electronic signals that gave full rein to the military penchant for inventing unpronounceable acronyms. The networks in question were extended on the ground, at sea, in the air, and even into outer space where satellites were used for navigation, communication, surveillance, reconnaissance, and target acquisition. Located at the heart of each system, like spiders in their webs, were command centers which could be stationary or mobile or even airborne in the form of AWACS (Airborne Warning and Control System) aircraft. There bank upon bank of computers were employed to "fuse" incoming information. There, too, officers found themselves trying to command—at one remove from reality, as it were—by sitting in front of multiple television screens, talking newspeak into microphones, and pressing buttons that supposedly made things happen.

Behind the tendency towards integration, a paradox increasingly revealed itself. Each successive weapon fielded was undoubtedly more powerful than its predecessor. Nevertheless, there were some indications that the inexorable drive towards integration was not only symptomatic of the declining effectiveness of each individual element but was, at the same time, acting as its cause. Late in

World War II, tanks and some types of aircraft such as heavy bombers already began to respond to increasing opposition by a process of integration. Rising simultaneously on both sides of the front, the resulting systems were less flexible than their predecessors and, as a result, engaged each other in prolonged struggles of attrition. During the decades since 1945 further integration, driven by similar causes, seems to have affected other weapons with similar results.

Specifically, the extraordinary effectiveness of the fighter-bomber both during the German *Blitzkrieg* campaigns, and later in the hands of the Allies, reflected the fact that it was a self-contained platform. A single pilot, requiring comparatively little outside assistance, was able to loiter above the battlefield, conduct reconnaissance, acquire a target, and hit it with the aid of the weapons carried aboard. Even as late as 1967 the Israelis (who, significantly, had rejected French advice to arm their planes with missiles rather than with guns) still gave devastating proof of the effectiveness of these methods. However, by that time a combination of the threat presented by modern antiaircraft defenses and of the pressure exercised by advancing technology as such was making itself felt. Over the next two decades tactical aircraft became increasingly dependent on cooperation with electronic navigation and communication systems, electronic warfare aircraft, and unmanned platforms known as RPVs or remotely piloted vehicles.

With the drive towards integration in full swing, another paradoxical result emerged. On the one hand, advancing technology subjected pilots to demands that verged on the limits of human capability, even to the point where the size of some air forces was determined by the availability of sufficient individuals of suitable quality. On the other, aircraft were turned into something very close to manned missiles. The feeling of autonomy which at one time had constituted one of the principal attractions of flying was largely lost. Pilots found themselves imprisoned in, indeed literally incorporated with, inconceivably complicated machines. The purpose of these machines was to hurtle through the air (often following a predetermined route) and fire their missiles at targets that the pilot would never see. In the skies of both Vietnam and Lebanon, the integrated systems approach helped the side who had mastered it to achieve something like complete command of the air; once achieved, however, its use turned out to be rather limited. At present, a new generation of even more sophisticated craft is under development, and already the writing is on the wall. More and more, the pilots' roles are being taken over by a variety of unmanned platforms.

To attempt a generalization from the case of the fighter-bomber, it is possible that the effectiveness of a new weapon often does not stem from its own inherent superiority. On the contrary, it may be due to the fact that, being new, it has *not* yet been integrated with all others and thus preserves a greater degree of autonomy and flexibility. Since no weapon has ever won a war on its own and without support, clearly some integration is always required. On the other hand, there exists a point beyond which integration, regardless of whether it was brought about by the strength of the opposition or by the inherent nature of technology itself, will lead to diminishing returns. The same, of course, applies to civilian industry. However, since war is characterized precisely by a very high level of uncertainty—which is partly the outcome of deliberate enemy action—that point is reached much sooner.

Another good example of the possibilities, and dangers, of integration is presented by the history of the tank. In World War I, the very novelty of the concept represented by the tank acted as one of the factors that prevented smooth cooperation between it and other arms. Therefore, during most of the period the tanks were unable to play a truly decisive role. Early in World War II, following a long period of technological and organizational development, the Germans discovered the ideal compromise between autonomy and integration. This compromise they built into the *Panzer* division, thereby acquiring the instrument with which to overrun a continent. Later, however, the balance was upset. One reason was that improved antitank weapons forced both the Germans and their opponents towards greater tactical integration. The second reason, however, was to be found not in the requirements of war but in the inherent qualities of technology in general, and of the rapidly-developing electronic technology in particular. Tanks, artillery, antitank weapons, motorized and foot infantry, and the rest were incorporated into the combined arms team. As tanks found it more difficult to survive in the open, the infantry was expanded until it included the very trench-digging engineers whom the tank was originally intended to defeat, an ironic reversal. Gradually, a situation arose where none of the team's members could so much as move without prior coordination with all the rest. Simplicity and flexibility, both of them vital principles of war, were lost. Consequently, though today's Abrams and Leopards and Challengers and T 72s are individually much more powerful than the Shermans and Tigers and Cruisers and T 34s of World War II, as instruments of war and conquest they may be less effective.

To conclude, the most important single outcome of technological progress during the decades since World War II has been that, on the modern battlefield, a blizzard of electromagnetic blips is increasingly being superimposed on—and to some extent substituted for—the storm of steel in which war used to take place. This development, in turn, opens the way to two possible scenarios. On the one hand, suppose a situation where one side operates much more sophisticated electronics and, as a result, is much more dependent on them. Under such circumstances, it is not inconceivable that the inferior side will be tempted to develop and use a weapon tailor-made to neutralize the other side's electronic circuitry more or less at a stroke, thus rendering him deaf, blind, and unable to operate or even to survive. Such weapons, in the form of nuclear warheads designed to emit a strong EMP (electromagnetic pulse) already exist. The literature suggests that they would be the more effective the more advanced, or the more miniaturized, was the electronic circuitry involved. Consequently, shielding is the order of the day.

The other scenario, by contrast, is an environment so teeming with electromagnetic pulses that the two sides' signals will neutralize each other. The danger exists that, with the proliferation of the systems employed by each side separately, the results will be very similar to those of heavy traffic coming in from different directions over an inadequate road network. Under such circumstances, the side whose dependence on sophisticated technology is the greatest may fall victim to older, simpler, ballistic weapons operating below what I shall call his sophistication threshold. Since the ability of electronic blips to represent a military situation is inversely related to the latter's complexity, everything else being equal the risk is greater at sea than it is in the air, and it is greater on land than at sea, and in a guerrilla-type conflict it is greater than in a conventional one.

As always in war, what constitutes a danger to one side by that very fact presents an opportunity to the other. The first scenario belongs to the future. The second has, in some instances at any rate, already been realized. Indeed, a case might be made that much, if not most, current modern military activity takes place below the sophistication threshold, and conversely that many kinds of military technology have become too sophisticated, too powerful, and too indiscriminate for use in real-life warfare. Partly as a result, such technology seems to be on its way to turning war itself into an empty, hollow game.

CHAPTER 19

Make-Believe War

IN WESTERN CIVILIZATION since the end of the Middle Ages, the predominant view of war has been political-utilitarian. From the days of Machiavelli to those of Kissinger, war has been defined as an act of force taking place between sovereign states. Sovereignty in turn was defined by Bodin in the second half of the sixteenth century as a characteristic possessed solely by political organizations, and not by all of those. Simply put, it means that the organization in question does not recognize any human authority above itself and no set of laws by which it is bound. However, this reasoning may also be turned upside down. Precisely because it is not subject to any rules, a sovereign political organization may be defined as one which has been recognized by other such organizations as possessing the *right* of using force and going to war. In other words, it has the right to be guided solely by expediency, or *raison d'état*.

Put in another way, war might be defined—indeed often has been defined—as an act of force which admits of no rules, and in which, consequently, all is fair. Such a view has much to recommend it in theory, and nobody in his right mind would deny that it also has a strong basis in practice. As often happens, however, when definitions derived from abstract reasoning are applied to the endlessly varied annals of mankind, it soon becomes clear that it does not cover the whole truth. Historically speaking, war very often has been waged according to a set of explicit or implicit rules which, one might add, were honored even in the breach.

It is even possible to argue, with Johan Huizinga and others, that the very concept of war as distinct from personal vendetta and simple murder already presupposes the existence of rules as to what things may be done to whom under what circumstances.

To the extent that war is not waged solely on the basis of utilitarian considerations, that it respects the rules, and does not involve the utmost use of force, it strongly resembles a contest or a game. A game could be defined as a struggle which, however violent the forms that it may take, proceeds according to a set of artificial rules and, to the extent that it does, stands apart from "ordinary" or "real" life. To allow the game to be played, these rules must be both fixed and acknowledged by the parties taking part. Where there are no rules there can be no game; the intimate connection between the two concepts is brought out with particular force by the fact that even a player who cheats by that very act admits the former's binding force. It is, consequently, not the cheat who ruins a game but the spoilsport. By refusing to recognize the rules, he either turns it into something else or brings it to an end.

Particularly when and where war is waged within a homogeneous civilization, against a common cultural background, and for ends which both sides regard as legitimate in themselves, it tends to be governed by rules, and to transform itself into something resembling a game. Depending on the historical period in question, these rules were said to be prescribed by God, justice, reason, nature, humanity, and what not; an inquiry into their origins would, in fact, be tantamount to a study of civilization itself. For example, a gamelike element was much in evidence in war as conducted during Hellenistic times. It was a period when a common language, *koine*, was spoken throughout the Eastern Mediterranean. There was little to choose between the various successor states; all of them were despotisms built around a single man and dynasty. Fighting among themselves for reasons of aggrandizement or prestige, they maintained armies made up of professionals who had no personal stake in the issue at hand. Accordingly, there applied among those states a fairly strict code which dictated what was and was not permissible in regard to the treatment of prisoners, the enslavement of the population of captured cities, the robbery for military purposes of temples dedicated to the gods (this was legitimate, provided restitution was subsequently made, or at any rate promised), and so on.

The application of rules to warfare was, however, extended further than this. While it would be imprecise to say that there existed an explicit international agreement concerning the types of military technology that might or might not be used, the various contestants shared a common material civilization and knew what to expect of each other. Since they fielded much the same weapons and equipment, but also because commanders and technical experts frequently transferred from one army to another, they found themselves operating on broadly similar tactical and strategic codes. The role of light infantry in opening the battle, the place of the phalanx in the center of the array, the function of the cavalry on the wings, were all more or less fixed. Consequently most Hellenistic battles unfolded according to a predetermined pattern, as it were, an excellent analogy being the opening moves in a game of chess. This fact was clearly recognized by both sides, even though they occasionally tried to circumvent it to their own advantage.

The period from approximately 300 to 200 B.C. was by no means the last in which technology, coupled with other factors, helped warfare turn into something akin to a game. An even better example of the same phenomenon is presented by the feudal Middle Ages when war and games, the latter in the form of tournaments, resembled each other so closely that they were sometimes almost indistinguishable. As we saw earlier in this study, during the Middle Ages war properly speaking, *la guerre* as opposed to *la guerre guerroyante,* was all but monopolized by an internationally homogeneous aristocratic class. Knights were warriors whose claim to membership rested in large part on the fact that they could afford certain well-defined implements of war including horse, lance, and armor. A common technology helped create common tactics which, as time went on, tended to become formalized and ritualized. Furthermore, they served as the basis behind a common military ethos that distinguished those who fought as knights from those who did not. The things that were, and were not, permitted in war among the former were fairly well-defined, even giving rise to a class of experts (the heralds) whose purpose was to define them. The tendency toward homogeneity and away from an all-out struggle was in part created by common equipment and was reinforced by the influence of a supranational Christian culture and a supranational feudal law.

The play-element often present in armed conflict was, however, probably never as pronounced as in the eighteenth century, when war became popularly known as the game of kings. It was an age in which, according to Voltaire, all Europeans lived under the same kind of institutions, believed in the same kind of ideas, and fornicated with the same kind of women. Most states were ruled by absolute monarchs. Even those who were not so ruled neither expected nor demanded the lump-in-the-throat type of allegiance later to be associated with the nationalist idea. Armies were commanded by members of an international nobility who spoke French as their lingua franca and switched sides as they saw fit. They were manned by personnel who, often enlisted by trickery and kept in the ranks by main force, cared nothing for honor, duty, or country. Warfare in general, and siege warfare in particular, came to be governed by an elaborate code that was partly customary, partly juridical. Once again a slowly developing, exceptionally homogeneous, military technology played a role in the taming process. It all but defined the weapons which might and might not be employed, thereby causing battles to unfold according to a fixed ritual. Consequently Count Wilhelm zu Schaumburg-Lippe-Bueckburg was even able to establish a sort of international military academy, where officers of all nations could receive training, pool their experience, and pass the rules of the game on to the next generation.

In each of the above three periods, as well as in many others which witnessed the same phenomenon, the transformation of war into something akin to a game did not pass without comment. What some people took as a sign of piety or reason or progress, others saw as proof of stupidity, effeminacy, and degeneration. During the last years before the French Revolution, Gibbons praised modern war for its moderation and expressed the hope that it would soon disappear altogether. Simultaneously, a French nobleman, the Comte de Guibert, was cutting a figure among the ladies of the *salons* by denouncing the prevailing military practices as degenerate and by calling for a commander and a people who, to use his own words, would tear apart the feeble constitution of Europe like the north wind bending the reeds. Both views, of course, represented extremes. Most contemporaries, including the statesmen and the generals who applied the rules, were mildly proud of the fact that civilized warfare was being ameliorated for the benefit of humanity. On the other hand, they would no doubt have taken offense at the suggestion that, as practiced by them, it had become so ensnared in those rules as to take on a game-like, make-believe character.

When Clausewitz around 1830 defined war as a pure act of force that is governed by expediency alone, he was therefore reacting to the situation actually prevailing at the time of his own early military service. As he himself was well aware, an examination of the historical record shows that there have been many times and places when war was governed by rules which were honored even in the breach. There have also been times and places when war was waged, not as an instrument of politics but for its own sake, as it were, thus further reinforcing its resemblance to a game. The tendency of war to be guided by a set of rules, rather than by utility and main force, is particularly pronounced whenever and wherever it takes place against the background of a common culture and civilization. Inevitably, these will be anchored in a common technology, which in turn will go some way in causing tactics, and even warfare itself, to unfold according to a predetermined pattern that is recognized and respected by both sides. The exception, of course, is civil war, when one or both sides disputes the other's *right* to resort to force of arms.

In light of these considerations, how are we to classify the period since 1945? The informed reader is well aware of the many important differences that in today's world separate the different states, regions, and power systems from each other. However, a case might also be made that, in the most advanced of those power systems, regions, and states, a common technology tends to overshadow these differences. That technology, in turn, is characterized precisely by the fact that it does not divide its operators into white or black, Christian or Moslem, right wing or left wing or liberal. Though dependence on technology cannot turn a "godless communist" Russian into a "right-thinking" American, up to a point it can and does impose a set of common procedures, methods, and styles. Even more important, the fact that it is produced and used—often at very great economic cost—is itself both cause and effect of a shared set of values. Central among those values is the belief in capabilities, innovation, superiority, and professionalism; briefly, everything necessary for technology to be effective in dealing with all kinds of social problems. Significantly for the argument at hand, these beliefs are not limited to those who actually possess the hardware. On the contrary, some of their strongest adherents are to be found precisely in technologically undeveloped countries.

For good and for ill, the belief in the effectiveness of technology is as pronounced in modern military life as it is in the civilian world and indeed represents one of the outstanding legacies of World War II. If only because the introduction of a weapon by one military power very often serves as the justification *par excellence* for its acquisition by all the rest, modern military technology tends towards homogeneity. This, of course, is not to deny that important differences often exist. It is a truism that, superficial resemblances notwithstanding, American tanks and ships and missiles and fighter-bombers, for example, are by no means identical with their Soviet opposite numbers. Far from being accidental, these differences often reflect considerable gaps in design philosophies which in their turn may have their origin not only in divergent military requirements but in the production methods favored by each country, and ultimately in their respective politico-socio-economic structures. Still, when all is said and done, it seems that the similarities between the military technologies fielded by East and West, the Warsaw Pact and NATO, are at least as important as the differences. This is also shown by the fact that the hardware in their hands is often capable of being analyzed on the basis of the same categories, more or less.

While the nature of the military technology in use today does not exercise a deterministic effect on the conduct of war, on the other hand it indubitably does have some effect. Where technologies are similar and where other circumstances are not too different, capabilities, methods, and missions are likely to converge. Even more important in the present context, the equation works the other way around. If similar military technologies in the hands of the principal states lead to a homogeneous style in the conduct of conventional war, it is no less true that no conventional war can take place unless the technology on both sides is sufficiently homogeneous to prevent a decisive margin of superiority in the hands of one. Such is the great paradox of our age.

Today's world differs from many previous ones in that a single, fairly homogeneous, military technology is recognized everywhere as dominant. The very fact that conventional war takes place already points to the existence of something like a technological balance between the belligerents. As historical examples show, homogeneous technology is one of the factors that may cause war to unfold according to something very like a predictable pattern. The existence of a pattern presupposes rules which, as usual, are sometimes honored even in the breach. Where both sides employ their weapons in accordance with a set of common rules, war can no longer be said to be governed by expediency alone or to involve the utmost exertion of force. In this sense, and to this extent, it takes on the character of a game.

The gamelike characteristics of much modern conventional warfare, one hastens to add, are not the result of technology alone. Precisely because it witnessed an unprecedented amount of senseless, mechanized slaughter, World War I was followed by widespread feelings of revulsion against armed conflict and everything pertaining to it. Those feelings could be interpreted either as a sign of progress or of decay. By and large, the victorious countries—even those which, like France, had been steeped in militaristic culture during the prewar years—took the progressive view. By the thirties, it led to widespread pacifist sentiments which found their political expression in appeasement and contributed to the defeats of 1940. Seen from this point of view, both Fascism and National Socialism now appear as desperate attempts to put back the clock and maintain, or revive, the military spirit. Whatever temporary success these movements did enjoy, and in this context it might be mentioned that not even Hitler was altogether satisfied with the warlike enthusiasm displayed by the German people, they were decisively defeated in 1945.

It is impossible here to follow postwar social attitudes to military affairs in any detail. Suffice it to say that considerable differences manifested themselves between the Soviet bloc and the Western world. In the Soviet bloc, the powers that be engaged in strenuous attempts to keep the spirit of warlike preparedness alive; to judge by current Moscow jokes concerning the need to keep one's nerve after a nuclear attack and proceed *slowly* to the cemetery, they were not altogether successful. In the West, in spite of many short term fluctuations, antimilitary feelings were generally allowed free rein. These feelings, in turn, affected Europe long before they did the United States, where Vietnam served as the turning point and where there currently seems to be a revival of interest in war and everything pertaining to it. The differences among the various countries should not blind us to the basic similarities. Though the status enjoyed by the Soviet armed forces differs from that of their Western counterparts, both sides of the Iron Curtain agree in regarding the adjective "militaristic" as a term of abuse. Exceptions to this truth only exist in a comparatively small number of developing countries. Even in a military-based monarchy such as Jordan, to be called "peace loving" is *de rigeur.*

Since 1945, the term "war" itself has acquired an unsavory connotation. Following the rules that govern the usage of all dirty words, it has tended to be taken out of the vocabulary and to give way to euphemisms. Beginning around 1950, and quite regardless of the nature of the ideology that they claimed to represent, most governments were no longer prepared to admit that they included a department, or office, or ministry, whose function was to take care of everything pertaining to war. Instead they spoke of defense or security, often in contexts that had nothing to do with the original meaning of those words. Next, and partly also as a result of the nuclear threat making itself felt, there was a change in the rationale under which these various ministries and offices and departments conducted their business. Previously, people prepared for war so as to be capable of fighting when it came. On a declaratory level at any rate, the new policy was to be able to fight in order *not* to have to. For many governments the need to prevent war by deterrence became almost the sole way to justify their military preparations, which of course did not in itself mean that the activity that took place under the smoke-screen of words was noticeably different from its predecessors.

Thus, changing the name of the thing represented one way by which military affairs could be made palatable to contemporary tastes. Another way, and to our purposes an even more important way, was to turn weapons into toys (the word "weapons" itself, incidentally, is increasingly being replaced by the term "systems" which are "optimized" for this mission or that). As our discussion of irrational technology indicated, this strange phenomenon is by no means without historical precedent. However, our age seems to be the first which systematically attempts to disguise the true nature of weapons even as it remains obsessed with their performance. From models and publications intended for boys of all ages, that attempt has spread to the so-called professional literature itself. To read any number of articles about modern military technology, and the advertisements published by the defense industry, one would never guess that the purpose of weapons is to do away with people in a variety of ways, most of them unpleasant. Instead they are presented much like stereo sets and lawn mowers and motorcycles. Like any other gadget, weapons are considered to derive their fascination from the sheer engineering skill that went into them, and of course from the power ("capabilities") which result from that skill.

The highly specialized, and often impossibly convoluted, terminology used in modern military parlance is another case in point. In this parlance, weapons, though they are sometimes described as lethal, never ever serve to kill. Instead all they do is give their owners the "antipersonnel capability" which, to be sure, they so desperately need. Rather than destroy enemy weapons, which after all consist of nice gadgets basically similar to our own, modern military technology "engages" targets, and "services," "neutralizes," or "suppresses" them. If a particularly vivid description is needed, it "defeats" them and "takes them out," the latter term being a direct derivation from children's games such as tag or hide-and-seek. As one would expect, the euphemisms become particularly hideous when it is a question of disguising the effects of nuclear devices. Here a "clean" bomb is one that kills people by blast rather than radiation, a "countervalue" attack is one that incinerates cities, and "colateral damage" stands for an incalculable, but certainly very large, number of dead men, women, and children.

As if to cap the irony, the object of the exercise—namely, the enemy who has to be beaten—has all but disappeared from the literature. Possibly because it is regarded as too personal, hence likely to give rise to feelings of guilt, the noun "enemy" has been largely replaced by the adjective "hostile." This, in turn, has given rise to the term "hostilian," an interesting Pentagon neologism, the real purpose of which is presumably to disguise the fact that, on the other side too, there are people made of flesh and blood, the euphemism making the whole thing easier by expiating any lurking sense of guilt. Or does this perversion of language have something to do with the fear lest, if only the realities behind it were plainly put, those who employ it as a basis for planning national policy would stand in danger of being declared insane?

Another example of disguise is the armed forces show. Traditionally, one of the functions of armed forces has been to display their power by organizing Army and Navy Days, Air Force Shows, and the like, all of which gave a prominent place to the technology in use. In the decades following World War II, the defense industry has joined the armed forces. It regularly advertises its wares in national and international bazaars, fairs, and exhibitions, some of which have turned into first-class tourist attractions. Often the excuse for holding the event consists of a few "shop only" days by which it is preceded. These over, the doors are thrown open to the public. The crowds are invited to admire the marvels on display to the accompaniment of bands, soft drinks, hot dogs, and sometimes displays by real-life soldiers operating real-life weapons. Everything is done to trivialize and disguise the deadly nature of the technology in question. This enables parents to admire it, and children to crawl over it, in good conscience. Before leaving the show, dad buys himself one of the innumerable illustrated books on weapons while the children, by way of a special treat, are presented with do-it-yourself plastic models of the equipment, complete with working parts. The very young, however, are by no means the only ones to feel the attraction of miniature weapons. Western armies very often use them as props in recruitment drives, and they are frequently found decorating the offices of military personnel of all nationalities.

The use of weapons as toys for grown ups playing a game of cops and robbers is not, of course, confined to the present age. However, unlike its predecessors of any age and place, more and more modern war takes place in the shadow of weapons that are too powerful to use. In the presence of these weapons, the parties possessing them are being compelled to develop a common set of rules in order to protect their mutual interest, namely, sheer physical survival. Fear of escalation is still causing those rules to spread downward and outward. Far from remaining limited to nuclear weapons only, they increasingly affect conventional warfare also. The point has now been reached where the most important potential belligerents have agreed not to hold large-scale maneuvers without giving previous notice to the other, allowing his officers to participate as observers.

Thus, instead of merely containing a game-like element as formerly, modern conventional war—particularly as prepared for by the superpowers—has itself been turned into a sort of game. Elsewhere this character is less pronounced, but still often falls short of what the Germans used to call *der Ernstfall,* the serious business of life. Though it is played with the aid of real-life conventional weapons, it proceeds according to certain rules. Explicit or implicit, the purpose of those rules is to limit the things that are, and are not, done so as to make them acceptable to the enemy and, even more important, to those of his allies who are armed with nuclear weapons and might become alarmed at the prospect of too-complete a victory. Only by subjecting itself to certain rules can the struggle take place without undue fear of mutual suicide. However, since it proceeds according to rules, it can no longer involve the utmost exertion of forces. Hence, once again, its similarity to a game.

Faced with the very real threat of global destruction brought about by nuclear weapons, conventional warfare has responded by thrusting its head into the sand. In many cases it has tended to become limited to powers that, by definition, are incapable of endangering the world by their squabbles. As the nuclear umbrella spread its shade not only over the superpowers but also extended it to their allies and clients, there was a decline in the number of places in which all out, real-life war could safely take place. A paradoxical situation manifested itself. Much of conventional war, and the preparations which it involved, assumed a make-believe character. Although, or perhaps because, it is waged with the aid of the most ingenious and expensive toys ever devised by man, it tended to take place in certain designated areas (the isolated and utterly unimportant Falkland Islands being a particularly good example) where it could only cause limited damage and did not affect the most important political issues of the day. Meanwhile, those powers that do have nuclear weapons in their arsenals for the most part stood by on the sidelines, permitting or encouraging the small guys to amuse themselves. Every now and then they snatched the ball and played awhile, but only while taking infinite precautions to ensure that their most vital interests—and those of their adversaries as well—were not put into serious jeopardy.

This argument can also be turned around. In practice, the difference between war and the deadliest games practiced by men consists precisely of the fact that, in war, the element of pure unbridled force is always present. Like a bolt of lightning coming out of a clear sky, it threatens to crash through the network of rules. Historically speaking, there have been many places and times when war began to resemble a game. Whenever this happened, there were people aplenty who chose to interpret the phenomenon as a sign that civilization was advancing, that eternal peace was possible, perhaps even that the millenium was about to arrive. On each of those occasions, however, sooner or later somebody came along who did not operate on the same code. Brandishing his sharp sword he tore apart the delicate fabric, revealing war for what it really was.

Nemesis, when it came, took different forms. The Hellenistic states, which had dominated the eastern Mediterranean, were laid low by the Romans who, to quote Polybius, were singularly inclined to use force (*bia*) in order to solve any problem. The jousts and other military games being played at the courts of France and Burgundy were rudely disrupted by Swiss pikemen and Spanish arquebusiers coming from "barbaric" countries on the fringe of civilization, nations that had never been properly feudalized. The European *ancien régime* was brought to an end when the French Revolution mobilized huge hordes of men and, unable to train them in the good old rules, hurled them forward at the enemy in formations that contemporaries regarded as crude but very effective. As might be expected, those who survived these eruptions often engaged in a spirited debate as to whether they involved progress or a reversion to barbarism. Though a disinterested historian writing long after the event might point out that they most probably represented both, this was scant consolation to the victims at the time.

To read the signs, our age also displays these symptoms. Partly because of the nuclear threat, partly because of the modern fascination with advanced technology *per se*, and partly for deeply rooted socio-ideological reasons, weapons are being turned into toys and conventional war into an elaborate, but fundamentally pointless, game. While games can be nice while they last, in our age too there is a real danger that they will be upset by barbarians who, refusing to abide by the rules, pick up the playing-board and use it to smash the opponent's head. Let him who has ears to listen, listen: the call *Lucifer ante portas* already reverberates, and new forms of warfare are threatening to put an end to our delicate civilization.

CHAPTER 20

Real War

THOUGH ADVANCING military technology has caused the conduct of war to change and change again, it does not seem to have affected the causes of armed conflict. Over the ages, the origins of warfare have been sought in factors ranging from God to the Devil and from the "objective" pressures of economic competition to the no less "objective" destructive drives supposedly found in each person's psyche. Nor has there been, particularly during the last few decades, a lack of attempts to blame war on technology itself.

Among the very numerous publications on the subject, few claim that swords or cannon or missiles act as the cause of war in the active, scientific sense of the word. It is argued, however, that the Military Industrial Complex—a loose term comprising the totality of the institutions involved with developing, manufacturing, and manning the hardware of war—by its very nature has a vested interest in the kind of bellicose atmosphere in which it can sell its wares. Furthermore, it is argued that the presence of those wares, the fact that they are being produced and kept in a state of readiness, helps create such an atmosphere. As World War I has shown, hardware can also help generate pressures which make the diffusion of crises more difficult. In the view of many, this problem is even more acute today when the world can be destroyed within half an hour of pressing the nuclear button.

While the above statements contain a large measure of truth, they do not represent the whole story. Technology helps shape

297

man's warlike activity, and demonstrates some of the countless ways in which it does so, but from another point of view, it is man who designs and produces and uses technology for the realization of his ends. Concerning the clash between determinism and freedom, one cannot improve on the great thirteenth century sage Maimonides who said that "everything is known *and* permission is granted." There, the argument rests.

To apply this to the issue at hand, there is no necessary contradiction between a deterministic view of technology and the belief, equally well founded, that wars have always been made by men. Depending on the occasion, there were many reasons why men went to war and many cases in which those reasons were not only hopelessly interwined but ill understood by the belligerents themselves. Sometimes war broke out because people saw themselves as specially appointed to carry out some divine mission. Sometimes it was because they wanted power, or because they envied their neighbors who had more to eat, or simply because they thought it would be fun. During the twentieth century, if not before, there have also been occasions when the decision-making processes of potential belligerents were influenced by the belief that technology was working for, or against, them. For example, early in the century there were officers on the German General Staff who thought that, since war with Russia was bound to come, it had better take place before that country could complete its strategic railway net. During the infamous Hossbach Conference of 1937, Hitler is reported to have said that war had better break out in 1943–45, or else the technological advantage which Germany had acquired by being the first country to rearm would be lost. Similar arguments are sometimes heard today. When voiced in the nuclear context, they sound scary indeed.

Whatever the causes of war may be, they cannot be eliminated simply by pulverizing cities. As of today, nuclear weapons by confronting man with the likelihood of his own annihilation have put the lid on global strategic warfare, and on much conventional warfare as well. Underneath, however, the pot continues to boil. It is even possible that putting on the lid may have caused the pressure to increase, but there is no way of proving this. However that may be, there have been many groups during the last four decades who were not content with the prevailing world order. Regarding the status quo as unjust or as inimical to their interests or both, they have looked for ways to change it without necessarily

298

running the risk of nuclear escalation and destruction. There may, in addition, have been some groups whose reason for resorting to violence was precisely the hope that it might lead to the end of the world as we know it.

Over the last 40 years, wars taking place below the nuclear threshold have assumed two main forms. Among countries that did not possess nuclear weapons or were not too tightly coupled to others that do, conventional war has been in many ways as serious, and as bloody, as any in history. Here and there, as in the case of Israel against the Arabs in 1967, these conflicts have ended in resounding victories. Thanks in part to the fact that modern warfare is so horrendously expensive in hardware, however, many others tended to peter out as both sides reached the bottom of their depots and their credit. Sometimes, as along the Iranian-Iraqi border, both sides started out with some of the most advanced equipment that had been supplied to them by the main industrial countries. Subsequently they found themselves unable to maintain and operate that equipment, with the result that a reversion to more primitive forms of warfare took place, in many ways resembling those of World War I. As part of that reversion, there have also been attempts to break the deadlock by unconventional means—mustard gas, used in the war between Iran and Iraq, being a good example.

Probably more far-reaching in their combined political effects than these conventional wars, however, and certainly more numerous, were conflicts of the subconventional type variously known as insurgency, terrorism, and guerrilla warfare. Both guerrilla warfare and terrorism constitute forms of armed conflict that are as old as warfare itself. The outstanding hallmark of both is that they are waged by groups who, whatever their precise identity, are not "authorized" to resort to armed violence by the legal system in force. Such being the case, their struggle is described as "irregular." It is conducted without reference to the system and, often enough, in crass disregard of the rules which apply to other kinds of conflict. Paradoxically, it is the fact that insurgents of every kind do not share the squeamishness characteristic of so much of modern military life that enables their opponents to deny that the conflict in question amounts to war. Instead, conflict as waged at their hands is called by a variety of names, among which "guerrilla" and "terrorism" are but some of the more recent and, incidentally, complimentary ones.

Apart from, and because of, their lack of political legitimacy, guerrillas and terrorists are usually weak in numbers, organization, and in the technology at their disposal. Consequently they have always required aid from the outside, such aid being a sine qua non for victory in virtually every case. Furthermore, as much reliance was placed on political warfare and propaganda as on physical violence proper. Victory, if and when it came, was usually the result not of outright military superiority on their side but of a crisis of confidence which caused the opponent's will and/or forces to melt away. Guerrillas and terrorists engage in a struggle against forces that are militarily much stronger than themselves. Hence they generally prefer continuous harassment to a direct clash, and long-term demoralization to a single powerful blow. Unable to defend themselves against a direct assault, their means for escaping destruction are dispersion, concealment, mobility, or all of these. These, in turn, force them to operate in small groups, make do without heavy weapons, and also without a large, permanent, logistical infrastructure.

These principles, brief as they are, apply to both guerrilla warfare and terrorism. The distinction between the two is often a fine one, and indeed cynics would say that it depends solely on the side one is on. As a matter of historical fact, guerrillas have often resorted to terrorism, while successful terrorist movements sometimes undertook to wage full-scale guerrilla warfare. Nevertheless, for the purpose at hand a useful dividing-line may be drawn according to the type of geographical area in which the conflict takes place. From the days of Judaeus Maccabeus to those of Mao Tze-Dong, guerrillas have always tended to establish themselves in remote, sparsely populated, and culturally backward regions such as mountains, forests, swamps, and deserts. Finding refuge in those, they attempt to create a local and temporal superiority of force to launch their attacks, a superiority which, contrary to Robin Hood–type romantic legend, is as important in irregular warfare as in any other.

Continuous harassment and small-scale attacks having carved out a reasonably secure "base area" which the regulars are afraid to enter, the guerrillas' next move typically is to try and disrupt the main arteries of communication by erecting physical obstacles and setting ambushes. This achieved, the country's demographic centers are subjected first to sporadic attacks and, later, to attempts at a military takeover by larger guerrilla units. As innumerable examples show, from Spain during the Napoleonic period to Vietnam, even the most dedicated guerrillas are usually unable to reach the stage at which they can risk a full-scale conventional confrontation without the benefit of massive assistance from outside. Even so, the process might take many years, so many indeed that some guerrilla movements have lost patience and, moving prematurely towards "the third stage," all but invited defeat. As the examples of China in 1949 and Vietnam in 1975 show, by the time the transition was completed, often they had become almost indistinguishable from a regular army.

During most of history, and with few exceptions, the weapons and equipment used by guerrillas were not especially developed for the purpose. On the contrary, it was precisely the fact that many implements ordinarily employed for work and for hunting could also, at a pinch, be used for armed resistance that made guerrilla warfare possible in the first place. Then, too, many weapons were sufficiently simple to be manufactured almost anywhere. Hence, it is only since the rise to dominance of precision-built, factory-manufactured, crew-operated weapons in the nineteenth century that one can speak of a separate guerrilla armory. For the most part it consisted of lighter, smaller, and weaker versions of weapons used by the regular forces, and occasionally included exotic devices not used them. Such being the case, one of the principal aims of all late-nineteenth and twentieth-century guerrillas has naturally been to acquire regular-issue weapons and discard their own. In a technologically-conscious world, it was inevitable that their ability to do so should itself often be regarded as a yardstick of their success.

The technological balance between regular forces and their guerrilla opponents being what it was, the regulars normally experienced few problems in dealing with the enemy if they could bring him to battle. Rather, the outstanding problem confronting "the forces of order" has always been their inability to operate and exist in economically undeveloped areas. This weakness was determined by their sheer size as well as by the nature of pre-mechanical means of transport and communication. They were therefore compelled to split up into smaller units, which were tactically vulnerable, and had to make do without their heavy equipment in which their principal advantage lay. Under such circumstances, the victory of the antiguerrilla forces has always hinged on their ability to isolate the guerrillas and pin them down, a process that could take many different forms. Often the first step, requiring an immense superiority in manpower and resources, was to erect a human or physical barrier around the affected regions, as the British did in South Africa and the French tried to do in Algeria. This accomplished, the next stage would be to deny the guerrillas logistic support by systematically destroying or removing anything that could be of use to him, the inhabitants often included. Stripped of resources, the guerrillas' former base area could then be carved up into smaller sections. The final stage usually consisted of clearing those parts one by one, employing mobile commandos to hunt down the guerrillas and bring them to battle in their last hideouts.

The change in the geographical incidence of guerrilla warfare during the last centuries emphasizes its dependence on the balance of technological factors. Before the eighteenth-century network of roads, canals, maps, statistical information, and semaphors covered Europe, guerrilla warfare had by no means been rare on the Continent. As late as the period of the French Revolution, a guerrilla movement was able to dominate the Vendée and hold off the French Army for several years. However, except for the struggles in the underdeveloped countries of Russia and Spain— it was the fighting in Spain which gave guerrilla its name—the Vendée episode proved to be almost the last of its kind. As railways and telegraphs spread, so did the ability of governments to send large forces into previously inaccessible regions. Once there, modern means of transport allowed them to be maintained indefinitely, thus putting an end to the typical preindustrial pattern where an army would penetrate a guerrilla area during the harvest season only to abandon it afterwards. Modern forces, arriving complete with all their heavy equipment and the crew-operated weapons which more and more dominated warfare, experienced no trouble making short shrift of the guerrilla opposition, which normally did not even try to make a stand. There was, instead, a tendency for guerrilla warfare to shift towards more remote, technologically less-developed areas. Even as late as World War II the mountains of Greece and Yugoslavia, and the forests of Poland and Russia, were still sufficiently inaccessible to afford considerable scope for guerrilla attacks against German-used roads, railroads, and communications. By contrast, no guerrilla movement of any significance was able to arise and maintain itself in any of the technologically advanced Western countries overrun by the Wehrmacht, criss-crossed as they were by modern roads and telecommunications.

The end of World War II created a situation where, partly because of technological factors, successful guerrilla warfare could no longer be waged in any of the more highly developed continents. It did, however, persist in Asia, Africa, and parts of Central and South America where, in one form or another, it had long served as an instrument in the hands of dissatisfied groups who sought to rid their countries of foreign or native oppressors. As employed by countless movements of national liberation from Malaya to Angola, guerrilla warfare took advantage of the usual jungles, swamps, mountains, and deserts. As compared to previous periods, when they had usually been defeated, their victories after 1945 were resounding. In the course of two or three decades, they made a decisive contribution to the collapse of empires that had taken centuries to establish themselves. Militarily, probably the most important single factor behind these successes was the ubiquity of outside support from the USSR, which over the years must have supplied literally hundreds of self-styled revolutionary movements with arms, equipment, and advisers. Other factors included the ideological reaction against imperialism taking place among the populations of the former colonial powers themselves, and perhaps also the codification of guerrilla doctrine at the hands of such men as Mao and Giap.

A very important technological consideration involved with the success of guerrilla warfare in Third World countries, one that links up with the emergence of integrated war, is the seeming inability of modern heavy military equipment to operate effectively in complex environments. As the Americans discovered in Vietnam, this inability is of a different order from the one confronting armed forces before the Industrial Revolution. Since modern weapons are powered and tracked, and since air power in particular is able to reach almost anywhere regardless of distance or topographical obstacles, only a shortage of resources can prevent their deployment and use even in the most difficult, remote areas. Rather, the difficulty stems from another factor. Major modern weapons systems are, for the most part, designed to fight machines rather than men. This, as well as their very power, range, and speed, makes them dependent on technological (electronic) means for surveillance, reconnaissance, target acquisition, range finding, gunlaying, damage assessment, and so on.

As of this writing, the sensors and computers to which these tasks are entrusted are for the most part good enough only for the simple environments presented by air and sea, though even there the use of weapons that fire indiscriminately at all comers is by no means without problems. They are decidedly not good enough for the extremely complex environment in which guerrilla warfare takes place; they are not sufficiently sophisticated to make out men from their background and friends from foes. Moreover, many of them are also easily vulnerable to rather simple countermeasures making use of the principles on which they themselves operate, a good example being the Viet Cong's use of urine-soaked rags in order to mislead the "people sniffer" developed by the Americans. Generally speaking, masking or modifying or faking the signature of a thing may well be easier than making the thing itself, and is certainly cheaper; hence it is questionable whether the sensors can ever be made sophisticated enough.

Another discovery that the Americans made in Vietnam, the Soviets in Afghanistan, and the Israelis in Lebanon, was that many modern weapons tend to act as parasols. Whereas their own electronically-supported firepower is wasted in antiguerrilla operations, they allow guerrilla warfare and terrorism to take place below the sophistication threshold that they themselves represent. Either the "elusive" targets (a favorite phrase of the Americans in Vietnam) are not hit at all, or hitting them inflicts such tremendous damage on the environment and on the civilian population as to render the entire exercise politically counterproductive. The regular forces are, of course, free to discard their heavy equipment and attempt to meet the enemy on equal terms. In that case, however, they are likely to forfeit much of their technological superiority, particularly if the guerrillas are not limited to home-manufactured weapons but have access to an outside source of supply.

Guerrilla warfare, to sum up, relies on harassment and attrition to achieve its goals. The guerrillas establish themselves in geographically remote, topographically difficult, regions where regular armies find the going hard and where their heavy weapons lose most of their effectiveness. Nevertheless, guerrilla operations resemble other forms of war in that they aim at achieving a superiority of force, however limited in duration and space. It stands to reason that, as urbanization and industrialization spread, the number of places where successful guerrilla warfare may be waged will decline, and indeed in many countries the guerrillas themselves seem to be perfectly aware of this.

Assuming such a development does take place, the other form of war left to those not content with the existing order of things will be terrorism. Terrorism resembles guerrilla warfare in many ways. The main difference between the two is that terrorists mount most of their operations in crowded demographic centers, rather than in remote rural areas. Such being the case, they cannot hope to attain even the limited local and temporary superiority often associated with successful guerrilla warfare. Instead, concealment and anonymity count for everything, a factor which terrorism shares with ordinary crime and which indeed constitutes one reason why the two are so often held to be indistinguishable.

Unlike guerrillas, who by definition conduct most of their operations in remote and backward areas, terrorists who are present in the main urban centers can attack the most critical targets, from the chief of state and his principal assistants downward. As countless episodes of tyrannicide show, this method has a long and honorable history, nor is it by any means dead today. However, in the most advanced countries many terrorist acts have been rendered futile by the fact that complex organizations, and the vast technological systems on which they rest, can absorb isolated attacks. Indeed, one of the most important hallmarks of modernity is precisely the fact that political and other organizations are no longer dependent on a single person and that, consequently, little can be accomplished by eliminating him. As countless examples from the assassination of Kennedy to that of Anwar Sadat show, in today's developed world a leader who is killed or incapacitated will promptly be replaced by another, and indeed one good index of modernity is precisely the extent to which this is the case. The new leader, hoping to escape his predecessor's fate, will persecute the terrorists by every means at his disposal.

Recognizing odds against successful terrorist attacks against prominent individuals in the modern world, from the second half of the nineteenth century terrorists began to switch over increasingly to another strategy. The aim now is not to achieve victory by a single blow against the center of government, but rather to try and disrupt normal functioning by a prolonged series of operations, creating an atmosphere of widespread uncertainty and fear. Sometimes, as in late nineteenth-century Russia, the impotence of the government was to be demonstrated by spectacular acts of terrorism aimed at its principal officials. As these tend to be heavily guarded, however, terrorism has very often gone in for indiscriminate killing, and indeed entire ideologies have been constructed by Bakunin and others to prove why anybody who is not actively on the terrorists' side deserves to die.

If only because an ideology that seeks to destroy everything can never attract a mass following, terrorist movements throughout history have tended to consist of a very small core of active members surrounded, perhaps, by a larger one of sympathizers. Since concealment is an absolute prerequisite, it goes far to determine their choice of technology. Even more than the guerrilla, the terrorist is limited to weapons which are small, light, and easily hidden from the authorities' eye. During the millenia before 1600 the dagger was by far the most popular of these weapons, as in the case of the Sicarii who are mentioned by Josephus and who were named after it. During the seventeenth century, the pistol and the bomb, the former easily acquired and the latter easily manufactured, joined the list of terrorist weapons. Even so, for another 300 years that list remained comparatively short. It was only during the twentieth century that technological advances made available a whole series of small, but extremely powerful, devices. Terrorist arsenals around the world now commonly include submachine guns, guided and unguided man-portable antitank and antiaircraft missiles with hollow-charge warheads; wire- and radio-controlled bombs that can be operated at a distance, and a variety of explosive materials that are stable, can be easily detonated, do not give off an electromagnetic signature, and can be molded into any desirable shape.

Though these are highly advanced weapons, many of them represent regular army issue. Provided a state can be found to back the terrorists and sponsor their actions, they are thus easily obtainable. The terrorists should also be able to make use of the normal means of communication and transportation available to any modern society. Since terrorist movements often count educated, technically qualified people among their members, they are able to freely employ technologies ranging from the telephone to the motor car to coordinate their actions, mount attacks, and make good their escape. Though this is not primarily a question of technology, they have also benefitted from the widespread coverage which Western media in particular often give to their operations. By enabling the terrorists to appear much stronger than they really are, the media often find themselves working *pour le roi de Prusse,* as the saying went.

A resurgence of terrorism, much of it state-sponsored, in advanced societies during the late 1960s, has expressed itself in countless attacks resulting in the death of thousands. The problem has been exacerbated by the fact that modern life abounds in situations, many of them created or made possible by technology, where large numbers of people are crowded together in narrow spaces without any possibility for self defense or escape. Under such circumstances a single hit, lucky or unlucky depending on one's point of view, may easily result in casualties wholly out of proportion to the number of terrorists. For example, a single portable antiaircraft missile fired at a jumbo jet during the plane's ascent or descent—which must take place along predictable routes—may kill as many as 400 people; in the previous century, this kind of lethal potential could only form the subject of wishful dreams by nihilists and anarchists.

Though modern technology may, in this way, have rendered present-day society more vulnerable to acts of terrorism than their predecessors, it is far from certain that this is also true in other ways. Much has been written concerning the dependence of advanced technological civilization on focal points such as telephone exchanges, power plants, fuel depots, and the like, the elimination of which would lead to dire consequences out of all proportion to the direct physical damage involved. There have also been scenarios, some of them written by experts, describing terrorists introducing poison gas into the air-conditioning systems of skyscrapers, and bacteria into the water supplies of cities. There is some merit to the view that sees large-scale technological systems as being particularly vulnerable to terrorism, especially those that are characterized by extreme specialization and interdependence. The mere fact that, to our knowledge, they have not yet been targeted does not mean that they never can or will be.

On the other hand, it might be argued that the outstanding characteristic of modern technological systems is precisely the presence of multiple, redundant, communication and transport networks. This makes it a comparatively easy matter to summon aid to the injured points, erect bypasses around them, and find substitutes for them. That great damage may be done by striking at well-chosen pinpoint targets is undeniable. However, nothing better illustrates the difficulty of disabling a modern country by such methods than the World War II Allied air campaign against the German economy, a campaign, incidentally, that was denounced as "terroristic" by Goebbels. At that time it took several years and millions of tons of bombs for the largest air forces that ever existed to bring about a state of collapse. The chances that a small terrorist group can achieve large-scale disruption by such means are therefore virtually nil.

On the whole, it would not be true to say that a society's widespread use of high-tech weapons and other devices helps the terrorists more than it does their opponents. On the contrary, antiterrorist squads should be able to make short shrift of their opponents, by employing technologies similar to those of the terrorists as well as specially developed devices such as stun grenades, incapacitating gasses, and remotely controlled robots for bomb-disposal work. Several conditions, however, must be met for this to be possible. There must be no reluctance to employ the normal surveillance apparatus of the modern state. The armed forces must be willing to do away not only with some, but possibly even with the majority of their favorite gadgets which are too powerful to use in what now constitute the majority of real wars. They must have appropriate political backing and legal freedom of action. Moreover, the public must be ready to accept some inconveniencies and recognize that, in some kinds of operations such as the freeing of hostages, some casualties may be inevitable and acceptable. Last but not least, some of our most cherished ideas as to what war is all about, and the things that are permissible in it, will have to go by the board. For reasons which have more to do with ideology than with technology, these conditions for successful antiterrorist warfare are seldom available in the West. They seem, however, to exist in Eastern Bloc states, which as of today have managed to hold terrorism within very narrow bounds.

The picture may change, however, once we contemplate the prospect that, given the inexorable proliferation of nuclear weapons and of nuclear expertise, sooner or later a terrorist group will either succeed in acquiring a nuclear bomb or in producing one of their own. That any government will take the risk of handing over a bomb to a group of state-sponsored terrorists is very unlikely but not completely out of the question. Equally, it is conceivable that one of the tens of thousands of nuclear warheads—many of them quite small—now in storage around the world will fall into unauthorized hands and the safety mechanisms with which they are ordinarily provided will be unlocked or neutralized. Much has been made of the hazards of stealing fissionable material and of the difficulties of constructing an operational device small enough to be concealed, and certainly those problems should not be underestimated. However, they do not necessarily appear insuperable. From a technical point of view, the terrorist use of nuclear weapons (or at least a plausible terrorist threat of using them) cannot be entirely discounted.

Assuming a terrorist group has got hold of a nuclear device, it might be used either for blackmail or to cause outright destruction on an immense scale. Nuclear blackmail (like the use of chemical and bacteriological weapons for similar purposes) as an instrument of terrorist policy would make sense only if the demands made were on a truly outrageous scale, and if the granting of those demands could not subsequently be reversed; two conflicting requirements which, between them, make that possibility appear rather unlikely. It is conceivable, however, that the bomb will be employed by an individual, or group, whose purpose is not to achieve some positive aim but simply to wreak havoc for its own sake. In the past there have been ideologies, some of them quite coherent, aimed at justifying precisely this goal. In the form of a nuclear device, they may now acquire the means for turning their dream into horrible reality.

Regardless of the state of technological development reached by society at large, it must be recognized that there exist today, and probably will continue to exist in the future, some states, some groups, and some people who are not content with the existing state of affairs or, indeed, with any conceivable state of affairs. Determined to use force in order to change the status quo, they will employ whatever means are available at the time. Even assuming that such people, such groups, and such states can forever be deterred from the full-scale strategic use of nuclear weapons in pursuing their ends, there is no lack of scenarios for the limited-theater use of nuclear weapons, small and large. Even assuming no such use takes place, and that the balance of terror will continue to spread as it has during the last few decades, it will presumably always be possible to find some places and circumstances where, albeit at perhaps great risk of escalation, conventional warfare can proceed as of yore. Even should this not be the case, guerrilla warfare and terrorism in particular will continue to provide instruments which, though not always very effective in achieving political ends, have repeatedly proved themselves quite capable of tearing apart entire societies.

While there is no doubt that advancing technology will continue to help alter the shape of war, there unfortunately appears to be little prospect that it will bring war to an end. Although the power of modern weapons may cause some forms of war to become extinct, others will take their place. The people who resort to these forms, particularly terrorists, are likely to find themselves aided rather than obstructed by the extraordinary power of much modern military technology which is not only too powerful to use but designed for make-believe war. Nor, presumably, will the terrorists be very impressed by any of the large inventory of dirty epithets hurled at them. Whatever form it takes, and whatever technology it employs, sooner or later war will break through the rules. It will remain what it has always been, namely a horrible, messy affair in which some people are killed and others mutilated. This is a fact that, for all the best efforts of our military industrial establishment, will not be altered by any kind of technology and with which, accordingly, society will have to come to terms.

Conclusions: The Logic of Technology and of War

LIKE A WALK in a garden where every path returns to the entry gate, the end of this book leads us back to its beginning. Our starting premise was that war is permeated by technology to the point that *every* single element is either governed by or at least linked to it. The causes that lead to wars and the goals for which they are fought; the blows with which campaigns open and the victories with which they (sometimes) end; the relationship between the armed forces and the societies that they serve; planning and preparation and execution and evaluation; operations and intelligence and organization and supply; objectives and methods and capabilities and missions; command and leadership and strategy and tactics; and even the very conceptual framework adopted by our brains in order to think about war and its conduct—all are and will be affected by technology.

If it is true that every part of war is touched by technology, it is no less true that every part of technology affects war. Indeed, technologies not ordinarily regarded as military, such as roads, vehicles, communications, and timekeepers, have done as much as weapons and weapons systems to shape the face of war. These technologies govern, and may indeed constitute, what we have called the infrastructure of war. That infrastructure goes a long way to dictate the character of organization, logistics, intelligence, strategy, even the concept of battle itself. Without it the conduct of armed conflict would be impossible, and its very existence, inconceivable.

Unlike these technologies, to date the effect of the vast majority of weapons has been limited mainly to tactics. Those weapons that can impact on strategy—namely, nuclear devices—are for that very reason too powerful to use; they are also well on the way to turning war itself into an exercise in make-believe, a game. Other things being equal, in the "conventional" world the importance of military versus nonmilitary technologies depends on the length of the conflict. The shorter the war, the greater the importance of weapons and weapons systems. The longer it is, the greater the role of military activities other than fighting pure and simple, and the greater the role of technologies that impinge on these activities or govern them.

However, even with the inclusion of nonmilitary devices of every kind, the scope of technology is not yet exhausted. As is already evident from common phrases such as "the fruits of" and "the products of," there is more to technology than hardware alone. Technology is perhaps best understood as an abstract system of knowledge, an attitude towards life and a method for solving its problems. There is no doubt that, just as the earliest Stone Age civilizations already had a technology of sorts, the conduct of war has always involved the use of technical devices. However, the idea that war is primarily a question of technology and so ought to be waged by technicians, that it should employ technologically-derived methods, and must seek victory by acquiring and maintaining technological superiority—that idea has been shown to be neither self-evident, nor necessarily correct, nor even very old. Nevertheless, the rise of this idea is one of the most significant developments brought about by the advance of technology since the Industrial Revolution; when taken to extremes, it can also be one of the most dangerous.

Finally, and peace to those who profess to look at the world in "rational" terms, it simply is not true that the impact of technology on war can be measured entirely in terms of the physical work it does. Rather, the relationship between the two involves additional—nonutilitarian and nonfunctional—aspects. Many of these are somewhat esoteric, and they may not be subject to an analysis based on calculations pertaining to cost-effectiveness or bang divided by buck. Nevertheless, they play a paramount role in an activity so permeated by psychological factors as war. Ignoring them, one runs the risk not only of a complete misunderstanding of the role played by technology in war but, even worse, the risk of defeat.

Given the sheer number of the points of contact between technology and war enumerated in the previous paragraphs, it is exceedingly difficult to discern long-time trends, the more so because a proper understanding of technology consists precisely of the realization that many of the things it can do to, and in the service of, war are connected, interacting, and interchangeable. To enumerate but a few simple examples of this truism, everybody knows that the various forms of transport may, up to a point, be substituted for each other. Similarly the power of many weapons can be traded against their accuracy, their range, their rate of fire, and even their moral effect. Mobility, dispersion, concealment, and armor can all be employed for protection. Mobility, in turn, may itself consist of speed, acceleration, range, cross-terrain capability, armor (which provides mobility where it matters, i.e., under fire), and other factors. Whatever the problem one confronts, there is almost always more than one way to attain a predetermined goal. For this reason, too, very often the same technology in different hands can be used in very different ways.

Though historical hindsight often reveals the "objective" pressures towards the adoption of this or that solution, there is no question that the interaction of technology and war at any given time has been as much the product of the arbitrary and the accidental as it was of the inevitable and the necessary. As a result, it is sometimes impossible to avoid the feeling that, the better and the more comprehensive one's understanding of that interaction, the more difficult it becomes to identify trends and make predictions.

Granting our inability to predict the form future developments will take, can we at least create a framework for thinking about it? Is it possible to identify in war some elements which are impervious to technological change, and that consequently remain constant over the ages? To answer this critical question, let us turn to the first paragraph on the first page in the first chapter of Clausewitz's *On War*. Here, armed conflict is defined as an act of violence where each side is out to destroy the other. This makes it into the province of hardship and of suffering, of stress and fear and pain and death. Hence its conduct, though it does involve an important intellectual element, is ultimately a question of nothing so much as the ability to cope with those factors.

When the chips are down, there is no "rational" calculation in the world capable of causing the individual to lay down *his* life. On both the individual and collective levels, war is therefore primarily an affair of the heart. It is dominated by such irrational factors as resolution and courage, honor and duty and loyalty and sacrifice of self. When everything is said and done, none of these have anything to do with technology, whether primitive or sophisticated. So it was at a time when war was limited to face to face clashes between hide-clad, club-armed cavemen, 50,000 years ago; so it will be when laser-firing flying saucers permit it to be fought over interplanetary distances 100, or 500, or 1,000 years hence.

Another aspect of warfare that technology has not changed nor will change nor can change is its functions. It is possible to argue about the exact nature of those functions; one pundit will distinguish between striking, protecting, and moving, whereas another will extend the list to include fixing or holding the enemy, intelligence gathering, communicating, supplying, and so on. Whatever the list we care to select, the critical point is that they are rooted in the very nature of war and thus immune to technology and the kind of change which it effects. Supplying (consisting, say, of gathering, registering, storing, transporting, and distributing) and communicating; gathering intelligence and securing against surprise attack; fixing the enemy, maneuvering, protecting and striking; each and every one of these were just as vital to a neolithic horde as they are to a modern army.

Finally, it seems that the logic of conflict, that logic which in turn dictates the essential principles of its conduct, is likewise immutable and immune to any amount of technology that is applied to or used for it. To explain the way technology relates to the logic of war, and hence should be used in it, is the last task of the present volume; and, quite possibly, it is the most important one.

Technology, then, to the extent that it is rooted in physical nature, might be described as linear. However primitive or sophisticated the hardware of which it consists, its ability to function depends on the existence of an "objective" physical world. In this world two plus two are four and results are directly proportional to the amount of effort applied. Furthermore, it is the world of again and again and again. In it, no matter how often a thing is tried and an action carried out, the same cause will always produce the same effect. Everything else being equal we expect what has worked yesterday to work today, tomorrow, and always.

Beginning in prehistoric times, it was this uniform, repetitive, predictable, character of physical nature which made technology possible. The only reason why even a simple technology, a hammer for example, can be constructed is because we are certain that its effect on a nail will always be the same; had this not been the case neither a hammer, nor any other tool, nor any machine, would even be conceivable. The division of work into tasks, and the construction of separate tools for each of them, constitutes the first step towards specialization. On this technological progress is largely, though not exclusively, based.

With work divided into many different tasks, and increasingly as civilization advanced, specialization in turn led to integration. The more numerous and differentiated the available tools or machines, the more important it became to sequence, dovetail, mesh, and synchronize every part with every other in order to create a system. Accordingly, from the time of the pyramids on, the most powerful technological enterprises have been those that are streamlined. In them, a perfect one-to-one fit is created between means and ends. Slack and waste must be eliminated, redundancy put aside, perfect timing and coordination achieved. Coordination hinges on the ability of management to predict the behavior of each and every part on the system. Ultimately what is involved is nothing less than an attempt to insulate the system from uncertainty by creating a perfectly controlled and perfectly stable— since change means disruption—artificial world. The result of this effort, however incomplete it may be in practice, is known under the name of efficiency, a quality that in a large steel manufacturing factory, or petrochemical plant, would be equated with effectiveness.

Thus the ideas which underlay technology, ideas so basic to our entire modern way of thought that we seldom even bother to take them for granted, might be summed up as a one-to-one link between cause and effect, repetitiveness, specialization, integration, certainty, and finally efficiency. To the extent that war consists in large part of the generation and application of brute destructive force, these methods are appropriate to it. Their objective would be, for example, to generate the greatest amount of firepower of which a battery is capable, or the largest number of sorties that an aircraft carrier can support. Contrary to the impression one might gain from much of the current technologically oriented literature, however, there is much more to war than simply applying force to targets. Nor is it true that the side with the greater force at its disposal always wins.

War, far from being an exercise in technology, is primarily a contest between two belligerents. The principles of its conduct are, accordingly, entirely different. As in any game from football to chess, each contestant is possessed of an independent will and can only be controlled by the other to a very limited extent. With each side seeking to achieve his objectives while preventing the other from doing the same, war consists in large part of an interplay of double-crosses. The underlying logic of war is, therefore, not linear but paradoxical. The same action will not always lead to the same result. The opposite, indeed, is closer to the truth. Given an opponent who is capable of learning, a very real danger exists that an action will not succeed twice *because* it has succeeded once.

Moreover, if the outcome of a conflict is predetermined it need never be fought. Not only is uncertainty inherent in war, as Clausewitz is at pains to point out, but it forms a necessary part of war and can be eliminated only at the cost of turning conflict into a charade. Accordingly, military standards of excellence are not only different from technological ones but constitute a class of their own. Although any commander worthy of the name will strive to maximize his knowledge concerning his own forces, the environment, and the enemy as a matter of course, ultimately that is not what war is all about. Rather, in armed conflict no success is possible—or even conceivable—which is not grounded in an ability to tolerate uncertainty, cope with it, and make use of it.

To illustrate the way in which these basic characteristics affect the harnessing of technology to the service of war, consider a logistic system operating in support of some large-scale military campaign. If efficiency were all that mattered, and if the goal were simply that of achieving the greatest throughflow of supplies (or generating the greatest firepower, or whatever) at the least cost in manpower, depots, vehicles, and so forth, then it is obvious that the system should be organized along technological principles.

It should consist of highly efficient components, which by and large means specialized components. It should not be allowed to contain any redundant or idle resources, and it should be subject to strict centralized direction, the objective of which is to mesh all the different components and make them work together with a minimum of waste and friction.

When fighting a war, however, such a solution would be useless or worse. The more centralized the system, the greater the danger that it will be paralyzed if enemy action causes the directing brain to be eliminated or communications with it to be impaired. The tighter the gearing of its various elements, the greater the likelihood that the destruction of any one of them will reverberate throughout the system and bring it to a halt. The more specialized those elements, the less their capability of taking over from each other. The kind of logic that underlies, for example, the design of an automobile factory is only relevant to that part of the conduct of war which consists of mobilizing and deploying and applying brute force. If, however, the logistic system in question is not to be hopelessly fragile and liable to catastrophic breakdown; if it is to function under changing circumstances and be capable of switching from one objective to the next; if, in short, it is to be capable of coping with the uncertainty that is the result of enemy action and, as such, inherent in war—in that case a certain amount of redundancy, slack, and waste must not only be tolerated but deliberately built in.

Moving from the supporting services to the actual interaction with the enemy, war differs from the physical world which constitutes the foundation of technology precisely in that two plus two do not necessarily equal four, and that the shortest line between two points is not necessarily a straight one. On the contrary, the more evenly balanced the opponents the more important it is to take the line least expected. That line may well prove to be not the shortest but the longest one between two points; the long line becoming the shortest because the enemy considers it the longest, and *vice versa*. This is not to say that "technological" considerations such as the length of the road, the difficulty of the terrain, and so on do not play an important role in war, much less that no such thing as "objective" reality exists. What it does mean, however, is that in a direct contest such as war (and many kinds of game) the "objective" length of the route often counts for little. What matters, instead, is the ability to cheat and deceive, to turn the expected into the unexpected and the unexpected into the expected. Victory is achieved by appearing like a thunderbolt at the right time and place, taking the enemy by surprise.

Contrary to the impression that one might get from many works on intelligence, cheating and deceiving do not come free of charge. Concealing one's intentions may mean that the advance has to be prepared at night, at the cost of a considerable reduction in efficiency and at greatly increased risk of disorder. Carrying out a feint on a scale sufficiently large to be noticed by the enemy will almost certainly involve a logistic outlay in supporting forces away from the principal combat area. Obtaining surprise often entails sending troops into terrain for which they are not really suited, a good example being the Germans in 1940 when they passed their armored forces through the Ardennes Forest. As if to highlight the nature of the paradox, the most important single means normally used for achieving the kind of coordination on which advanced technology is based—namely, communication— may have to be the first to go. Enforced radio silence is an extreme but historically common method of doing this.

Whichever way one looks at it, the conclusion is always the same. The conduct of war against an intelligent opponent differs from the management of a large-scale technological system precisely in that efficiency and effectiveness, the concentration and employment of the greatest possible force on the one hand and military success on the other, are not the same even in the short run, or (one might well argue) particularly in the short run. On the contrary, there are any number of occasions when military effectiveness is not only compatible with diminished efficiency but positively demands that it be sacrificed.

Much the same consideration, namely, the need to balance technological efficiency *against* military effectiveness, also applies to some of the other methods by which efficiency is achieved. Thus, cost/benefit calculations may very well indicate the superiority of a single large platform (such as a battleship) to several smaller ones because, ton for ton, crewmember for crewmember, and dollar for dollar it can put more tons of high explosive on a target in a given period of time. In war, however, this advantage has to be balanced against the fact that putting all one's eggs in a single basket is dangerous, is likely to lead to a loss of flexibility, and may even given rise to the kind of timidity which, often in history, has prevented precisely the mightiest platforms available from being used at all. Or take that other mainstay of technological efficiency, standardization. However desirable and even necessary it may be from the point of view of efficiency, in war its result is to make things easy for the enemy. The amount of uncertainty with which he is confronted is diminished. He is put in a position where resources and attention can be focused on countering a single threat, instead of many different ones. Finally, he is spared the dilemma of having to do two contradictory things at once, which probably represents the most important single way of using technology (or anything else) in order to obtain victory in war.

Since technology and war operate on a logic which is not only different but actually opposed, nothing is less conducive to victory in war than to wage it on technological principles—an approach which, in the name of operations research, systems analysis, or cost/benefit calculation (or obtaining the greatest bang for the buck), treats war merely as an extension of technology. This is not to say that we should start fighting war with our bare hands (although that might be desirable if diminishing its destructiveness were the objective), nor that a country that wishes to retain its military power can in any way afford to neglect technology and the methods that are most appropriate for thinking about it. It does mean, however, that the problem of making technology serve the goals of war is more complex than it is commonly thought to be. The key is that efficiency, far from being simply conducive to effectiveness, can act as its opposite. Hence—and this is a point which cannot be overemphasized—the successful use of technology in war very often means that there is a price to be paid in terms of deliberately *diminishing* efficiency.

Since technology and war operate on a logic which is not only different but actually opposed, the very concept of "technological superiority" is somewhat misleading when applied within the context of the war. It was not the technical sophistication of the Swiss pike that defeated the Burgundian knights, but rather the way it meshed with the weapons used by the knights at Laupen, Sempach, and Granson. It was not the intrinsic superiority of the longbow that won the battle of Crécy, but rather the way in which it interacted with the equipment employed by the French on that day and at that place. Using technology to acquire greater range, greater firepower, greater mobility, greater protection, greater whatever, is very important and may be critical. Ultimately, however, it is less critical and less important than achieving a close "fit" between one's own technology and that which is fielded by the enemy. The best tactics, it is said, are the so-called *Flaechen-und Luecken* (solids and gaps) methods which, although they received their current name from the Germans, are as old as history and are based on bypassing the enemy's strengths while exploiting the weaknesses in between. Similarly, the best military technology is not that which is "superior" in some absolute sense. Rather it is that which "masks" or neutralizes the other side's strengths, even as it exploits his weaknesses.

The common habit of referring to technology in terms of its capabilities may, when applied within the context of war, do more harm than good. This is not to deny the very great importance of the things that technology can do in war. However, when everything is said and done, those which it *cannot* do are probably even more important. Here we must seek victory, and here it will take place—though not necessarily in our favor—even when we do not. A good analogy is a pair of cogwheels, where achieving a perfect fit depends not merely on the shape of the teeth but also, and to an equal extent, on that of the spaces which separate them.

In sum, since technology and war operate on a logic which is not only different but actually opposed, the conceptual framework that is useful, even vital, for dealing with the one should not be allowed to interfere with the other. In an age when military budgets, military attitudes, and what passes for military thought often seem centered on technological considerations and even obsessed by them, this distinction is of vital importance. In the words of a famous Hebrew proverb:

The deed accomplishes, what thought began.

BIBLIOGRAPHICAL ESSAY

General

Surprising as the fact may appear to modern eyes, none of the classical military writers paid much attention to technology. Neither Sun Tzu in his *Art of War*, nor Thucydides in his *History of the Pelopponesian War*, nor Caesar in his *Commentaries*, give the subject more than a fleeting mention. The same is true in regard to Machiavelli in *The Art of War*, and de Saxe in *Dreams about the Art of War;* both of them do, however, come up with some quaint ideas. Neither Jomini in his *Summary of Great Operations of War* nor Clausewitz in *On War* included weapons among the decisive factors in war, let alone among those that affect its principles and nature. Von Moltke in his collected *Military Writings,** like Schlieffen in his collected *Works,** has interesting things to say concerning individual technologies such as railways and rifles, but nothing on technology as such. Foch only gave technology a brief mention in the preface to the fifth, and last, edition of *The Principles of War* (1918). Between the wars, Ludendorff in *Total War* (1936) argued that modern technology would necessarily cause all future wars to resemble the one in which he had exercised supreme command. Taking the opposite tack, B. H. Liddell Hart in his many publications proposed to use technology in order to avoid another total war; he was behind the times, however, in that he still thought of technology as consisting of tanks and vehicles and aircraft rather than of much more extensive systems of development, production, transportation, maintenance, and communication.

In the military "classics," then, little of value can be found on the subject. The one exception is J. F. C. Fuller, whose brilliant if idiosyncratic study, *Armaments and History*, was published in 1945, just too soon for

---

*NOTE: with very few exceptions, the present bibliographical essay includes only works available in English. Where this is not the case the translation is my own; such works have been marked with an asterisk.

321

him to take note of nuclear weapons in anything but a highly pertinent footnote. Fuller's thesis can be summed up in two points. First, in the modern world, no army can survive unless it keeps technologically abreast. Second, "weapons, if only the right ones can be found, form ninety nine percent of victory." The first of these points has become trite, whereas one of the aims of the present book has been precisely to examine the truth of the second. Nevertheless, as a history of the interaction of war with technology, politics, economics, social development, religion, literature, culture, and many other factors, his work remains in a class of its own.

Among general works on technology and war written in the postwar era, B. Brodie in *From X Bow to H-Bomb* (1962, revised edition 1973) is nice. The year 1973 also saw the publication of a new and updated edition of T. Wintringham, *Weapons and Tactics*, which, thought-provoking though it was at its first appearance in 1943, has now become dated. J. Weller, *Weapons and Tactics: Hastings to Berlin* (1973), and T. N. Dupuy, in *The Evolution of Weapons and Warfare* (1981), are straightforward; the latter makes an attempt at quantifying the effect of weapons on tactics. Finally, W. H. McNeill, *The Pursuit of Power; Technology, Armed Force and Society* (1982), has made a heroic attempt to link together technological, military, social, economic, and cultural themes under the rubric of command economies versus free ones, to my mind not altogether with success.

As is frequently the case, Marxist and Soviet writings on technology and war diverge considerably from their Western counterparts. Friedrich Engels was one of the first writers to grasp the importance of the problem; his *Anti Duehring* of 1878, where he suggested that war was decided primarily by industrial prowess and only secondarily by the generals' genius, was far ahead of its time. Trotsky in his collected *Military Writings* (English edition 1969, but dating mostly to the years before 1930) thought deeply about what technology does and does not do to war, but did not formulate a comprehensive theory of the subject. To Stalin the quality of weapons and equipment was one of the "five permanently operating factors" in war. During the years since 1945, two of the most comprehensive attempts to deal with the question have come from Soviet pens: these are G. I. Pokrovsky, *Science and Technology in Contemporary War* (1957), and N. A. Lomov, ed., *The Revolution in Military Affairs* (1973). Unlike the majority of postwar Western writers, both of these men were high-ranking officers. Unlike the majority of postwar Western writers, too, they have much to say not only on the latest developments in weapons but, more pertinent to this part of our bibliographical essay, concerning the politico-socio-economic foundations of war and the role of technology among those foundations.

To sum up this part of the survey, it is no accident that the majority of general works on the subject belong to the post-1945 era, when its critical importance was becoming obvious to all. Nevertheless, a systematic, comprehensive theory of the relationship between technology and war is still not available. It would be highly desirable, and writing it would present an appropriate challenge for a new Clausewitz.

Part I
The Age of Tools, from Earliest Times to 1500 A.D.

Chapter 1. Field Warfare

Information on the weapons in use in the ancient Middle East may be found in Y. Yadin, *The Art of Warfare in the Lands of the Bible* (1963), a rather popular work by an archeologist who also happened to serve as Israel's second chief of staff. Equally popular is A. Ferril, *The Origins of War* (1985), which argues that no important changes took place in war from Gaugamela to Waterloo. There is no comprehensive study, in English, of ancient military technology, but see chapter "Military Technology" in C. Singer *et al.*, *A History of Technology* (1956), vol. ii. Many readers may find A. M. Snodgrass, *Arms and Armor of the Greeks* (1967), too technical, and the same is true for M. C. Bishop, ed., *The Production and Distribution of Roman Military Equipment* (1985). However, the last-named book contains an excellent bibliography.

Much the best general introduction to medieval warfare is Ph. Contamine, *War in the Middle Ages* (English trans., 1984), which has several chapters on equipment; see also J. F. Verbruggen, *The Art of Warfare in Western Europe during the Middle Ages* (1977). C. H. Ashdown, *Armor and Weapons in the Middle Ages* (1925), is comprehensive but old. Medieval military archery is dealt with by S. T. Pope, *Bows and Arrows* (1962). A broader perspective is taken by R. Hardy, *The Longbow, a Social and Military History* (1976). The crossbow is the subject of R. Payne-Gallwey, *The Crossbow, Medieval and Modern, Military and Sporting, its Construction, History, and Management, with a Treatise on the Balista and Catapult of the Ancient World* (London, 1903, reprinted 1981), which tells you everything you always wanted to know about that weapon and never dared to ask.

Chapter 2. Siege Warfare

S. Toy, *A History of Fortification from 3000 B.C. to A.D. 1700* (1955) is popular but apparently the only general study of the subject. Yadin's work, mentioned earlier, also has considerable information on ancient Middle Eastern, particularly Assyrian, siege techniques. The earliest known stone fortifications surrounding a city are described in M. Wheeler, *Walls of Jericho* (1956). On fortification in the classical world, see F. E. Winter, *Greek Fortifications* (1971), and A. W. Lawrence, *Greek Aims in Fortification,* (1979); E. N. Luttwak, *The Grand Strategy of the Roman Empire* (1976), is very good on the concepts underlying the Roman *limes.* For ballistae, catapults, etc., see the highly technical works by E. M. Marsden, *Greek and Roman Artillery* (1975), and J. G. Landels, *Engineering in the Ancient World* (1978); however, there seems to be no comprehensive study of siege warfare as such.

W. Anderson, *Castles of the Middle Ages* (1970), is a good introduction to the subject. Ph. Warner, *Sieges of the Middle Ages,* (1968), is weak. R. C. Smail, *Crusading Warfare 1097–1193* (1956, reprinted 1972), ch. 7, has much to say on the construction of Crusader castles and even more concerning the role that they played in strategy.

Chapter 3. The Infrastructure of War

On early methods of transport, see M. A. Littauer, *Wheeled Vehicles and Ridden Animals in the Ancient Near East* (1979). Little has been written on the logistic problems of armed forces before mechanical transport, but a good start may be found in D. W. Engels, *Alexander the Great and the Logistics of the Macedonian Army* (1978), ch. 1. G. Perjes, "Army Provisioning, Logistics and Strategy in the Second Half of the 17th Century," in *Acta Historica Academiae Scientiarium Hungaricae,* No. 16 (1966), and M. van Creveld, *Supplying War, Logistics from Wallenstein to Patton* (1977), ch. 1. The reader who is not a specialist will find K. D. White, *Greek and Roman Technology* (1984), enlightening on such aspects of classical technology as power sources, civil engineering, surveying, and land transport, including both vehicles and roads. Medieval vehicles, horseshoes, saddles, and much else are discussed in L. White, *Medieval Technology and Social Change* (1961), a provocative work; on power resources see the equally interesting study by J. Gimpel, *The Medieval Machine* (French edition 1976, first English edition 1977), ch. 1.

On cartography in the ancient world see O. Dilke, *Greek and Roman Maps* (1985), which is up-to-date and authoritative; also the popular but enlightening work by P. D. A. Harvey, *The History of Topographical Maps* (1980). The "information base" available to Roman emperors for military and other purposes is discussed by F. Millar, "Emperors, Frontiers and Foreign Relations, 31 B.C. to A.D. 378," *Britannia,* vol. xiii, 1982, pp. 1–23. A. Gurewich, *Categories of Medieval Culture* (English trans. 1985), is very strong on concepts of time and space but has comparatively little to say about the way in which they were related to, and determined by, technology.

Chapter 4. Naval Warfare

There are many works on ancient naval warfare, of which the most comprehensive is probably W. L. Rodgers, *Greek and Roman Naval Warfare* (1937). This should be read together with W. W. Tarn, *Hellenistic Military and Naval Developments* (1930), as well as V. Foley and W. Soedel, "Ancient Oared Warships," *Scientific American,* 244, April 1981, pp. 148–63, which is up-to-date. Arab naval power is the subject of a book by D. Ayalon, *The Mamluks and Naval Power* (1975). R. W. Unger, *The Ship in the Medieval Economy* (1980), is excellent and crammed with information on technical aspects in a period when civilian and military shipping were hardly differentiated from each other; whereas the special northern tradition is covered by I. Atkinson, *The Viking Ships* (1979). J. F. C. Fuller in *The Decisive Battles of the Western World* (1954), vol. i, ch. 8, offers as good an analysis of a medieval naval battle (the one at Sluys) as may be found. Finally, the role of oar-based maritime technology during the early modern period is discussed in depth by F. Guilmartin, *Gunpowder and Galleys* (1974), a book which sets out to prove that Mahan's theories on seapower do not apply to oared warships, but which later digresses into highly technical, almost esoteric, matters.

Chapter 5. Irrational Technology

Though knowledgeable hints concerning the importance of irrational factors on the evolution of technology may be found in many places, to my knowledge the only modern student who even tries to get a hold on the problem is R. L. O'Connel, "Putting Weapons in Perspective," *Armed Forces and Society,* vol. ix, Spring 1983, pp. 441–54, a real eye-opener to which the present book owes much. U. Nef, *War and Human Progress* (1954), is one of the few authors who has something to say about the connection between weapons and art. Perhaps understandably, the problem of unfair technology has attracted the attention of lawyers rather than of military historians. A few pertinent remarks may be found in G. Best, *Humanity in Warfare* (1980); however, of the many works on the law of war which appear in his bibliography none is devoted specifically to this question. J. R. Hale, "Gunpowder and the Renaissance," in C. H. Carter, ed., *From Renaissance to Countereformation* (1966) discusses the "chorus of disapproval" directed at the gun as an effective, all-too-effective, weapon in fifteenth-century Italy. J. Keegan, *The Face of Battle* (1976), has interesting things to say on why some weapons are more feared than others. The possibility that beliefs concerning what was fair and what was not may, during the period 1919–39, have contributed to the concentration on aircraft and tanks rather than on gas is discussed in B. C. Hacker, "The Military and the Machine; an Analysis of the Controversy over Mechanization in the British Army," (U. of Chicago Ph.D. thesis, 1968). See also E. Gray's teasing *A Damned Un-English Weapon, the Story of British Submarine Warfare 1914–18* (1971). However, I know of no work specifically devoted to discussing modern weapons in aesthetic terms.

Part II
The Age of Machines, 1500–1830
Chapter 6. Field Warfare

A good modern account of the origins of artillery, which emphasizes the methodological difficulties involved in research, is J. R. Partington, *A History of Greek Fire and Gunpowder* (1960). H. W. L. Hime, *The Origin of Artillery* (1915), and A. W. Wilson, *The Story of the Gun* (1944), though old, are still valuable. Th. Esper, "The Replacement of the Longbow by Firearms in the English Army," *Technology and Culture*, No. 6, 1965, argues that the advantage of the arquebus consisted in that it required less training. B. P. Hughes, *Firepower: Weapons Effectiveness on the Battlefield 1630–1850* (1975), is concerned with the details of the performance of firearms and the formations in which they were employed; see also R. Quimby, *The Background to Napoleonic Warfare* (1957), which, though less narrowly focused on technology, examines the impact of firearms on tactics with the kind of detailed attention worthy of a medieval scholastic. For the early eighteenth century, D. Chandler, *The Art of Warfare in the Age of Marlborough* (1976), offers a meticulously documented introduction, whereas H. Koch, *The Rise of Modern Warfare from the Age of the Mercenaries through Napoleon* (1981), extends the story to the battle of Waterloo.

Chapter 7. Siege Warfare

A good general introduction to the problems of siege warfare in this period, profusely illustrated, is I. V. Hogg, *Fortress* (1975); even better is C. Duffy, *Siege Warfare* (1979). The transition from medieval to early modern fortresses is covered by J. R. Hale, *Renaissance Fortification* (1961), as well as by S. Pepper and N. Adams, *Firearms and Fortifications* (1986), which is superbly researched and very detailed. B. H. St. J. O'Neil, *Castles and Cannon* (1960), has much more to say about castles than about cannon. Vauban has been the subject of several biographies, among which M. Parent, *Vauban* (1982)* may be the best; in English, however, nothing more recent than R. Blomfield's *Sebastien le Prestre de Vauban* (1938), is available. A general work on the strategic as distinct from the tactical impact of technological changes in siege warfare remains to be written.

Chapter 8. The Infrastructure of War

For works on the logistic problems of armies prior to the introduction of mechanical transport, v. the present essay, *supra,* part I, 3. Though primarily concerned with administration rather than with technology, G. Parker, *The Army of Flanders and the Spanish Road 1567–1659* (1972) is enlightening. On the diffusion of information, including military information, during the early modern period see C. A. J. Armstrong, "Some Examples of the Distribution and Speed of News in England at the Time of the Wars of the Roses," in R. W. Hunt *et al.,* eds., *Studies in Medieval History* (1948). J. Koren, *The History of Statistics* (1918), and H. Westergaard, *Contributions to the History of Statistics* (1932), are among the few works devoted to that subject; Koren is particularly interesting on the period under consideration. While there has been no systematic work done on the problems of timekeeping in relation to war, there are some interesting remarks in D. Landes, *Revolution in Time, Clocks and the Making of the Modern World* (1983), part II, ch. 5. Since the subject has been neglected by military historians, those interested in the general technological background of war during the three centuries before the Industrial Revolution will have to look to economic and social histories of that period; among the ones that this author found most useful were Ph. Deane, *The First Industrial Revolution* (1965), C. M. Cipolla, *Before the Industrial Revolution; European Society and Economy 1000–1700* (1976), and F. Braudel, *Capitalism and Material Life 1500–1800* (1977).

Chapter 9. Command of the Sea

The outstanding role played by European naval technology in imperial expansion during the early modern period is brilliantly dealt with by C. M. Cipolla, *Guns and Sails in the Early Phase of European Expansion, 1400–1700* (1965). G. Mattingly, *The Spanish Armada* (1965), J. H. Owen, *War at Sea under Queen Ann* (1938), and G. J. Marcus, *Heart of Oak; a Survey of British Sea Power in the Georgian Era* (1975), all have much to say about the interaction of technology and maritime conflict. D. W. Waters, *The Art of Navigation in Elizabethan and Early Stuart Times* (1958), is authoritative in its field. So is C. J. Corbett, *Fighting Instructions 1530–1816* (1904), which, though specialized, offers excellent insight into tactical problems of naval warfare during the centuries that it covers. A broad if fragmentary naval perspective on the period is presented by P. Padfield, *Tides of Empire 1481–1763* (2 vols., 1979, 1981); Padfield also wrote *Guns at Sea* (1973), which is not only much the best work on that subject but carries the story almost down to the present. Finally, A. T. Mahan, *The Influence of Seapower upon History 1660–1793* (original edition 1890, innumerable reprints), though not primarily concerned with the technology of shipping, is worth reading in the present context because of the many insights it contains on the ways in which the technology of sailing men-of-war affected tactics and strategy.

Chapter 10. The Rise of Professionalism

Q. Wright, *A Study of War* (1941, 1965), is good on the relationship between military technology and forms of military organization; see also S. Andreski's classic *Military Organization and Society* (1968). A fascinating case study of the connection between the technology of war and its ethos, in this case feudalism, is offered by D. Ayalon, *Gunpowder and Firearms in the Mamluk Kingdom* (1978). McNeill's work, listed above, deals briefly with the role of technology in the development of military professionalism during the seventeenth century. So does M. D. Feld in "Middle Class Society and the Rise of Military Professionalism; the Dutch Army 1589–1609," *Armed Forces and Society*, i, 1975, pp. 419–42. F. B. Artz, *The Development of Technical Education in France 1500–1850* (1966), has several chapters on the origins and development of the French armed forces' most important military-technological colleges. T. N. Dupuy, *A Genius for War* (1977), does not focus primarily on technology and is also unsatisfactory in many other respects; however, it is the closest thing we have to a study of professionalism in what was perhaps the world's most important single army between 1866 and 1945. M. Janowitz, *The Professional Soldier* (1960, many reprints), is the standard modern work on the U.S. forces and has served as a model for many others. H. Wool, *The Military Specialist* (1968), documents the splintering effect of advancing technology on military organization.

Part III
The Age of Systems, 1830–1945
Chapter 11. Mobilization Warfare

W. R. Plum, *The Military Telegraph during the Civil War* (1882, rep. 1974), seems to be the only English-language study of military telegraphy going beyond mere technicalities; also, see this author's brief chapter in *Command in War* (1985). E. A. Pratt, *The Rise of Rail-Power in War and Conquest* (1916), is dated and should be supplemented by D. S. Showalter, *Railways and Rifles* (1977). J. Westwood, *Railways at War* (1980), focuses on what railways did *in* war rather than *to* it. Before World War I the fact that modern technology would result in total war was only understood by a handful of people; on which problem see C. Trebilock, "War and the Failure of Industrial Mobilization," in J. M. Winter, ed., *War and Economic Development* (1975), pp. 139–64, as well as M. van Creveld, "The Origins and Development of Mobilization Warfare," in G. H. McCormick and R. E. Bissell, eds., *Strategic Dimensions of Economic Behavior* (1984), ch. 2.

Though they do not focus on technology in particular, the rise of total war is very much the theme of such books as C. Falls, *The Art of War from the Age of Napoleon to the Present Day* (1961), and J. F. C. Fuller, *The Conduct of War 1789–1961* (1961, reprinted 1972), the latter especially being an excellent piece of work. E. Ludendorff, *Total War* (1936), analyzes the lessons of World War I and offers it as a model for the future. Probably the closest thing to a study of the "total" character of World War II is A. S. Milward, *War, Economy and Society 1939–1945* (1977), which cannot be recommended strongly enough. A. Marwick, *War and Social Change in the Twentieth Century* (1974) explores that relationship. Finally, P. Bracken in "Mobilization in the Nuclear Age," *International Security*, 3, 1978, pp. 74–93, deals with the role of mobilization in our time.

Chapter 12. Land Warfare

A good general account of nineteenth-century warfare, land warfare included, which also has much to say on the development of military technology, is W. McElwee, *The Art of War from Waterloo to Mons* (1974). More recent accounts are H. Strachan, *European Armies and the Conduct of War* (1983), and L. H. Addington, *The Patterns of War since the Eighteenth Century* (1984), both of which carry the story down to the present.

Showalter's *Railroads and Rifles*, mentioned earlier, analyzes the attempts of mid-nineteenth-century armies to come to terms with quickfiring weapons, and much else besides. J. Ellis, *The Social History of the Machine Gun* (1975), is a superficial work on an important subject. M. Howard, "Men against Fire; Expectations of War in 1914," in S. E. Miller, ed., *Military Strategy and the Origin of the First World War* (1985), is authoritative. J. Wheldon, *Machine Age Armies* (1968), offers a more general account of the impact of technological developments since 1914.

The rise, and subsequent decline, of armor has been the subject of innumerable monographs, of which R. Ogorkiewicz, *The Design and Development of Fighting Vehicles* (1962), H. C. B. Rogers, *Tanks in Battle* (1965, 1972), and D. Orgill, *The Tank* (1970), probably remain the best in spite of being rather old. C. Messenger, *The Blitzkrieg Era* (1976), is weak. The story of anti-armor combat is told in a monograph by J. Weeks, *Men against Tanks* (1975), which is somewhat lowbrow but very entertaining.

Chapter 13. Command of the Air

The best short guide to war in the air is probably R. Higham, *Airpower* (1972), which, however, carries the story only as far as the Vietnam War. The origins of aviation are covered by L. T. C. Rolt, *The Aeronauts; a History of Ballooning 1783–1903* (1969), and C. H. Gibbs-Smith, *The*

Invention of the Aeroplane 1793–1909 (1966). There is no comprehensive history of air power in World War I; however, J. Slessor, *Air Power and Armies* (1936), covers the Western Front while the American side is described by J. L. Hudson's *Hostile Skies* (1968). Again, there is no single history of military aviation during the interwar years. Theoretical developments are dealt with most comprehensively in R. Flugel's dissertation, "United States Air Power Doctrine; a Study of the Influence of William Mitchell and Giulio Douhet at the Air Corps Tactical School, 1921–1935" (1968). There are many studies of the Luftwaffe, among which W. Murray's *Strategy for Defeat* (1983), is the most recent and the best. U. Bialer, *The Shadow of the Bomber* (1980), is good but should be read together with M. Smith's more recent *British Air Strategy between the Wars* (1984). R. J. Overy, *The Air War 1939–1945* (1980), is much the best general work on the subject, based on an impressive range of source material and with something to say about almost everything; Overy, however, does not mention airborne operations even in his index, so that the reader is referred to B. Gregory and J. H. Batchelor, *Airborne Warfare 1918–1945* (1979). As compared to the official histories, A. Verrier's *Bomber Offensive* (1968), enjoys the advantage of brevity.

Chapter 14. Sea Warfare

J. P. Baxter, *The Introduction of the Ironclad Warship* (1933), is very detailed not only on technology but on the politico-military-economic debates that accompanied the transition from sails to steam. B. Brodie, *Naval Strategy* (1941, 1965), remains the best general introduction on the development of seapower since the onset of the Industrial Revolution. R. W. Daly, *How the "Merrimac" Won* (1957), is good on technology but biased on strategy. P. Padfield, *The Battleship Era* (1972, reprinted 1975), is excellent on the interaction of technological and operational considerations pertaining to his subject. A case study of one naval technology that was unspectacular but very important is J. T. Sumida, "British Capital Ships, Design and Fire Control in the Dreadnought Era," *Journal of Modern History*, 51, 1979.

G. Jordan, ed., *Naval Warfare in the Twentieth Century* (1977), has several good chapters on technology including aircraft and submarines. C. G. Reynolds, *The Fast Carriers* (1968), and N. Polmar, *Aircraft Carriers* (1969), together offer enough technical detail on these ships to satisfy anyone. E. P. Hoyle, *The Carrier War* (1972), is a good account of the Pacific Theater in World War II in which carriers took a particularly prominent part. A. R. Hezlet, *The Submarine and Seapower* (1967), is a somewhat popular introduction to that subject, whereas R. E. Kuenne, *The Attack Submarine* (1965), is strong on the period from the beginning of World War II to the early sixties.

Chapter 15. The Invention of Invention

M. Kranzberg, *Technology in Western Civilization* (1967), vol. i, has a chapter on this subject which, however, is not limited to military technology. V. Bush, *Modern Arms and Free Men* (1948, reprinted 1968), argues that democracy is as good as, or better than, totalitarian states in developing new military technology, a point which was interesting at the time but has become trite since. The question as to whether military technology helps civilian technological development has given rise to a vast literature. L. Mumford in his many publications, particularly *The Myth of the Machine* (1932), and *The Pentagon of Power* (1970), says yes. Precisely the opposite opinion is advanced in the previously-mentioned work by J. U. Nef, who is determined to show that no kind of progress, including technological progress, has ever resulted from war, and succeeds in doing so to his own satisfaction. M. Kaldor, *The Baroque Arsenal* (1982), argues that modern military technology by diverting resources away from civilian R&D tends to hinder, rather than advance, technological development and economic growth; a thesis with which those who have watched Japanese economic growth in recent years may be inclined to agree.

M. R. Smith, *Harper's Ferry Armory and the New Technology* (1980), is a very detailed case study which looks into the process by which new military technology is diffused. E. E. Morison, *Men, Machines and Modern Times* (1966), investigates social obstacles to military-technological progress in a somewhat one-sided way. For a man who is himself a scientist, R. V. Jones, *Future Conflict and New Technology* (The Washington Papers, No. 88, 1981), displays a remarkable lack of imagination in his survey of contemporary science which is intended to show that no revolutionary developments are (or were then) on the horizon.

Possibly because its utility is taken for granted, there is no systematic study of the effect of technological superiority on war; some kind of case in favor of technology is, however, made by former U.S. Secretary of Defense H. Brown in *Thinking about National Security* (1983), ch. 14. In recent years, the view that modern military technology is often too expensive to afford and too complex to work is presented by M. Handel, "Numbers Do Count; the Question of Quality versus Quantity," *The Journal of Strategic Studies*, vol. iv, September 1981, and, at greater length, by F. Spinney in *Defense Facts of Life* (1986).

Part IV
The Age of Automation, 1945 to the Present

Chapter 16. Computerized War

In spite of an enormous body of literature, there seems to be no single work on the effect of cybernetics on war. Perhaps the closest anyone has come is V. V. Druzhinin, *Concept, Algorithm, Decision* (originally published in Russian in 1972, English translation 1976), which is unrivaled in its treatment of the automation of military decision-making. R. J. Bastiani, *Computers on the Battlefield* (1983), is too limited to do justice to its subject. Two books, R. Lewin *Ultra Goes to War* (1976), and R. Bennett, *Ultra in the West* (1979), cover that subject very well. P. M. S. Blackett, *Studies of War* (1962), offers examples of the use of operations research in war, as does C. H. Waddinton's *Operations Research in World War II* (1973). This author's *Command in War*, ch. 7, describes the way in which computers and numeracy affected military command as exercised by the Americans in Vietnam, a subject on which J. Ewell's *Sharpening the Combat Edge; the Use of Analysis to Reinforce Military Judgement* (1974), is also valuable. The case in favor of reducing war, particularly nuclear war, to microeconomics supported by computers, is made by A. C. Enthoven, *How Much is Enough? Shaping the Defense Program, 1961–1969* (1971); whereas scathing critiques of that approach are presented by I. L. Horowitz, *The War Game* (1963), and by Ph. Greene, *Deadly Logic* (1968). Finally, J. Andriole, ed., *Artificial Intelligence and National Defense* (1987), is an up to date survey of that field, which probably promises more than it can deliver.

Chapter 17. Nuclear War

Among the more comprehensible general works on the sometimes bizarre world of nuclear strategy, including technology, are K. Tsipis, *Arsenal, Understanding Weapons in the Nuclear Age* (1983), and D. Schroeer, *Science, Technology and the Nuclear Arms Race* (1984), both of which aim at technical literacy rather than technical expertise. The successful construction of the American atomic bomb is covered in R. Rhodes, *The Making of the Atomic Bomb* (1980), which puts everything else in the shade. The development of the hydrogen bomb is covered by H. F. York, *The Advisors; Oppenheimer, Teller and the Superbomb* (1975); see also H. Morland, *The Secret that Exploded* (1981). The development of the earliest ballistic missiles is described by M. Y. Armacourt, *The Politics of Weapons Innovation; the Thor-Jupiter Controversy* (1969), whereas H. H. Sapolsky, *The Polaris System Development* (1972), and R. I. Tammen, *MIRV and the Arms Race* (1973), do the same for their respective subjects. Though it has less to say on the politics of development and more about strategic implications, R. K. Betts, *Cruise Missiles; Technology, Strategy, Politics* (1981), is excellent. As against these (and countless other) publications on specific delivery vehicles for nuclear weapons, little has been published about the technical details of command in nuclear war. However, what has been published is conveniently summarized in P. Bracken, *The Command and Control of Nuclear Forces* (1983), whereas the danger of nuclear war breaking out by accident is discussed by D. Frei, *Risks of Unintentional Nuclear War* (1982).

Among the very numerous contemporary discussions of the Anti-Ballistic Missile debate of the late sixties, the most comprehensive is J. J. Halls, ed., *Why ABM?* (1969); for a retrospective view of this issue see E. J. Yanarella's excellent *The Missile Defense Controversy; Strategy, Technology and Politics 1955–1972* (1977). A. B. Carter and D. N. Schwartz's *Ballistic Missile Defense* (1984) does an excellent job in discussing not just ABM but every conceivable defensive technique, including space-based particle-beam or laser-operated weapons.

I. Clark, *Limited Nuclear War* (1982), presents a critique of that possibility. K. N. Waltz, *The Spread of Nuclear Weapons; More May be Better* (Adelphi Papers No. 171, 1981), advocates a minority view according to which more nuclear devices in the hands of additional countries may be good for the safety of the world. Tactical nuclear war is discussed in F. Barnaby's *Tactical Nuclear Weapons* (1977), R. L. Fischer, *Defending the Central Front* (Adelphi Paper No. 127, 1976), and S. Zuckerman, *Nuclear Illusions and Reality* (1982).

Chapter 18. Integrated War

A systematic, comprehensive, rather technical survey of new weapons appearing year by year is being brought out by Jane's but is really suitable only for the specialist or the afficionado. Shorter, more superficial but in some ways more useful accounts of the most recent weapons can be found in the *RUSI and Brassey's Defense Yearbook* which, year by year, contains articles on this subject. E. N. Luttwak, *A Dictionary of Modern War* (1971), brilliantly summarized many aspects of modern military technology at the time of its appearance but is now badly dated. L. Martin, *Arms and Strategy* (1973), much of which consists of an attempt to assess the impact of modern arms on the conduct of war, was valuable at the time of publication. S. J. Deitchman, *Military Power and the Advance of Technology* (1979, revised edition 1983), has many interesting details but, as far as I can see, no clear thesis.

The origins of electronic warfare as conducted during World War II are discussed in nontechnical language by D. E. Gordon, *Electronic Warfare* (London, 1981); but see also A. Price, *Instruments of Darkness* (1967). P. E. Walker, "Precision Guided Weapons," *Scientific American*, vol. 245, No. 2, August 1981, pp. 36–45, provides a succinct explanation of how these contraptions are supposed to work. That they often fail to work in practice is proved by R. A. Beaumont, "Rapiers versus Clubs; the Fitful History of Smart Bombs," *Journal of the Royal United Services Institute*, 1981, No. 3. The present study has taken the view that the similarities between the military technologies used by today's most advanced armed forces outweigh the differences between them; however, see J. W. Kehoe and K. S. Brower, "US and Soviet Weapon System Design Practices,"

International Defense Review, No. 6, 1982, pp. 705–20, for the opposite standpoint.

Although the division of military affairs into land, air, and sea makes little sense in the period of integrated warfare, the literature for the most part is still organized on these lines. Concerning the land, the best discussions are probably R. Simpkin, *Mechanized Infantry* (1980), and his *Race to the Swift* (1985). The future of air warfare is discussed in E. J. Feuchtwagner and R. A. Mason, *Airpower in the Next Generation* (1979), that of seapower in G. Till, *Maritime Strategy in the Nuclear Age* (1984). The military uses of space are discussed in T. Karmas, *The New High Ground* (1984), an excellent introduction to a fascinating subject.

Chapter 19. Make-Believe War

This is a subject on which, understandably, military men have been loath to write. A good starting point is provided by the works of a great historian who was no expert on technology, J. Huizinga in *The Waning of the Middle Ages* (1919, first English edition 1924), and *Homo Ludens* (original edition, 1936), which represent war, and some of the technology used in it, in terms of play, games, and toys. An attempt to refute Huizinga on these points was made by M. Vale, *Warfare and Aristocratic Culture in England, France and Burgundy in the Middle Ages* (1981). This is a somewhat pedestrian book not at all comparable to the master's brilliant exposition.

A general work on contemporary attitudes to war, which in turn help shape contemporary attitudes to weapons, is P. Fussell, *The Great War and Modern Memory* (1975), which represents 1914–18 as the great turning point; see also J. Keegan, *The Face of Battle,* already mentioned. A journalist's account of the arms industry's attempts to present its products as harmless gadgets may be found in A. Sampson, *The Arms Bazaar* (1977), ch. 1. E. Cohen, "Slick'ems, Glik'ems, Christmas Trees, and Cookie Cutters; Nuclear Language and How We Learnt to Pat the Bomb," *Bulletin of the Atomic Scientists,* June 1987, offers some fine insights into military euphemisms. The abovementioned study by M. Kaldor, one of whose main points is precisely that complexity in weapon systems is often being pursued for its own sake, is also valuable. L. Mumford in his disorganized way has many fascinating things to say on weapons as deadly toys, but the reader who is interested in the subject will have to look them up for himself.

Chapter 20. Real War

Though the possibility that technological progress may play a role in causing wars is mentioned in many publications, R. N. Lebow, "Windows of Opportunity," in S. E. Miller, ed., *Military Strategy and the Origins of the First World War* (1985), pp. 147–86 seems to be one of the few systematic discussions of that important subject. A good historical introduction to the problem of guerrilla warfare and terrorism is available in the form of W. Laqueur's *Guerilla; a Historical and Critical Study* (1976), and the same author's *Terrorism* (1977); each of these volumes comes complete with companions filled with readings that are almost more valuable than Laqueur's texts. For reasons that are partly ideological (terrorist weapons are not *real* weapons, after all) and partly practical (not many people are willing to tell terrorists how to go about their bloody business), little has been written about the technological aspect of the problem; however, see C. Dobson and R. Payne, *The Terrorists, their Weapons, Leaders and Tactics* (1979), as well as D. Dean ed., *Low Intensity Conflict and Modern Technology* (1986). A. de Volpi, *Proliferation, Plutonium and Policy: Institutional and Technological Impediments to Nuclear Weapons Propagation* (1979), explains, among other things, why it would be hard for terrorists to obtain such weapons, and one can only hope he is right.

Conclusions: The Logic of Technology and of War

Sun Tzu, *The Art of War* (S. B. Griffith trans., 1963), is the classic work on the need to conduct war by deception, surprise, meshing with the enemy, *ying* and *yang*. A modern discussion of much the same problems, gathered under the heading of the "paradoxical" logic, is E. N. Luttwak, *Strategy; the Logic of War and Peace* (1987), which is brilliant.

Index

Index

Index

Hossbach, F. von, 298
Huizinga, J., 286
Huns, 22
Huygens, C., 128
Hydraulic civilizations, 16; and fortifications, 26
Hydrogen bomb, development of, 254
Hyksos, the, 22

Icarus, 183
Illiad, the, 67
Incendiaries, at sea, 58; and gunpowder, 82, 89; dropped from balloons, 184
Inflexible, 203
Innovation, technological, 4; before 1830, 217–9; and the military, 220–1; and qualitative arms race, 223–4; and the nature of war, 225; and victory in war, 226–30; problems of, 231–2; and the complexity of war, 235–6; new form since 1945, 278–9; belief in, 290
Intelligence, methods used in obtaining, 120; and computers, 241
Intercontinental Ballistic Missile (ICBM): *See* Missile Iron, discovery of, 14; in middle ages, 20; as material for siege engines, 30; as material for cannon, 133; as material for ships, 200–1
Irrational technology, nature of, 4–5, 67; manifested in decoration, 68; in size, 69; in names, 69–70; in complexity, 70; in unfair weapons, 71; role in war, 76–8, 292
Itineraria, 43; in middle ages, 44; in early modern age, 117

Javelin, primitive, 10, 14, 15; in Roman use, 17; drops out of use, 20
Jeep, 240
Jena, battle of, 123
Jet engine, 220, 228, 275
Jeune école, 204
Jodphat, siege of, 75
John II, of France, 99
Johnson, S., 222
Joinville, J. de, 76
Jomini, A. H., 48, 94, 164, 167, 219
Judaeus Maccabeus, 300
Junks, Chinese, 52, 136
Justinian, 18
Jutland, battle of, 207, 216

Kennedy, J. F., 224, 305
Kipling, R., 172
Kissinger, H. A., 285
Kitchener, H. H., 162, 229
Koniev, I. S., 180
Königgrätz, battle of, 226
Kriegsakademie, 145
Krupp, A., 220

Lance, 15, 20; size of, 68, 88, 229, 287
Lanchester, F., 244
Landing craft, 214
Langley, S., 185
Larrey, D. J. B., 95
Laser, 272, 273, 314

Lateran Council, 71
Laupen, battle of, 319
Lavoisier, A. L. de, 119
Leather gun, 87
Legion, 17, 26
Leiden Jar, 156
Leipzig, battle of, 113
Lepanto, battle of, 61
Levée en masse, 113, 147, 167
Liddell Hart, B., 5, 164, 277
Limes, Roman, 27, 154
Lind, J., 132
Lippershey, H., 154
Lissa, battle of, 203
List, F., 158
Livius, T., 142
Lloyd George, D., 162, 164
Logistics, 46; and the campaigning season, 47; at sea, 57, 65; during siege warfare, 107; early modern, 116; of armored warfare, 181; and computers, 240, 246, 247, 316–7
Longships, 62–4
Louix IX, 76
Louis XIV, 68, 109, 118, 144, 145
Louis XV, 118
Louis XVI, 118
Loxodromes, 129
Ludendorff, E., 160, 164; and total war, 166, 227, 277

Mace, 15; persistence of, 21
Machiavelli, N., 21, 74, 89, 91, 102, 165, 285
Machicolation, 29
Machine gun, 177; carried by aircraft, 187; invented, 220, 223, 228; in colonial warfare, 229, 274
Mack, 97
Magellan, F., 126
Magic, 238
Mahan, A., 210
Mahdi, the, 229, 230
Maimonides, 298
Malplaquet, battle of, 113
Mamluks, 89
Mangonel: *See* Ballista
Manhattan Project, 221
Mantelet, 30, 31
Mao Tze-Dong, 300, 303
Maps, 2; before 1500, 43–5; at sea, 56; early modern, 116–8; for navigation, 129
Maraldi, G., 117
Marcelinus, Ammianus, 17
Marcellus, M. Claudius, 54
Marconi, G., 267
Marignano, battle of, 91
Marius, C., 139
Marlborough, John Churchill, Duke of, 94
Marne, battle of, 271
Martinet, J., 94
Marx, K., 5
Mary Rose, 69
Maxim, H., 220
Maxwell, C., 267
McNamara, R. S., 224; and computers, 245, 246

MP12T